FOOD FOR THOUGHT

Compiled by
PHILLIP DAY

 Credence Publications

TABLE OF CONTENTS

INTRODUCTION

Welcome to *Food For Thought*, the companion recipe book for Credence titles. I am delighted to have been part of this project because it has given me an opportunity to brush up on the practicalities of food and what it means to lay eyes on good, wholesome nutrition. Like many reading this, I love food, and in the past, this love has led me into overweight, ill-health and a fair degree of misery. Today my life is very different. I am strong, vital, disease-free (approaching 18 years) and my life is immensely satisfying as I see the Principles  of Longevity that do for me working for the many who try them for themselves. The bottom line is that I must be doing something right. My job as a reporter and health researcher has been to catalogue these and other amazing features of health and pass them on to as wide an audience as I can reach.

As many know, I do a lot of travelling as part of my speaking tours (around ten months of the year) and I rely more than I should for food on restaurants, hotels and foraging for myself in foreign, as well as domestic climes. Getting fed properly some of the time can be a real trial, both abroad and in the UK, and I have discovered over the years the variation of people's beliefs in what constitutes proper food for the public. In many cases, the food is not really 'food' at all, but highly processed commercial material palmed off on the public as edible matter. And British motorway services? Some of those people (and their food) should be in jail.

In *Health Wars*, *The Mind Game* and other Credence titles, we examine key features of the body's metabolic requirements for food. These axiomatic truths have been confirmed through the outstanding nutrition and physical condition of certain peoples on Earth who, in their native state, do not suffer the same legacy of disease and ill-health currently plaguing industrialised societies. Put simply, as we become more technologically advanced, so increases our temptation to fiddle with our food, water and air in our efforts to bring 'science' to a new plane of understanding and profitability. That this tinkering is one of the chief causes of disease and misery today is widely ignored or trivialised by the arrogance of industry and our (mostly unhealthy) scientific peers, who seem to ignore the fact that while our world changes constantly around us (and often not for the best), the human body still craves the same nutrients it always did.

But nutritional information today is a minefield of contradictions. I make no bones about the differences that exist between the principles expounded in this book and those promoted by other authors. In *Health Wars*, we examine the devastating role played by excessive consumption of meat, dairy and sugary foods in causing ill-health in the population. Yet some diets advocate heavy meat and dairy consumption. Other authors decry the need for vitamin and mineral supplementation, declaring them to be 'a con', a 'health fad', and a pernicious way to part the public from its pennies. These ones state that you can get all your nutritional requirements from the 'four food groups'. And yet a cursory examination of the situation will clearly reveal that the average member of the public needs no education on how to scarf down the four food groups by the bushel box-load, and yet these same folk are suffering grievously from food-abuse diseases and general incapacitation through obesity and *malnutrition*, in spite of the amount of tucker they skilfully skewer with their fork.

Health Wars shows how, in the absence of our political and scientific peers giving any practical guidelines on how to eat properly, millions die each year from nutritional deficiency diseases, dehydration, auto-immune problems and toxins. Tens of millions of Americans pour hundreds of millions of gallons of cows' milk down their throats every year after being sold the bogus story that drinking the white stuff gives them more than sufficient calcium to ward off the dreaded osteoporosis. But what has been the result of this catastrophic wrong turn? *A higher rate of osteoporosis than in any other nation.*

I think you are a pretty rotten expert if you die from the very disease you are trying to prevent in other people, and I have seen some government health experts who look so sick I feel like ringing for the ambulance immediately. And what of our doctors? Many of them look so ill I am amazed they have the energy to climb out of bed in the morning. Next time you visit your doctor – *examine him (or her).* How well do they look? After all, aren't these the ones who are supposed to keep us well?

The answer actually is no. The medical industry sees its role in repairing the sick, NOT educating the public to exercise disease prevention. This is given as the reason why doctors are not trained in nutrition. You can always tell the ones who are. They look great. They treat their patients' diseases with simple, wholesome foods and leave almost all the old drugs and potions in the rubbish bin behind them. These nutritionally trained doctors are our future, and I support and applaud these men and women wholeheartedly. I scorn the medical establishment that hounds these brave ones and castigates them for going against the religion of worn-out, discredited drug medicine.

In *Health Wars*, we examine the fascinating subject of entrenched scientific error in some detail, and I encourage you to become thoroughly familiar with the facts. Find out how drug-based medicine has now become at least the third leading killer in our societies today. Discover the simple answers to major diseases, both in prevention and treatment with nutrition. Learn what you can do to qualify for a long and healthy life. Discover the Principles of Longevity and apply them, so that your healthy existence may not only benefit you, but be a life-saving inspiration to others.

The method underlying *Food For Thought* is to identify key truths in the body's requirements for food, water and air, and put forward practical solutions to these requirements. These are known as the Principles of Longevity. As I am always stating in my seminars, if you want to live to a hundred, then go talk to those people who routinely live that long, see if you can discover what they are doing (or not doing) and then copy them. Thankfully, you don't need to board a rickety plane bound for the Himalaya valleys to find this out. The research was done many years ago by able scientists and nutritionists who have reported their findings back to the ailing West, which has mostly ignored them in the scramble for the last cream doughnut.

In the sections that follow, we will be examining these Principles and discussing them, along with their associated recipes, as an extension to the work we did, and are still doing, at Credence. Whether you are a healthy individual looking for further information on diet and nutrition, a bodybuilder going for the max, an elderly lady trying to combat arthritis, a cancer patient looking to bring the full arsenal of nutrition to bear on your body, a 'mentally ill' patient looking for answers to your problems in nutrition, or a youngster looking for some 'fun food', *Food For Thought* will spark up your imagination, fire the boilers of your gastronomic curiosity, and have you dribbling with anticipation as you get to look at your physical You-Ness from a whole new and inspirational direction.

And welcome to the revolution. A new healthcare system is being born – one fit for the 21st century with nutrition and prevention at its helm. Almost as if in response to the people's disgust at the failures of traditional, drug-based medicine, the UK's *Daily Mail* headline read on 19th July 2001: *"THE END OF DOCTOR KNOWS BEST"*.

Yes. And welcome to the start of *"DO IT FOR YOURSELF!"* And what better way than to start with the Principles of Longevity, because there is some fabulous food from some of the world's top experts waiting in the following pages for you, and I wouldn't want you to miss a mouthful.

So here's to some food fun. Let bellies rumble in hearty anticipation. Let hospitals scrap their sorry excuses for what passes for food and turn over a fresh new lettuce leaf for their patients. May governments fall in scandalous ruin if they fail to encourage their fellow citizens to chow down as follows. And may the British Motorway Services, and indeed all others around the world who are poisoning their customers at ruinous profit, read the following... and weep those decaf tears.

Phillip

Notes on Recipes

Great care has gone into ensuring that the following recipes are suitable for all ages. Some recipes however may require the addition of a 'forbidden' component, such as sucrose or an ill-chosen food combinant. This must be left to the discretion of the reader.

The following recipes are intended only as a guide towards expounding the principles laid out in *Health Wars*. In the interests of not becoming 'food fascists' however, the reader is invited to try their own variations along the themes contained in this cookbook.

The idea is to have fun with these foods, but also be mindful of the general direction in which we must all head in order to lay hold of suitable health for our future.

Please note: if you suffer allergies of any kind, or are seriously ill, please contact a healthcare professional before embarking on any diet or supplement regime.

KEY
tsp – teaspoon
tbsp – tablespoon
food item in **bold** – contains vitamin B17, The valuable nitrilosidic food group expounded upon in my book *Cancer: Why We're Still Dying to Know the Truth*. See also the section in this book entitled *An FDA Toxicologist on Vitamin B17*.

THE PRINCIPLES OF LONGEVITY

1) Live in a toxin-free environment
2) Strive to be an alkalised body system
3) Be well hydrated
4) Eat natural, properly constituted food
5) Be active
6) Maintain an overriding optimism and positive spiritual outlook for the future

Health Wars embraces these principles, from which flow all the good sense measures that you are bursting at the seams to tell others. Let's have a brief look at each:

LIVE IN A TOXIN-FREE ENVIRONMENT
The Principle: Cultures surviving to long lifespans simply do not have the toxic overload to contend with, which weighs down those of us living in the industrial societies. Many would not really want to live in these pristine environments of the Hunza and Karakorum, since to do so would mean going without many of the technological luxuries we cannot do without. Many believe that cleaning up the world is a hopeless task, but I do not subscribe to that view at all. A toxin-free environment begins at home and works outward as we educate others on what it feels like to be clean. The more people want to live clean, the cleaner the environment will become.

The Problem: Many are absolutely staggered when they learn the extent to which their lives have become contaminated through the use of electro-magnetic technologies, seemingly innocuous food additives, chemical preservatives, personal care and household products which have not been tested *impartially* to ensure their safe use by the public. Toothpaste's sodium fluoride, antiperspirant's aluminium, shampoo's sodium lauryl sulphate, make-up's propylene glycol and ethanolamines (MEA, DEA, TEA, etc.) are examples of how our governments and industry have utterly failed the public in warning about potentially life-threatening cumulative side-effects arising from constant use of these chemicals.

The Solution: Eat properly constituted[1], organic food to avoid insecticides, pesticides, bovine growth hormones and estrogens, steroids and chemical additives. Change out personal care and household products for safe, uncontaminated alternatives. These products will include shampoo, conditioner, shaving foam, moisturiser, toothpaste, make-up, skin cream and oil. Antiperspirants are an abomination and should be exchanged for safe deodorants.

Where Do I Go To Get These? Neways International is the company I choose. They manufacture a whole range of 'safe' personal care and household products. Neways is a direct marketing company available in over forty countries. Find a representative close to you and enquire how to purchase the products (also see the *Contacts!* section at the back of this book for further details). Neways represents a transfer spend. You simply stop buying the junk from supermarkets, and commence purchasing safe products direct.

STRIVE TO BE AN ALKALISED BODY SYSTEM

Principle: Nobel Laureate Otto Warburg dramatically proved in the 1930s that alkalised bodies are healthy oxygenated bodies and acidic bodies are prone to degeneration, oxygen deprivation and parasites/*Candida*. Warburg was severely contested and maligned by his peers for promoting this amazing information, but was entirely correct. The body likes to maintain a pH of 7.4, a slight alkali. When moved into acid, the body responds by using water and minerals, such as calcium, magnesium, potassium, sodium and iron to regain the alkali balance.[2] As most of us in the industrialised nations are dehydrated, the body has scant water to play with, and so has no choice but to use minerals stripped from the body, including the bones, to restore the alkali balance.

---

[1] 'Properly constituted food' means unprocessed, whole food with a normal or superior mineral and nutrient content. As discussed in *Health Wars*, most soils used to grow food in these production-intensive times have had the minerals farmed out of them. Thus most food, even some organic produce, is minerally deficient. The answer therefore, until this error can be redressed, is to supplement wholesome diets with vitamins, minerals and antioxidants in their most absorbable forms.

[2] **Morter, M T**, *pH – Your Potential For Health*, Morter HealthSystem, 1000 West Poplar, Rogers, AR, 72756 , USA

The Problem: The average western diet comprises foods very prone to generating acidic residues. These are meats, refined sugars and grains, chocolate, fizzy drinks, coffee, tea, breads, milk, butter and cheese. Also alcohol, smoking and other 21st century activities guarantee the abuser an acidic system, which will repel oxygen and become a haven for degenerative problems.

The Solution: If you are 'not sick' but wish to become healthier than you 'feel' at present, change out your existing eating habits with those in the **Maintenance Recipes** section. Here, the watchword is 80% alkali ash foods to 20% acid ash foods (see acid/alkali charts at the back of this book). These foods should be organic and eaten soon after harvest. If you are sick, suffering from cancer or other degenerative ailments, you need the **Detox Recipes**, which place a heavy accent on alkali ash foods WITHOUT the acidic components, such as meat, grains, sugar and dairy. Note that both sections are essentially natural peasant or fisherman diets which have been given a little inspiration!

Please note that the Detox Recipes section is not recommended for exclusive long-term consumption, although of course you may use the recipes you like in this section any time you like. The Detox Recipes are designed to do just that – help the body detoxify the junk held captive in our systems to restore them to optimal function over a 60-90 day period. The Maintenance Recipes are designed to ensure a balanced and superior intake of essential food factors *for life*. Please note though that vitamin, mineral and certain other nutrient supplementation is recommended FOR LIFE to optimise nutrient intake. This would of course NOT be necessary if our soils were properly constituted.

BE WELL HYDRATED
The Principle: The body requires water in two different formats: nutrient-laden water from high water-content natural, whole foods and fresh drinking water with a measure of natural mineral content. The body is a complex electro-chemical organism at the heart of which is water to ensure that billions of chemical reactions occur and soluents (minerals and nutrients) get to where they're going around the system. Medicine teaches doctors that water is essentially inert, whereas the truth is that water is absolutely pharmacologically active in the body, meaning that if governments were intellectually consistent, water

would have to be regulated by the government as a drug! But watch for the future. Water has always been very political, but is now set to become 'the new oil' and sold for profit in Big Corp's new agenda for the 21st century.

The Problem: If the body is starved of water, the brain uses the neurotransmitter histamine to regulate the water shortage by prioritising essential systems while curtailing others. Over time, chronic dehydration will begin interfering with cellular processes and the net result will be degeneration. Water deficiency complaints such as asthma, heartburn, colitis and constipation will turn into more severe diseases if allowed to continue unchecked. Notice that probably the last thing in a physician's mind is to prescribe water to his patient! He has never been trained on its incredible medicinal properties.[3]

The Solution: The body requires at least 4 pints (2 litres) of water every day. I can lead you to water but I cannot make you drink it. Filtered tap water is fine (carbon filters work well to produce good tasting water). In areas where the public water system has been deliberately contaminated with raw industrial waste fluorides, such as H_2SiF_6 (hexafluorosilicic acid), then water purified by reverse osmosis filters, or alternatively water purchased in glass (not plastic) bottles should be consumed.

EAT NATURAL, PROPERLY CONSTITUTED FOOD

The Principle: Our bodies are comprised approximately 74% water, 18% gaseous carbon compounds and the rest solids. Minerals are essential so that our bodies can form the myriad complex compounds required to sustain life. These minerals cannot be manufactured by our body and so have to come into us via the food we eat. If this food is depleted of minerals, we will suffer a metabolic deficiency disease which is linked to the depletion or deficiency of a particular nutrient. Almost all the diseases we suffer are related to metabolic or toxin complaints (and sometimes a combination of the two). Cultures living long lifespans in toxin-free environments have an abundance of these minerals at their disposal in their food and water. We do not.

---

[3] **Batmanghelidj, F** *Your Body's Many Cries For Water*, Tagman Press, 2001

The Problem: Is supplementation with vitamins and minerals a 'quaint health fad'? Absolutely not. Here's the important news: *One should eat properly constituted, organic foods as a first priority. But one must also supplement*, in order to ensure the body has access to the correct nutrients it is not receiving from even organic produce supplied through the centralised food production system. An example is fruit. Fruit is often picked unripe and then cold-stored before trans-shipment to the supermarkets. Plucking fruit before it has had a chance to ripen will guarantee that the fruit in question has not had a chance to develop its vitamins, which lead to the ripening state. Fruit left alone once ripened and picked will commence a degeneration of its vitamin C content. This was not always the way. In earlier days, we simply plucked the ripe fruit and ate it. Sadly, things are not that simple any more.

Vitamin C, for instance, needs to be supplemented. Try *not* doing it and many of us will wind up with heart disease, the No. 1 killer, in one of its various forms, as we discuss in *The ABC's of Disease* and *Health Wars*. And that's just C-complex. What about the other essential nutrient factors? How can we be sure we are getting those as well?

Our soils are greatly depleted of nutrients due to increasingly excessive demands placed on them by the food and agriculture industries. In our desire to plunder the land to produce food at an ever increasing rate, soils are not only NOT replenished with nutrients, but chemical fertilisers and other artificial constituents are compelled upon farmers in an effort to meet impossible quotas. The net result? The land is rapidly becoming empty of the raw materials our bodies require to maintain health. Worse, our bodies are under increasing, toxic attack and require an abundance of vitamins and minerals to carry out damage control. Antioxidants especially are required to neutralise and detoxify unstable chemical agents which enter our bodies and then seek to stabilise themselves. These oxidation or 'free radical' compounds are a leading cause of ageing and degenerative disease.

The Solution: Supplementation with ionised minerals, together with vitamins and antioxidants, will ensure maximum protection, along with the other Principles of Longevity. Ensure that the products you are using have maximum bioavailability and are not packed with

16

gimmicks and fillers. Some companies' products are far better than others and have been tested to show efficacy and absorption. Avoid metallic minerals packed into a pill, which have very poor absorbability.

Where Do I go To Get These? I am a big fan of the Neways supplements **Maximol** and **Revenol**, in view of their superior construction and ease of absorption into the body. **Maximol** provides 67 minerals, 21 amino acids, 17 vitamins and includes essential enzyme proteins for health.[4] **Revenol** is an extremely powerful, broad-spectrum antioxidant, which helps to clean up rogue oxidation in the body due to pollution, bad food metabolism and other causes.

BE ACTIVE
The Principle: The body is designed to move and function as an integrated unit. If a person is sedentary over a long period, problems will arise.

The Problems: A lack of exercise will produce a lowering of the body's immune defences and its ability to absorb oxygen and keep circulation flowing freely. Today 8 out of 10 people are physically inactive, smoke cigarettes or have a sedentary lifestyle. This is all having appalling repercussions in the realm of health and longevity.

The Solution: As our special chapter on exercise in *Health Wars* demonstrates, a consistent, moderate amount of exercise, combined with a healthy diet, fresh air and plenty of rest, gives us the optimum shot at health and long-life. *Do not ignore this principle!*

MAINTAIN AN OVERRIDING OPTIMISM AND POSITIVE SPIRITUAL OUTLOOK FOR THE FUTURE
The Principle: Much has been made recently of the new science of psychoneuroimmunology, or, put more simply, the ability of the mind to influence the physical health of the body through the bolstering of the immune system. While almost nothing is known at present on exactly how this works, from time immemorial, active, cheerful and positive people have always had the longevity edge over their angst-ridden compadres.

---

[4] Mary vary by country.

The Problem: Worry, stress, fear and loneliness, along with feelings of rage and jealousy, alter the body's responses to stress via neurotransmitter hormones. A person who is, for instance, constantly in a state of adrenalin flux will consume prodigious amounts of vitamin C, as this nutrient complex is required as a catalyst for adrenalin production. Later on, a chronic deficiency of vitamin C will lead to heart complications and eventually to an attack.

The Solution: Well, it's 'Think Positive!' But you know as well as I that this is easier said than done. I think one of the great starts in reducing stress is to try and find something you love doing. Everyone is great at something, and this should be the pastime or career you look forward to doing each day. We need to realise that a career change might be, not just desirable, but a matter of life and death for some people, whose careers or stress-loads are surely going to be the death of them unless they change.

Recent studies in medicine, reported on Dr Joseph Mercola's website at www.mercola.com, also state that those who have a belief in God and pray regularly have fewer serious health problems, as they do not seem to 'bottle things up' as much as their non-believing counterparts. They say that faith can move mountains! What mountains are you trying to scale these days? Are you in 'Fight or Flight' syndrome ALL THE TIME? Need some help?

I am, as many of you know, not an advocate of drug-based psychiatry *at all*, but rather see our friends, family and work colleagues as those who can help us balance our lives and put things into perspective when we need someone close by to talk to. Nothing is worth killing yourself over – not the bank manager, not a relationship, not a career, and certainly not a boss.

Stressed out? Do what I do and go lie on a beach for 10 days and write a book (or read one!). Stand back from the whole of your life and use the time to see where you are and how you fit into life's bigger picture. There's a mission for you somewhere that you are going to love and enjoy. Find it.

It's a beautiful life, despite all the world's problems, and most importantly, it's *your* life. And things are never *that* bad that something can't be done about them. I always find that regular exercise helps me maintain my physical and mental perspectives on things. I was fortunate to be given a strong and abiding faith in God too, which has helped me through many a dark hour. And so my mood is almost always upbeat, in spite of life's trials. Standing your ground in the face of adversity is a great character-builder.

A positive attitude and firm faith is essential for combating illnesses of all kinds, and I have seen extremely sick, but stentorian men and women balk some terrific odds to be disease-free and active today. Many of these inspirational stories are carried in my books. These people are remarkable. They have the ability to overcome. Have courage! As the famous saying goes: "Being brave is not being without fear. It's being frightened and having the courage to go on."

I am sure a positive outlook for the future and a great spirit will help you immensely too. For here is the good news. You <u>do</u> have a future and a hope.

NATURAL HYGIENE

Embodied in the Principles of Longevity is the Science of Natural Hygiene. The science of Natural Hygiene revolves around the following topics:

- Understanding The Body's Natural Digestive Cycles
- Correct Consumption of Fruit
- The Concept of High Water-Content Food
- Correct Food Combining
- Detoxification

THE BODY'S NATURAL DIGESTIVE CYCLES

The basis of Natural Hygiene teaches that the human body's digestive system goes through three eight-hour cycles every twenty-four hours:

Noon – 8pm: **Appropriation** of food (eating and digestion)
8pm – 4am: **Assimilation** of food (absorption and use)
4am – Noon: **Elimination** (excretion of waste products)

It is not hard to see these cycles in action. It is also uncomfortably clear when these cycles are thrown into confusion and turmoil by, for example, eating a pizza late at night or eating a big breakfast.

APPROPRIATION (12 noon – 8pm)

The body prefers the Appropriation Cycle to happen on time, commencing at noon. Those who rise late in the morning can easily make it through to noon without any food, because the body is currently in the Elimination Cycle and isn't yet ready for food. After the commencement of the Appropriation Cycle however, once afternoon arrives, we become uncomfortable if we do not eat anything. Our body craves nourishment during Appropriation and lets us know of its needs in no uncertain terms if we are remiss in supplying the necessary fodder. The most important rule during Appropriation is *to eat only when your body (not you!) is hungry.*

ASSIMILATION (8pm – 4am)

The Assimilation Cycle mostly occurs at night, and ideally must, like Britain's RailTrack, leave on time. Assimilation (nutrient extraction and use) at night makes all the sense in the world as the body is resting and the digestive system can crank into gear and do its thing with the minimum of interruption. Night-time is naturally not a good time for Appropriation (eating and digestion) because of the horizontal angles involved. During Assimilation at night however, the body extracts nutrients in our intestines, which are ten times the length of our trunks, designed as they are to keep high-water-content, high-fibre, unrefined plant dietary food in their clutches until all the nutrients are withdrawn. If you leave three hours between your last meal and when you go to bed, a properly combined supper, along the lines we will be examining, will already have left the stomach and be well on its peaceful way through the alimentary tract for its squeezing and extracting by the time you lay your precious head down on your pillow. During the night, your body is putting all those nutrients to work replenishing your systems, replacing damaged cells and allowing the blood and lymph systems to pick up waste and take it to the garbage collection points in preparation for the truck the following morning.

If however you commit the cardinal sin and wolf down your pepperoni and pineapple pizza (with the obligatory jalapenos) immediately prior to going to sleep, you will go to bed feeling like you have swallowed a horse. Your body is horizontal which means that gravity is working against your stomach and everything therein, inevitably resulting in the desperate need to throw down half a bucket of antacids at 2:30am to douse the mighty conflagration, or else prop your head up on a pillow in a vain attempt to stop the resultant hydrochloric acid reflux bringing those jalapenos and cheese up for a chat.

ELIMINATION (4am – 12 noon)
At 4am, Elimination cuts in and the garbage truck arrives to take out the junk. Your body has sorted through the food it has processed, and has rejected the food debris that cannot be absorbed and satisfactorily metabolised into constituent nutrients for further use. Elimination is simply the removal of waste matter from the body, be it from fibrous, non-metabolised food or other waste products the body generates, which we will examine in a minute. The human body has very efficient systems to accomplish the shedding of waste, using the bowel and urine to excrete the junk the body no longer wants to be involved with. The body also eliminates metabolic toxins, which have

accumulated in the body, shunting them out via the underarm, the bowel, the urine, glands at the backs of the knees, glands behind the ears, from the groin area, from the nose, the mouth, the ears and the skin.

Elimination is the most thwarted digestive cycle of the three - an abuse that has led to chronic obesity in our populations and catastrophic ill-health. *The reason is because the Elimination Cycle is almost always sabotaged by us unwittingly eating big, badly combined, low-fibre breakfasts, preventing the body from executing its essential daily function of getting waste out of the body.* Thus the junk stays put and gets filed in all the parts of our bodies where it can do the least harm. We look at our naked bodies in the mirror with horror: *"Good grief, my butt DOES look big in this. I look like a beached whale."* Your body is naturally offended at the insult being aimed in its general direction, and caustically replies: *"Then unplug me, Einstein, and let's get rid of the whale...."*

The following recipes are ideal for Natural Hygiene detoxification measures and should be adhered to. Notice that the breakfast component is FRUIT, not Heart-Attack-on-a-Plate (fried eggs, fried bread, sausages, etc.). In the event that you have a *Candida* condition or other, which necessitates a cutback in fruit, then a light garden salad in the morning will do nicely, thank you.

FRUIT
(FOR BREAKFAST)

At the heart of Natural Hygiene is the science of energy. The great news is that you can manipulate your body's energy usage very simply by the sort of food you consume, and you can start right now. As we have already seen, to assist the body in eliminating toxins and waste during its morning cycle EVERY

DAY, the idea is not to introduce anything during the Elimination Cycle that will divert the body from doing its life-saving housework. No traditional breakfasts. No Aunt Lily's Arkansas Pancakes. No grits or muesli. No British Heart-Attack-on-a-Plate, with the fried eggs, fried bread, sausages, tomatoes, and bacon. The problem is, many folks are culturally prepared to eat a herd of wildebeest in the morning, since it was hammered into us by our obese grannies time and time again that a healthy, farm-fresh breakfast was essential to our optimum welfare. Unfortunately this dangerous rubbish which our grannies fervently believed and took to their eventually failing hearts, is why many of them remained the size they did, up until they died of a toxin-related food-abuse disease, such as coronary heart disease, stroke or cancer.

If you want the Queen's telegram, and wish to achieve a happy and healthy longevity, bouncing your great-granddaughter upon your firm and functioning knee, then you must admit you aren't going to make it with the West's current food *modus operandi*. The frightening legacy this dietary treachery will give you will be a heart attack, cancer, and the other nightmares we examine in *Health Wars* and *The ABC's of Disease*. If you want to live to be a healthy hundred, find those who routinely live to these ages, and do what they do.

Making the change means making a decision to avoid completely unnecessary tragedy, pain and heartache, both for your benefit and for those who love you and want you around for as long as possible. I remember having dinner with a preacher and his wife in America. His wife unfortunately had suffered a stroke and was wheelchair-bound. During the meal, the pastor was explaining how he believed his wife's condition was God's way of communicating a message to them both. I heartily agreed with him. God was certainly communicating a message. It was: *"My lovely children. You are killing yourselves with your troubled interaction with nourishment."* The meal we had that night consisted of a huge sidewalk of beef and an Everest of mashed potatoes slowly eroding into an Atlantic Ocean of gravy. Upon enquiry, I learned that this gastronomic profanation, together with some other close offshoots, was their regular evening munch.

Fruit is your man. Clean, light and more mobile than an SAS infiltration unit. Fruit digests in the intestinal tract, not the stomach, and charges through your system in 30 minutes like the 5:15 from Paddington. Fruit contains the monosaccharide sugar fructose, which is completely metabolised into ATP, the energy form the body uses to sustain its life-systems. Your brain runs on nothing but glucose, and fruit is your most efficient source of this essential blood sugar without provoking excess insulin. Besides, blood sugar levels rise and normalise after adequate fruit consumption, meaning that your hunger switch is turned off and you eat less food.

Fruit (uncontaminated with pesticides, of course), is rich in hard-working enzymes, vitamins, amino acids, minerals and fibre, and is an extremely low-taxing amino acid source in the morning, which makes it ideal for breakfast. And what do amino acids build? That's right. Proper human proteins. *This is by far the body's preferred way of constructing protein – from the human body's amino acid pool.* Fruit is alluring with its shapes and colours, has the most exotic tastes, and is loved by almost everybody. Those few who hate fruit are usually addicted to heavy, processed foods, which they indiscriminately combine with fruit into an apocalyptic jam-preserve, which will produce fermentation, putrefaction, acid residues and the resultant graveyard gas and corpse-like breath. If your breath smells like something has died... it has. And guess what sometimes gets the blame? Fruit! Naturally this is a no-no, and we'll have a look at why there are set rules for fruit consumption, which, if followed, clear up all the bad press in which fruit has been embroiled over the years.

Raw fruit has been described as 'a perfect food' because humans have been found in the past to survive for long periods on it. Within the past seventy years however, commercially grown fruit, cereals and vegetables have lost a significant part of their vitamin and mineral content due to harvesting before the fruit is ripe, and those chemically laden, over-farming techniques. Fruit-only diets should be avoided because they lack a spectrum of nutrients contained in other foods, which must be consumed.[5] The mineral deficiency in fruits and other organic matter can be easily and simply remedied using mineral supplementation, which shall be discussed later.

Here are the Ten Fruit Commandments. Tattoo them on your cookie jar:

- *Eat fruit <u>on an empty stomach</u> any time during the day*
- *Always leave 30 minutes after fruit consumption before eating foods other than fruit*
- *Leave at least 3 hours after a properly combined meal before consuming fruit. This allows the previous meal to leave the stomach and avoids putrefaction and fermentation of the previous meal*
- *Before noon, consume only fruit*
- *Never combine fruit with any other foods*
- *Never eat fruit AFTER a meal as a dessert*
- *Steer clear of bananas, avocados and dates <u>in the morning</u> (but not at other times). These are heavier on the digestion, but can be eaten, properly combined, during the Appropriation Cycle, after noon*
- *If you get hungry during the morning, eat another piece of fruit and keep munching until the blood sugar levels normalise and your hunger abates*
- *Eat organic fruit only where possible*
- *Do not eat processed, canned or cooked fruit, which normally contain sugars, e-additives and other aliens*

---

[5] **McCance & Widdowson** "The chemical composition of foods", special report series no. 235/297, Medical Research Council, & MAFF, 1940, 1946, 1960, 1976 &1991

Fruit is the perfect food when eaten on its own. Although sometimes described as an acid, malic acid from apples, for example, actually yields an alkali ash in the body, unless it is combined with other foods, whereupon the usual acid gunk is produced. During the morning Elimination Cycle, fruit is invaluable in assisting in detoxification and the elimination of toxins. The fruit consumer, properly following the above rules, will experience a rapid return of energy, a steady and satisfying weight-loss as toxins and detritus leave (sometimes resembling diarrhoea), and an overall feeling of health and well-being, as these nutrients use the vital juices of fruit to gain instant access to the energy processes of the body. All these benefits just from consuming fruit the right way? YES!! And we haven't even got to the really good tools yet.

If fruit is eaten with, or even after other foods, problems will more often than not result. This is because the Fruit Express is trying to get through to its destination quickly, and its clear path is blocked by a Chicken Fried Rice Goods Train lumbering through at walking speed. The resultant wincing collision causes the liquefied fruit juices to combine with China's finest and this fruity morass will begin to spoil. Proteins in the chicken putrefy and the rice carbohydrates ferment, resulting in the usual problems. Culturally we have come to view fruit as a dessert, which is nutritional heresy, in that fruit will always charge down the tunnel before hitting the back end of the Beef Risotto you chose to wolf down half an hour earlier. Once again, fruit should always be consumed on an empty stomach for happy smiles and care-free miles.

BREAKFAST FRUIT IDEAS

(and other juices and smoothies for the rest of the day)

BREAKFAST SMOOTHIES

A special breakfast combination is:
225 g cherries
1-2 small punnets (small tray containers) **strawberries**
1 punnet **redcurrants**
1 punnet **raspberries**
1 punnet **blueberries**
5 g of **apricot kernels**
juice 1 lemon

Prepare the fruit in a bowl and sprinkle the kernels on the fruit and mix. If you should feel hungry mid-morning, tuck into more fresh fruit. Have three or four pieces of fruit between breakfast and lunch. <u>The idea is to eat only fruit until midday</u>. Avoid bananas and avocados until lunch. These should be consumed, properly combined, any time after noon.

Another breakfast combination is:
Small handful of seedless green grapes
A small handful black or other **sweet cherries**
1 sweet or semi-sweet dessert apple (including **seeds***)*
1 ripe nectarine or peach

Again, if you feel hungry during the morning, a few grapes and cherries will increase blood sugar levels and normalise hunger pangs. Follow the Fruit Commandments and do not eat any fruit within 30 minutes of a main meal or three after.

Any of these combinations can be liquidized to form a refreshing juice drink.

MELON COMBINATION JUICE

Peel and de-seed half a watermelon and add a peeled and de-seeded cantaloupe melon. Chop into cubes and blend together in a juicer. Different varieties of melon can be experimented with in order to ring the changes.[6]

OTHER JUICE COMBINATIONS

Apple, *dates and banana (This one's for a snack during the afternoon. Avoid bananas for breakfast because of their concentrated composition)*
Apricots, plums and seedless grapes
Banana, **apple** *and peach (afternoon only)*
Watermelon and **raspberries**

And when available fresh, as they often are in larger supermarkets, try lychees, mangoes, paw paw and kiwi fruit, all prepared and juiced. **Apricot kernels** can always be ground up in a coffee grinder and added to smoothies or juices for added taste.

HOW TO SPROUT WHEATBERRIES FOR WHEATGRASS JUICING

Hard organic wheatberries
Wide-mouthed glass jar
Nylon mesh or muslin
2 plastic trays 30 x 35 cm (12 x 14 in)
peat moss, compost or topsoil

Fill a cup with wheatberries. Wash and rinse them thoroughly to remove any dirt. Put wheatberries in a jar filled with water and leave them to soak overnight. Drain and rinse the berries. Cover the jar with muslin and leave the berries to sprout for 12 hours.

Put an inch of soil in one tray and scatter the seeds on top. Water the seeds and cover with the other tray. After about 3 days, remove the top tray of sprouting berries onto a window ledge. Make sure you do not put them in direct sunlight as this may dry out the berries. Keep the berries moist, but not too wet. Cut the wheatgrass when it is about

---

[6] **Lee, W H** *Getting the Best Out of Your Juicer.*

18cm/7inches high. Try to cut the wheatgrass as close to the soil as possible, as this is where the greatest concentration of nutrients is found.

TROPICAL FRUIT SALAD

1 1/4 cups of apple juice
1 ripe mango
*1 punnet **blackberries***
1 passion fruit
1 small fresh pineapple
2 star fruit
2 kiwi fruit
1 pomegranate

Pour the juice into a container with a lid. Peel the mango, mark into small cubes, cutting through to the stone. Cut the flesh off the stone. Halve the passion fruit and scoop the seeds into the container. Cut the green top off the pineapple, then cut off the peel. Cut into chunks. Add these and the blackberries to the container. Peel and slice the kiwi fruit. Quarter the pomegranate. Bend back the skin, and carefully loosen the seeds and add to the container. Discard any white pith. Cover the container and chill for 1 hour to allow the flavours to develop fully. Turn into a glass serving dish and serve very cold.

VEGGIE JUICE

A great starter is to prepare a juice made from 2 parts of carrot to 1 part of celery. Any green leaf vegetable can be added. Another starter uses:

6 tomatoes
3 carrots
5 celery stalks
2 red peppers, seeded
¼ beetroot, cooked
a squeeze of lemon

Always wash the vegetables thoroughly. Cut all the ingredients into suitable slices for your juicer and combine thoroughly. Can be served with a celery stick.

MELON WITH MINTED RASPBERRY

1 honeydew melon
1 punnet of **raspberries**
1 tbsp chopped mint
A few sprigs of mint to decorate

Cut the melon into eight wedges. De-seed and peel. Cover and chill. Puree the raspberries into a blender with the chopped mint. Pass the puree through a sieve and into a measuring jug. Chill until ready to serve. Lay the melon on serving plates. Pour the raspberry juice sauce over the centres of the melon wedges and decorate with the sprigs of mint.[7]

FRUIT IDEAS FOR THE AFTERNOON

The following recipes are ideal for a quick and nutritious snack in the afternoon or before 8pm in the evening. Bear in mind that these preparations, because of the bananas, will not digest as quickly as high water-content fruit itself, and so longer should be left between consuming these and eating a main meal.

FRUIT SMOOTHIE

1 cup of fresh orange or apple juice
1 banana
¼ papaya, 1 **apple (inc. seeds)**, *1 peach or 1 cup of* **strawberries**

Place the juice, banana and fruit in a blender.[8]

BERRY SMOOTHIE
(great for kids)

1 cup fresh orange, apple or tangerine juice
1 cup fresh berries – **strawberries, raspberries** *or* **blueberries**
1 or 2 large bananas

---

[7] **Humphries, Carolyn** *7-Day Low Cholesterol Diet Plan,* Foulsham, 1999
[8] **Diamond, Harvey** *Fit For Life*, Bantam Books, 1985, p.242; also **Diamond, Marilyn** *Fit For Life Cookbook*, Bantam Books, 1991

Combine all the ingredients in a blender until smooth and thick.

MELON AND BLUEBERRY SUPREME

½ cantaloupe, diced, or in balls
2 peaches, peeled and sliced
1 cup of **blueberries**
1 small banana, sliced

Mix all the fruits together. Great on a hot summer day.

DATE OR STRAWBERRY SHAKE

1 cup fresh almond milk (see below)
2 frozen bananas
6 pitted dates or 6 fresh or frozen **strawberries**

Place almond milk and fruit in a blender. Blend until thick and creamy. If you like a thinner shake, use 1½ bananas.

FRESH ALMOND MILK

¼ cup raw almonds
1 cup cold water
2 tsp pure maple syrup (optional)

Nut and seed milks were used for centuries in Europe, Asia, and by the American Indians, and they are still used throughout the world as easily digestible substitutes for cows' milk. Those made from almonds or sesame seeds are excellent sources for easily assimilated calcium and they are delicious! – Harvey Diamond

Blanch almonds by adding them to a large skillet containing ½ inch of boiling water, allowing them to sit in water as it boils for about 30 seconds. Drain and pop skins off. Place blanched almonds in a blender with 1 cup of cold water. Run blender at high speed for 2-3 minutes, until a thick white milk has formed. If you are going to drink almond milk straight, strain it through a fine sieve. If there is a lot of pulp, you have not blended long enough. If you are going to use the milk in a shake, there is no need to strain.[9]

---

[9] Diamond, Harvey, *Fit For Life*, op. cit. pp.249-250

WATER – THE STUFF OF LIFE
by Phillip Day

Another important point is water. Once again traditional medicine believes water is largely nothing more than an inert solvent the body uses to transport the soluent (minerals, proteins, enzymes, etc.) around the body. Yet water is far from inert. The blood is made up of a large percentage of watery serum. Our cells literally owe their life to an adequate supply of fresh, clean water. When the body does not receive a constant, reliable supply of water, it has to ration what's available and cut back on certain functions in order to make the supply go round. Essential systems like the brain are prioritised, others are impaired or cut back until the brain has decided a reliable source of water has been garnered.

Here's the rub. Most citizens have become CHRONICALLY AND DANGEROUSLY DEHYDRATED (especially the elderly), since we decided water was too bland to drink and axed it in favour of tea, coffee, beer, wine, sodas, flavoured water and other chemical-laced water alternatives. This has proven a disastrous and dangerous move for the body and society's health in general, and we have been reaping the whirlwind in terms of disease and death as a result. Many doctors today cannot readily identify the many water-deficient diseases and associated pains, and so the inevitable prescribing of drugs to treat the symptoms usually results.

The body needs in excess of four pints of water daily (2 litres). Water is used by the body for digestion, detoxifying cells, watering the lungs, keeping the body alkalised and a host of cleaning duties. Water expert Dr Fereydoon Batmanghelidj maintains that asthmas, allergies, diabetes, arthritis, angina, stomach upsets, chronic intestinal complaints and certain other degenerative illnesses are the body's many cries for water, complaints which are dramatically improved with a consistent and long-term intake of fresh, clean water.[10] Dr Batman's best-selling book has helped thousands quash long-term health problems effortlessly and inexpensively. Coffee, tea, diet sodas, beer and a host of other liquids do not qualify as 'clean, fresh water' for the

---

[10] Batmanghelidj, F, *Your Body's Many Cries for Water*, op. cit.

body and should not be consumed by the cancer patient. Many of these are diuretic (water expelling) in their effect because of their chemical compositions. Cancer patients especially should be consuming 4 pints of water a day[11] as part of their intake of vital nutrients, provided they do not have any renal (kidney) damage or disease that will cause complications with urine production resulting from the intake of additional water. Flushing the body with CONSISTENT, long-term water consumption is a superb way to assist with detoxification and hydration and is especially important for cancer patients. Drink a glass half an hour before a meal and then two glasses around two and a half hours afterwards for optimal digestive effects.[12] The remainder of the day's intake of water can be throughout the day.

An indication of dehydration is if the urine is thick, dark yellow and rank in smell. Here the body is cutting back on water usage throughout its various systems due to a chronic shortage.[13] The resultant urine the kidneys make is thus thick with waste consisting of less water than normal, giving rise to a more concentrated urine solution. The body can take several weeks to use water to full effect, so ensure that this vital health bonus is used consistently and effectively.

---

[11] A carbon filter attached to a tap/faucet is adequate for producing chlorine- and soluent-free water to drink. This is preferable to plastic-bottled water which can be contaminated with chemicals from the plastic. Water in glass bottles is fine. In the event that you live in a fluoridated area, reverse osmosis or backwash filters should be used to remove the fluoride poisons.
[12] For heartburn, drink water! Every time you feel the pain starting, drink some water. The symptoms usually pass within a few minutes. Constipation too is a sure sign of water starvation, as the body's intestinal peristaltic action extracts every precious drop of water from your food to save losing it, creating gridlock.
[13] Note that B vitamin intakes can also darken the urine. An ammoniac smell to the urine may also indicate depletion of freely available alkalising minerals to neutralise acid residues (ash) in the body, leading to the kidneys producing ammonia to render the solution alkali.

A FEW 'JUICY' TIPS

Heart Disease
4 medium tomatoes
1 small sweet potato, unpeeled
1 oz fresh root ginger
2 sticks celery with leaves
2 tsp kelp powder

This little circulatory boost to the system will aid function of white cells and stimulate the thyroid.

Hepatitis
16 oz cherries, stoned
*16 oz **strawberries**, topped*

Very fast and effective in neutralising uric acid. Super-rich in vitamin C bioflavonoids and vitamin A.

Infections
3 unpeeled apples
2 celery sticks with leaves
1 medium beetroot, with leaves
½ small round cabbage

Powerful tonic and bone-builder.

Skin Problems
4 unpeeled organic carrots
2 asparagus spears
½ iceberg lettuce
***spinach**, large handful*

The blood builder – which means more skin nutrients are carried to the surface where they are needed.

Good Mouthkeeping
6 radishes with leaves
4 unpeeled carrots, remove top and bottom

4 tomatoes
1 spring onion
leek, cut lengthways in strips
Worcester sauce, optional

Sexual performance
Ginger 1 oz fresh root
watermelon ¼, with seeds and skin.

Dilates the blood vessels and improves circulation.[14]

---

[14] Van Straten, Michael, *Super Juice*, Mitchell Beazley, 1999

DETOX RECIPES

The purpose of the following section is to provide recipes that will assist the body in cleansing itself. These recipes are ideal for someone who is ill and wishes to cleanse and alkalise their body to assist in the regeneration of health. These recipes are not recommended for a permanent dietary plan and should be used with adequate intakes of minerals and vitamins as part of a basic supplementary program. Please consult your health practitioner if you have a serious illness before embarking on any change in diet. For a healthy selection of recipes for an on-going dietary regimen including 80% alkali ash and 20% acidic ash foods (tables at the back), please see the Maintenance Recipes in the next section.

SOUPS

PARSNIP AND GINGER SOUP

*3 tbsp **apricot kernel oil***
2 medium onions
500 g parsnips
3 cm fresh ginger, peeled and grated
grated zest and juice of two oranges
1 litre of vegetable stock
sea salt and freshly ground pepper

Heat the oil and sauté the onions gently until they are soft and transparent. Add the parsnips and ginger and cook for a further five minutes. Add the orange rind and the stock and bring to simmering point. Simmer for about 40 minutes until the parsnips are tender. Allow to cool a little, then liquidise and sieve into a clean saucepan. Add the orange juice and seasoning to taste. Reheat gently.[15]

TOMATO, LEMON & CARROT SOUP

3 tbsp olive oil
2 medium onions, skinned and finely chopped
500 g carrots, peeled and chopped
500 g tomatoes, skinned, seeded and chopped
grated zest of 2 lemons and juice of one lemon

---

[15] MacDonald, Claire

36

1 litre stock (home-made if possible or Marigold organic vegetable stock)

Heat the oil and sauté the onions until soft and transparent. Add the carrots and cook for 5 minutes then add the tomatoes, lemon rind and stock. Bring to simmering point and simmer for about thirty minutes until the carrots are tender. Cool and liquidise and then sieve for a smoother texture into a clean saucepan. Stir in the lemon juice and season with sea salt and freshly milled black pepper. Reheat gently and pour into soup bowls. Decorate with a small slice of lemon and finely chopped parsley.

PUMPKIN SOUP

3 lb pumpkin
2 leeks, trimmed and sliced
1 ¾ pints chicken or vegetable stock
¼ tsp grated nutmeg
1 tsp ground **apricot kernels**
Sea salt and black pepper
1 oz petit pois
8 oz **spinach leaves,** *finely chopped*

Cut out the flesh from the pumpkin, discarding the seeds and fibres. Cut into chunks (2 cm). Grease the saucepan with butter. Add the leeks and cook gently, covered for 10 minutes. Add the stock, pumpkin chunks, nutmeg, apricot kernels and salt and pepper to taste. Bring to boil, cover and simmer for 30 minutes. Puree the soup in a blender until smooth. Return to the pan. Stir in the petit pois and spinach, heat through and serve immediately.[16]

MINT AND MUNG BEAN SOUP

1 bunch spring onions
1lb fresh shelled peas
¼ pint coconut milk
2 tsps freshly chopped mint or tarragon
sea salt and pepper to taste
mung bean sprouts

---

[16] **Berry, Mary** *Soups, Starters and Salads*, Dorling Kindersley, 1995

Clean the spring onions and chop the white and green parts finely. Take a medium-sized saucepan and add the peas, chopped spring onions and water. Cook until the peas are tender, which takes about 20–25 minutes for fresh peas. Let this cool slightly and then stir in the coconut milk and fresh mint or tarragon. Season well with sea salt and pepper. Sprinkle mung bean sprouts on top.

WATERCRESS SOUP

2 potatoes, coarsely chopped
1 onion, finely chopped
*4 oz **watercress**, tough stalks removed*
1½ pints of vegetable or chicken stock
¼ pint milk (preferably goat's), ¼ pint water
1 bay leaf
sea salt and black pepper, to taste
Dash cream to garnish!

Grease a saucepan with butter. Add the onion and cook gently for 1-3 minutes until soft. Add the potatoes and the watercress and cook for about 5 minutes until the watercress is wilted. Pour in the chicken/vegetable stock and milk/water, add the bay leaf, and salt and pepper to taste.

Bring the mixture to a boil, cover and simmer gently for 15 minutes until the potatoes are tender. Remove the bay leaf and discard. Puree the soup in a blender until smooth. Return the soup to a clean pan, reheat and taste for seasoning.[17]

HOT AND SOUR SOUP

2 dried Chinese mushrooms
¼ head Chinese cabbage, sliced
2 ½ pints chicken or vegetable stock
2 oz Chinese noodles, such as rice sticks
*3 oz **bamboo shoots,** sliced*
3 oz cooked chicken, diced
*1 oz **bean sprouts***
3 tbsp corn flour mixed with 3 tbsp water

---

[17] Ibid.

2 eggs, beaten
2 tbsp white wine vinegar
1 tbsp dark soy sauce
¼ tsp each, white pepper and cayenne pepper
2 tsp sesame oil
2 spring onions, thinly sliced
coriander sprigs

Put the mushrooms into a bowl, cover with hot water, leave to soak for 30 minutes. Meanwhile, put the sliced cabbage into a large saucepan, add the stock and bring to the boil. Simmer for about 15 minutes. Break the noodles into pieces. Simmer in boiling, salted water for 3-4 minutes until just tender. Drain and set aside.

Drain the mushrooms, reserving the soaking liquid. Pour the liquid through a sieve lined with a paper towel to catch any grit. Squeeze the mushrooms dry, then cut them into thin strips. Reserve the mushrooms and their liquid.

Add the bamboo shoots, chicken, bean sprouts, noodles and the mushrooms and their liquid to the cabbage and stock. Heat until almost boiling, then stir in the corn flour mixture. Simmer until the soup thickens slightly, then drizzle in the beaten eggs to form strands.

Combine the vinegar, soy sauce, white and cayenne peppers, and pour into the soup. Taste for seasoning. Drizzle a little sesame oil over each serving, and garnish with spring onion slices and coriander sprigs. Serve at once. [18]

TOMATO, LEMON AND CARROT SOUP
3 tbsp **apricot kernel oil**
2 medium onions skinned and finely chopped
500 g carrots peeled and chopped
500 g tomatoes, skinned, seeded and chopped
grated zest of 2 lemons and juice of 1 lemon
1 litre of stock (home-made if possible or Marigold organic vegetable stock)

---

[18] Ibid.

Heat the oil and sauté the onions until soft and transparent. Add the carrots and cook for 5 minutes. Then add the tomatoes, lemon rind and stock. Bring to simmering point and simmer for about thirty minutes until carrots are tender. Cool and liquidise and then sieve for a smoother texture into a clean saucepan. Stir in the lemon juice and season to taste with sea salt and freshly ground pepper. Reheat gently and pour into soup bowls. Decorate with a small slice of lemon and finely chopped parsley.[19]

VEGETABLE JUICE COCKTAIL

If you have a juicer, try a vegetable juice cocktail for a pre-lunch or supper drink:

8 carrots
2 stalks of celery
¼ small beetroot
1 tomato
1 red or green pepper
fresh parsley

Prepare the vegetables as usual and put through the juicer.

NEUTRALISE THE LEAD IN YOUR BODY

Lead can be sealed in the bones permanently without risk of ever leaking by making sure that your body receives an adequate daily intake of those few minerals known to harden the bones. Boron can be obtained in the food supply by frequently eating celery, cauliflower, turnips and potatoes with the skin intact. Beets can also be juiced along with their skins. Sometimes they need to be slightly cooked first. The next two recipes are ideal for this.

RED CABBAGE AND BEET BEVERAGE

¼ cup cranberry juice
*¼ cup **fresh cranberries** or whole cranberry sauce*

---

[19] Lee, W.H., op. cit.

½ cup red cabbage, steamed until tender
½ cup canned beets, with a tsp of beet juice
¼ tsp tarragon vinegar
½ cup ice cubes

Place all ingredients in a blender or juicer until smooth. Serve warm or cold.[20]

BEETS WITH BERRY MEDLEY

¾ cup cold cranberry juice
*¼ cup whole cranberry sauce or **fresh cranberries***
1 small beet, steamed
*¼ cup fresh s**trawberries***
1 or 2 tsp honey
2/3 cup ice cubes

Blend until smooth.[21]

MISO SOUP

People may think that miso is a high-sodium food. Actually, there are 2,200 milligrams of sodium in a tablespoon of dark brown miso. But you can choose a less salty variety. The easy way of distinguishing is by looking at the colours. Avoid the dark brown type; light-brown (2,160 milligrams sodium per tablespoon) or white miso (1,000 milligrams sodium per tablespoon) would be less salty. Also, *mugi* miso has 1,800 milligrams of sodium per tablespoon. Another secret of making less salty miso soup is to add a lot of ingredients. Most of all, the ratio of soup per cup will be decreased if you use plenty of vegetables, compared with selecting only wakame seaweed. Making thick *dashi* (Japanese style soup stock) is also a good way to create tasteful miso soup without adding too much miso.

You can find miso in Oriental stores or health food stores. Ready-made miso soup might be more common on a regular supermarket shelf, but most of these include fish ingredients. Furthermore,

---

[20] **Heinerman John** *Encyclopedia of Vitamins and Minerals*, Prentice Hall, 1999
[21] Ibid.

convenient miso soup is not as delicious as one you would make yourself.

Miso soup is very simple to cook. Boil ingredients in the *dashi* (stock), then add miso. That's it. If you want a good soup however, you should remember some secrets behind the simplicity, just as with cooking other Japanese dishes. Here are some tips to help you make great miso soup.

- When you add miso into *dashi*, put miso in a ladle and stir it with some *dashi* at first. If you skip this process, the miso won't dissolve well.
- Add miso little by little. I found that the miso sold in the US is saltier than Japanese miso (this means VERY salty), so be careful, especially if you want a low-sodium soup.
- Never boil the soup after putting miso into the *dashi*. It spoils the flavor of the miso.
- Make sure to serve miso soup hot.
- Create a good combination of ingredients. Seasonal vegetables are preferable.
- Consider the possible combinations of miso and other ingredients.
- If possible, add *suikuchi*, a condiment, which is used for adding to the aroma. *Suikuchi* may be thinly cut long green onions or welsh onions, grated ginger, thinly cut Japanese basil (*shiso*), *yuzu* (a sort of citron) peel, *shichimi* (seven-spice chili), or roasted sesame seeds. Most of these are available in Oriental stores. *Suikuchi* is not necessary, but it increases miso soup flavour double, triple, or more!
- There are recommended combinations of miso soup and *suikuchi*, so please refer to the following recipes if you are a beginner at miso soup cooking.
- Avoid leaving miso soup overnight, because 'fresh' miso soup is definitely the best. If you are eating left-over miso soup, add a little more *suikuchi* than usual.
- If the package is not opened, miso can be preserved at room temperature. Once you use miso, keep it in a refrigerator and

seal the package with plastic wrap. Finish miso as soon as possible.[22]

BASIC JAPANESE SOUP STOCK
(vegan-style dashi)
(serves 4-5)

Though Japanese usually make soup stock with *kombu* and *katsuobushi* (shaved dried bonito fish), or *niboshi* (small dried fish), this Zen Buddhist style soup is satisfying enough. *Kombu* (kelp) seaweed and dried *shiitake* mushrooms are great for making tasty soup. We recommend keeping dashi in the refrigerator or freezer, to use anytime you want.

5 cups water
5 pieces kombu seaweed (each about 1 inch long), cut in thirds crosswise, and cleaned with a slightly damp paper towel or cloth. For making delicious soup stock, you should buy high quality dashi-kombu, thick and straight, as much as possible
5 dried shiitake mushrooms, cleaned and rinsed

Place water in a saucepan. Soak the *kombu* and *shiitake* mushrooms in the water for at least 15 minutes, until they become tender enough. (If time permits, more than three hours to overnight is much better.) Heat the water over high heat and reduce heat once it boils. Remove *kombu* just below boiling point.

After around five minutes, remove saucepan from the heat. The boiling time depends on the size of *shiitake* mushrooms and the soaking time. Remove the *shiitake* mushrooms from the water, and save them for use in other recipes.

Notes: *Kombu* and dried *shiitake* mushrooms are available in Oriental stores. You can make dried *shiitake* mushrooms by drying raw shiitake mushrooms in the sun for a couple of days.

You can make the soup stock with one ingredient, *kombu* or dried *shiitake* mushrooms. In this case, double the portion of the chosen

---

[22] *Vegetarian Journal*, Jan/Feb 2000. "It's Japanese Soul Food" by Hiroko Kato

ingredient and soak longer. If you cook with only *shiitake* mushrooms, it's better to soak them in warm water. For making thick *dashi*, increase the ingredients or soak them longer.

MISO SOUP WITH DAIKON
(serves 4)

Especially good for a winter dish. Oriental people believe miso and daikon make the body warm, and we believe it really works!

4 cups of vegan style dashi (see first miso recipe above)
2/3 pound of daikon*, julienned
1-3 teaspoons of miso (all types can be used, but in winter, shiro miso would be the best)
Recommended suikuchi: Grated ginger, thinly cut welsh onion, thinly cut Japanese basil (shiso), yuzu peel, shichimi (seven-spice chili), or roasted sesame seeds

Place dashi in a saucepan. Put daikon into dashi and boil them together. Remove scum. When daikon becomes tender, reduce the heat and add 1 teaspoon of miso at first. Taste and if you need more miso, add it little by little. Remove the pan from the heat before the miso soup boils again. Put a pinch of suikuchi on miso soup. Serve hot.

Recommended arrangement of ingredients: Daikon and wakame, daikon and **spinach**, daikon and satoimo (Japanese taro), etc.

*You can find daikon at supermarkets or Oriental stores. If you can get daikon with leaves, use the leaves, too. In this case, cut daikon leaves into bite size pieces and first lightly stir-fry them with a little apricot kernel or sesame oil. Add them to dashi before adding miso.

MISO SOUP WITH POTATO AND ONION
(serves 4)

Typical American vegetables can make savory miso soup too!

4 cups of vegan-style dashi (see first miso recipe above)
½ pound potato, peeled and cut into small pieces
½ pound of onion, sliced
1-3 teaspoons of miso (any type can be used)
Recommended suikuchi: Thinly cut welsh onion, thinly cut

Japanese basil (shiso), shichimi (seven-spice chili), or roasted sesame seeds

Place dashi in a saucepan. Add potato and onion to dashi and boil them. Remove scum. When the vegetables become tender, reduce the heat and add 1 teaspoon of miso at first. Taste, and if you need more miso, add it little by little. Remove the pan from the heat before the miso soup boils again. Put a pinch of suikuchi on miso soup. Serve hot.

Recommended arrangement of ingredients: Potato and wakame, potato and snow peas, onion and wakame, etc.

MISO SOUP WITH TOFU AND WAKAME
(serves 4)
This is the most basic style of Japanese miso soup. Master it first!

4 cups vegan style dashi (first miso recipe above)
1 ounce wakame (dried seaweed, available at Oriental specialty stores)
10 ounces tofu (any type), diced
1-3 teaspoons of miso (any type except shiro miso)
Recommended suikuchi: Thinly cut long green onion or welsh onion, grated ginger, thinly cut Japanese basil (shiso), yuzu (Japanese citron) peels, shichimi (seven-spice chili), or roasted sesame seeds

Place dashi in a saucepan and boil. Add wakame to dashi. Next, put tofu into dashi. When dashi boils, reduce the heat and add 1 teaspoon of miso at first. Taste, and if you need more miso, add it little by little. Remove the pan from the heat before the miso soup boils again. Put a pinch of suikuchi on miso soup. Serve hot.

Recommended arrangement of ingredients: Tofu and snow peas, tofu and chopped green long onions, tofu and chopped Chinese chives, wakame and snow peas, wakame and potato, wakame and onion, wakame and green onion, wakame and bean sprouts, wakame and **spinach**, wakame and daikon, wakame and Chinese chives, etc.

MISO SOUP WITH EGGPLANT
(serves 4)

Eggplant miso soup is recommended for the summer season or the beginning of autumn. In Oriental medicine, eggplant has the function of cooling down the body heat. Just for this miso soup, simple is best. I suggest not mixing any other ingredients with eggplant, except suikuchi.

4 cups of vegan style dashi (first miso recipe above)
1/3 pound of eggplant, caps removed and cut into bite size pieces.
If possible, grill lightly.
1-3 teaspoons of miso (all types except shiro miso. Brown miso would be the best)
Recommended suikuchi: Grated ginger, thin- ly cut Japanese basil (shiso), shichimi (seven-spice chili), or roasted sesame seeds

Place dashi in a saucepan and boil. Add eggplant to dashi. When eggplant becomes tender, reduce heat and add 1 teaspoon of miso at first. Taste, and if you need more miso, add it little by little. Remove the pan from the heat before miso soup boils again. Put a pinch of suikuchi on miso soup. Serve hot.

GARAM GARBANZOS

*1 can of **chickpeas (garbanzos)** drained*
1 tbsp garam masala
sea salt

Dry the chickpeas on kitchen paper. Spread on a non-stick baking tray. Mix the garam masala with a pinch of sea salt, coat the chickpeas thoroughly. Bake in a pre-heated oven at 180C/350F/Gas Mark 4 for about 50 minutes, until crisp and golden. Cool and store in an airtight tin.

GREAT GUACAMOLE

1 avocado
½ tsp Spike or Parsley Patch Mexican Seasoning (or similar)
½ tsp cumin
½ tsp dried oregano

Cut avocado in half, remove seed and scoop out pulp, reserving seed. In a small bowl, mash with fork, mixing in seasonings. Whip with fork until creamy. If you are not going to serve guacamole immediately, return seed to bowl to prevent discoloration, cover tightly, and refrigerate until ready to use. Serve as a dip for natural corn chips, celery stalks, or other raw vegetables.[23]

DRY ROASTED NUTS
Unsalted peanuts, almond, hazelnuts or **cashews** are best.

Put 3 tbsp raw shelled nuts in a heavy non-stick frying pan and toss over a moderate heat until golden.

HOT SPICY NUTS
Prepare the nuts as above only add a small amount of organic soy or Worcester sauce to the nuts before frying. Remove from heat and sprinkle with chilli powder and apple spice. Toss thoroughly and allow to cool before storing.

SNAPPY CUCUMBER AND STRAWBERRY SERVINGS
½ cucumber
*1 punnet of **strawberries***
*ground **apricot kernels***
French dressing
fresh ground black pepper

Peel ½ a cucumber, halve lengthways and remove the seeds, cut into chunks. Hull and halve the strawberries and toss in French dressing. Sprinkle with ground black pepper and apricot kernel dust.

---

[23] Diamond, Harvey, *Fit For Life*, op. cit. p.226

SALADS - THE BEST

Raw foods are best. They reserve their full complement of enzymes without the heat of cooking (anything over 45C) destroying them. For those suffering debilitating illness, the majority of foods consumed should be raw. Enzyme superfoods or capsules may also be taken, the latter consumed on an empty stomach. Briefly steaming foods appears not to disrupt enzymes. Bear in mind cooking damage whenever you prepare foods.

SPINACH SALAD

*1lb organic **spinach***
1 medium sized red cabbage
1 medium onion
4 oz apricots (optional)
2 tbsp French dressing
2 oz toasted sunflower seeds
ground apricot kernels

Tear the spinach leaves into bite-sized pieces and place in a serving dish. Add the sliced cabbage, sliced apricots and chopped onion. Pour over the French dressing and mix thoroughly. Sprinkle with the sunflower seeds and ground apricot kernels and serve.

MILLET SALAD

*8 oz **millet***
16 oz filtered water
sea salt
large carrots, sliced into very thin matchsticks
*1 cup **fenugreek sprouts***
¼ cucumber chopped
*4 oz **garden peas***
black pepper
a few sprigs of mint or coriander or lovage

Place the millet into boiling salted water. Stir once and cover with the lid. Reduce the heat and simmer gently until all the water is absorbed and the millet soft. Leave to cool. Fluff up the millet with a fork and mix with all the remaining ingredients.

MILLET AND CELERY SALAD

*¾ cup **millet***
sea salt and fresh ground black pepper
½ green pepper
4 sprig onions
2 sticks celery
1/3 cup sunflower seeds
2 tbsp extra virgin olive oil
1 tbsp cider or wine vinegar
2 tbsp fresh parsley, chopped

Cook the millet until tender in three times its volume of water, with a little sea salt added, for about 20 minutes. Chop the green pepper, spring onions and celery. Toast the sunflower seeds under the grill until lightly browned. Fluff the millet with a fork. Add the oil and vinegar and mix. Stir in the chopped vegetables and parsley and the toasted sunflower seeds. Adjust the seasoning as required.[24]

FRESH TOMATO, BASIL AND PINE-NUT SALAD

12 Roma or plum tomatoes, chopped
*250 g/8 oz/1 cup **pine nuts,** soaked for 30 minutes, then drained*
365 g/12 oz/1 ½ cups fresh basil
½ tsp sea salt
cayenne pepper to taste

Mix ingredients together and enjoy.

BIG BEAN SALAD

6 oz fine green beans, topped
*1 can red **kidney beans**, rinsed and drained*
*1 can of **fava** (butter beans)*
*1 packet of **beansprouts***
1 packet of cherry tomatoes, halved

FOR THE DRESSING:
1 shallot, peeled and finely chopped

---

[24] **Leneman Leah** *Easy Vegan Cooking,* Harpers and Collins, 1998

2 oz roasted chopped hazelnuts
*1 oz **cashew nuts***
*ground **apricot kernels***
2 tbsp red wine vinegar
1 tbsp wholegrain mustard
4 tbsp olive oil
sea salt and fresh ground black pepper

Blanch the green beans for 3 minutes in boiling water. Drain then plunge into cold water and leave for 5 minutes. Drain thoroughly and place in a large bowl. Stir in the red kidney beans, fava beans, beansprouts and cherry tomatoes, then set aside. In a small bowl, combine all of the dressing ingredients and mix together well. Just before serving, add the dressing to the salad and toss thoroughly to coat.[25]

SPROUTED LENTIL SALAD

8 oz broccoli florets
*8 oz sprouted **lentils***
1 red pepper
2 oz raisins
1 tsp freshly grated ginger
4-6 tbsp olive oil mixed with lemon juice and fresh or dried herbs

Cover the broccoli florets with boiling water and leave to stand for 5 minutes. Drain and cool. Core and de-seed the pepper and dice roughly. Arrange sprouted lentils on a serving dish. Mix together the broccoli florets, pepper and raisins and pile in the centre. Mix the ginger with the dressing and pour over the salad. Serve at once.

SIMPLE COUSCOUS SALAD

120 g couscous
120 ml filtered water
1 tbsp extra virgin olive oil
*1 small can of **chickpeas***
2 strips unwaxed lemon peel
1 tsp sea salt

---

[25] *Tesco Recipe Collection*, June 1996

Place the couscous in a bowl, pour the boiling water on top, and add the salt, lemon peel and olive oil. Leave for about an hour. The couscous should have swelled to about twice its original size. When cool, fork over and add small can of chickpeas well drained and rinsed, a handful of ready to eat dried apricots roughly chopped, 1 chopped mint, moisten with 1 tbsp olive oil.

Couscous prepared as above can also be mixed with grilled Mediterranean vegetables such as red peppers, courgettes (zucchini) plus mixture of your favourite fresh herbs, mixed with a simple lemon and oil dressing.

TABBOULEH

150 g bulgur or cracked wheat
2 bunches flat leafed parsley, chopped finely
8-9 spring onions, trimmed and finely sliced, including some of the green parts
6 organic tomatoes
10-12 tsp olive oil
juice 2-3 unwaxed lemons
2 tbsp chopped mint

Put the bulgur wheat in a bowl, cover with water, leave to soak for 30- 60 minutes. Drain in a sieve and place in a serving dish. Add the lemon juice, 10 tsp olive oil, sea salt and freshly ground pepper. Dice tomatoes and add to the bulgur. Taste and adjust the seasoning. This is good on its own or with other salads.

APPLE-WALDORF SALAD

*1.3 kg/2 lbs/4 cups apples, peeled, cored, and cut into bite-sized pieces (keep the **seeds!**)*
500 g/1 lb/2 cups celery, chopped into bite sized-pieces
*250 g/8 oz/ 1 cup **walnuts** (soaked 8 hours)*
250g/8 oz/1 cup raisins (soaked 4 hours)

Combine nuts and fruit together and enjoy as is, or add creamy Sweet Date Dressing for a more traditional Waldorf salad.

SWEET DATE DRESSING:

Add ½ cup of date cream, made by blending 4 soaked dates with ½ cup soak water until creamy.[26]

MIXED GREEN NUT SALAD

Choose from a variety of lettuce, **alfalfa sprouts**, **spinach**, **watercress**, celery, cucumber, avocado, rocket, lambs lettuce. Add some ground sesame seeds, chopped **walnuts** and **apricot kernels** along with your favourite dressing (*see below*).

Combine salad leaves, washed, dried and torn into small pieces. Add in a handful of spinach leaves, some diced cucumber, plus any of the raw vegetables above. Sprinkle over sunflower and sesame seeds plus some ground **apricot kernels**. This can be dressed with:

3 tbsp extra virgin olive oil, olive or unrefined sunflower oil
1 clove crushed garlic (ok for telephone operators!)
1 tbsp lemon juice
sea salt and freshly ground pepper to taste

Whisk altogether and pour over salad and toss lightly.

SALAD NICOISE

1 lettuce
2 large tomatoes
1 green pepper
1 clove garlic
5 tbsp French dressing
8 oz cooked fresh/frozen French beans
¼ cucumber, peeled & diced
2 sticks celery, chopped
8 black olives

---

[26] Brenda Cobb, from *Get Fresh*, The Fresh Network Ltd. PO Box 71, Ely, Cambs, CB6 3ZQ, UK

FRENCH DRESSING:
¼ tsp French mustard
pinch of sea salt
freshly milled black pepper
1 tbsp vinegar
2 tbsp olive oil

FRESH TOMATO SALAD

Peel tomatoes. Slice and place in serving dish. Mix the basil with a French dressing. Pour over the tomatoes and add finely chopped onion.

VARIATION:
Omit the basil. Add:

2 tsp of chopped parsley
2 tsp chopped chives
Add garlic clove to French dressing

TOMATO BASIL SAUCE

750 g/1lb 8oz/3 cups fresh tomatoes
750 g/1lb 8oz/3 cups sun-dried tomatoes (soaked 1-2 hours, then drained)
365 g/12 oz/1 ½ cups fresh basil (3 tbsp if dried)
4 cloves garlic, chopped
3 tbsp lemon juice
1 tsp sea salt
3 tbsp olive oil
9 pitted dates (soaked 1 to 2 hours and drained)

Place garlic in food processor and chop. Add dates and blend well. Add sun-dried tomatoes and blend. Add remaining ingredients and blend until smooth. Use immediately or refrigerate overnight so flavours meld together.[27]

FRESH SPINACH NUTS SALAD

2 lbs **spinach**
¼ cup olive oil
1 red onion, sliced thinly
5 garlic cloves, chopped
3 tbsp pine nuts
4 tbsp basil
3 tbsp lime juice, freshly squeezed

Wash and chop the spinach. Drain well. Heat the oil in a frying pan, sauté the onion until translucent. Add the garlic, pine nuts and basil, sautéing over a medium heat. Add the spinach, stirring to coat it with the flavoured oil. Season to taste and serve immediately.[28]

STRAWBERRY-KIWI SALAD

(serves 2)

2 oranges, peeled and sliced across the sections
2 cups **strawberries***, sliced*
2 large kiwi fruit, peeled and sliced
1 small banana, peeled and sliced
1 tbsp **currants**

---

[27] Brenda Cobb, from *Get Fresh*, The Fresh Network Ltd., op. cit.
[28] **Mercola, Joseph** *The Mercola Cookbook*, www.mercola.com

On a small platter, make a bed of orange wheels. In a large bowl, combine strawberries, kiwi fruit, and bananas. Add currants. Mix gently and mound on oranges. Make Fruit Dip (see below) and pour it over salad, or serve separately.

PINEAPPLE, RED PEPPER AND BROWN RICE SALAD

250 g/8 oz/1 cup cooked wholegrain brown rice
1 ¼ tbsp olive oil
1 ¼ tbsp lemon or lime juice
½ tsp hot chilli oil
250g/8 oz /1 cup diced fresh pineapple
115 g/4 oz/1/2 cup diced red pepper
115 g/4 oz/ ½ cup green spring onions
1 tsp sesame oil

Take a large bowl and stir in the pineapple with the cooked rice. Add lemon juice, chilli oil, red pepper, onions and sesame oil. Toss to mix. Adjust the seasoning to taste by adding ground black pepper and a little sea salt.

FRUIT DIP
(five different suggestions)

1) Puree in blender or food processor:
½ papaya, ¼ cup fresh orange juice, and ¼ tsp nutmeg; or
2) 1 persimmon and 1 banana; or
3) 1 banana and ½ cup strawberries; or
4) ½ cup fresh orange or apple juice, and 6-8 pitted dates; or
5) ½ cup pineapple cubes and 1 banana

Serve on or with fruit salad.[29]

---

[29] Diamond, Harvey, *Fit For Life*, op. cit. p.219

BABY COURGETTES WITH PINENUTS

1 oz pine nuts
1 level tsp cumin seeds
2 tbsp extra virgin olive oil
1 lb baby courgettes (zucchini), halved
1 garlic clove, crushed
juice of 1 lemon

Heat a non-stick wok or frying pan and dry-fry pine nuts until golden. Add cumin and heat until you can smell the cumin cooking. Tip into a bowl to cool. Heat the oil into the same pan and add the courgettes and garlic. Stir-fry for 3-5 minutes or until golden. Add lemon juice, cumin and pine nuts and serve.[30]

WATERCRESS AND RADISH SALAD
(can be used for a starter)

*2 bunches **watercress**, washed and trimmed*
5 small radishes
*sprouted **mung beans***
apricot kernel oil
juice of 1 lemon

Place the watercress in a large bowl and add the diced radishes and mung beans. Sprinkle over sufficient oil to cover the leaves and then add the juice of one lemon. Sea salt and pepper to taste. Mix lightly and arrange attractively on a flat dish.

POTATO SALAD

800 g small new potatoes
3-4 trimmed spring onions (leave some green)

DRESSING:
1 tbsp filtered water
1 tbsp white wine vinegar
100 g groundnut oil
chopped parsley

---

[30] *Good Housekeeping*, April 2001

Scrub but not peel the small new potatoes. Simmer in sea-salted, filtered water for about 20 minutes. While they are cooking, mix the whites and some green of the trimmed spring onions in the serving bowl, finely chopped. For the dressing, mix the water, white wine vinegar and groundnut oil. Season well.

Drain the cooked potatoes, cut into chunks and mix in the dressing whilst still warm. Sprinkle with the chopped parsley.

BEETROOT AND WATERCRESS SALAD
2 large beetroot, cooked in plenty of sea-salted water
*1 bunch **watercress**, washed and roughly chopped*
50 ml extra virgin olive oil
1 tsp white wine vinegar
1 shallot, finely chopped

Dice the beetroot into a bowl, whilst still warm pour over the oil and vinegar. Add the chopped shallot and watercress mix well and season to taste.

SPROUTED SALAD
Mix your favourite tubs of sprouting seeds (**alfalfa, lentils, mung, chickpea**, etc. or you can easily grow your own). Sprinkle with pumpkin seeds and 1 tsp **ground apricot kernels.** Dress with 4 tbsp extra virgin olive oil, plus juice of 1/2 unwaxed lemon and 1 tsp Dijon mustard. Season to taste. A chopped tomato can be added together with 2-3 finely chopped spring onions and some finely chopped parsley.

CRUNCHY WINTER SALAD
Make a dressing in your salad bowl with 3 tbsp olive oil, 1 tbsp wine vinegar, salt, 1 tsp runny honey, and freshly ground pepper. Add 2 heads of trimmed chicory sliced diagonally, 2 carrots peeled and grated, 1 green apple (Granny Smith has tartness and crunch), washed, cored and sliced. Toss salad in the dressing. Add 6-8 spring onions trimmed and finely chopped and a handful of chopped flat leaf parsley.

THE SHADOW OF SOY

or

How I stopped loving and learned to worry about the bean

by Sean McNary Carson

You've joined an army of thousands committed to being all you can be. You rise at dawn to pound the pavement, or climb the Stairmaster to heavenly buttocks while listening to Deepak Chopra on your Walkman. Or, maybe you contort yourself into yoga asanas in rooms hotter than a Korean chutney. You drink only purified water as you toss a handful of the latest longevity pills into your mouth. You're hungry, hungry for health, and no doubt about it, you're no stranger to soy.

Faster than you can say *"isoflavone,"* the humble soybean has insinuated itself into a dominant position in the standard diet. And that shouldn't be a surprise. Cheap, versatile, and karma-free, soy in the 1990's went from obscurity as vegan-and-hippie staple to *Time* magazine. With mad cows lurking between whole wheat buns, and a growing distrust of conventionally-produced dairy products, soy seemed like the ideal choice, the perfect protein.

But like all seemingly perfect things, a shadow lurked. By the final years of the last decade, a number of soy researchers began to cry foul. Soy Good? Soy Bad?

As the soy industry lobbied the Food and Drug Administration for a cardiovascular health claim for soy protein, two senior FDA scientists, Daniel Sheehan and Daniel Doerge - both specialists in estrogen research - wrote a letter vigorously opposing such a claim. In fact, they suggested a warning might be more appropriate. Their concern? Two isoflavones found in soy, genistein and daidzen, the same two promoted by the industry for everything from menopause relief to cancer protection, were said to *"demonstrate toxicity in estrogen sensitive tissues and in the thyroid."* Moreover, *"adverse effects in humans occur in several tissues and, apparently, by several distinct mechanisms."* Sheehan also quoted a landmark study (Cassidy, et al. 1994), showing that as little as 45 mg of isoflavones could alter the length of a pre-menopausal woman's menstrual cycle. The scientists were particularly concerned about the effects of these two plant estrogens on foetuses and young infants, because *"development is recognised as the most sensitive life stage for estrogen toxicity."*

It wasn't the first time scientists found problems with soy, but coupled with a Hawaiian study by Dr. Lon White on men, the controversy ended up on national television. While industry scientists criticized both the White study and the two FDA researchers (who are now disallowed from commenting publicly on the issue), other researchers weighed in on the anti-soy side. The tofu'd fight had begun.

WHAT ABOUT ASIA?
One of the favourite mantras of soy advocates is that the ubiquitous bean has been used *"safely by Asians for thousands of years."* With many soy *"experts"* (often with ties to the soy industry) recommending more than 250 grams of soy foods - and in some cases, more than 100 mg of isoflavones each day - it's easy to get the impression that soy plays a major role in the Asian diet. If you saw it on TV or read it in a magazine, it must be true, right? Well, not exactly.

Sally Fallon, president of the Weston A. Price Foundation (www.westonaprice.org) and author of *Nourishing Traditions*, responds that the soy industry and media have spun a self-serving version of the traditional use of soy in Asia. *"The tradition with soy is that it was fermented for a long time, from six months to three years and then eaten as a condiment, not as a replacement for animal foods,"* she says.

Fallon states that the so-called Asian diet - far from centring around soy - is based on meat. Approximately 65% of Japanese calorie intake comes from fish in Japan, while in China the same percentage comes from pork. *"They're not using a lot of soy in Asia - an average of 2 teaspoons a day in China and up to a quarter cup in some parts of Japan, but not a huge amount."*

Contrast that with modern America, home of *"if a little is good for you, more must be better."* Walk into any grocery store, especially the health-oriented variety, and you'll find the ever-present bean. My recent, limited survey of Marin, California food stores found soy in dozens and dozens of items: granola, vegetarian chilli, a vast sundry of imitation animal foods, pasta, most protein powders and *"power"* bars, and even something called *"nature's burger,"* which, given the kind of elaborate (and often toxic) processing that goes into making soy isolate and TVP, would make Mother Nature wince. There's even a bread - directly marketed to women - containing more than 80 mg of soy isoflavones per serving, which is more than the daily dose in purified isoflavone supplements. All of this, in addition to the traditional soy fare of tempeh, tofu, miso, and soy sauce. It's no wonder that Californians are edamame dreaming.

So, while Asians were using limited to moderate amounts of painstakingly prepared soy foods - the alleged benefits of which are still controversial - Americans, especially vegetarians, are consuming more soy products and isoflavones than any culture in human history, and as one researcher put it, *"entering a great unknown."*

Oddly, nowhere in industry promotion does anyone differentiate between traditional, painstakingly prepared "Asian" soy foods and the modern, processed items that Fallon calls *"imitation food."* And therein lies the rub. Modern soy protein foods in no way resemble the traditional Asian soy foods, and may contain carcinogens like nitrates, lysinoalanine, as well as a number of anti-nutrients which are only significantly degraded by fermentation or other traditional processing.

"People need to realise that when they're eating these soy foods - and I'm not talking about miso or tofu - but soy "burgers," soy "cheese," soy "ice cream," and all of this stuff, that they are not the real thing. They may look like the real thing and they may taste like the real thing, but they do not have the life-supporting qualities of real foods," Fallon says.

THERE'S NO BUSINESS LIKE SOY BUSINESS

"The reason there's so much soy in America is because they started to plant soy to extract the oil from it and soy oil became a very large industry," says lipid specialist and nutritionist Mary Enig, PhD. *"Once they had as much oil as they did in the food supply they had a lot of soy protein residue left over, and since they can't feed it to animals, except in small amounts, they had to find another market."*

According to Enig, female pigs can only ingest it in amounts approximating 1% during their gestational phase and a few percent greater during their lactation diet, or else face reproduction damage and developmental problems in the piglets. *"It can be used for chickens, but it really has limitations. So, if you can't feed it to animals, than you find gullible human beings, and you develop a health claim, and you feed it to them."*

In a co-written article, Enig and Fallon state that soybean producers pay a mandatory assessment of ½ to 1 percent of the net market price of soybeans to help fund programs to *"strengthen the position of soybeans in the marketplace and maintain and expand foreign markets for uses for soybeans and soy products."*

They also cite advertising figures - multi-million dollar figures - that soy-oriented companies like Archer Daniels Midland or ADM spend for spots on national television. Money is also used to fund PR campaigns, favourable articles, and lobbying interests. A relaxation of USDA rules has lead to an increase in soy use in school lunches. Far from being the *"humble"* or *"simple"* soybean, soy is now big business - very big business. This is not your father's soybean.

There's been such a rush to market isoflavones that the before-mentioned multinational corporation, ADM, in 1998, petitioned the FDA for GRAS (generally recognized as safe) status for soy isoflavones. For those who don't know GRAS, the designation is used for foods, and in some cases, food additives, that have been used safely for many years by humans. For those who didn't know - like a number of protesting scientists - that soy isoflavones had been widely used by generations of Americans before the late 1950's, it was a revelation indeed. Ahem.

Dr. Sheehan, in his 1998 letter to the FDA referenced earlier, states *"that soy protein foods are GRAS is in conflict with the recent return by CFSAN to Archer Daniels Midland of a petition for GRAS status for soy protein because of deficiencies in reporting the adverse effects in the petition. Thus GRAS status has not been granted."* And what about those safety issues?

REQUIEM FOR A THYROID

One of the biggest concerns about high intake of soy isoflavones is their clearly defined toxic effect on the thyroid gland. You don't have to work too hard to convince Dr. Larrian Gillespie of that. Dr. Gillespie, author of *The Menopause Diet*, in the name of scientific empiricism, decided to run her own soy experiment - on herself. She notes that she fits the demographic soy isoflavones are most marketed to: borderline hypothyroid, menopausal females.

"I did it in two different ways. I tried the (isoflavone) supplements (at 40mg), where I went into flagrant hypothryoidism within 72 hours, and I did the 'eat lots of tofu category,' and it did the same thing, but it took me five days with that. I knew what I was doing but it still took me another 7-10 days to come out of it."

In the current issue of the *Whole Earth Review*, herbalist Susan Weed tells the story of Michael Moore - no, not that Michael Moore, but the founder of the Southwest School of Herbal Medicine. In an e-mail to Weed, Moore declares that *"soy did me in."* Weed describes how Moore, in his own experiment, ate a large amount of manufactured soy products - protein powders, "power" bars, and soy drinks, over a period of three weeks. Weed writes that Moore ended up in a cardiac care unit because the action on his thyroid had been so pronounced.

Harvard-trained medical doctor Richard Shames, MD, a thyroid specialist who has had a long time practice in Marin, says that *"genistein is the most difficult for the metabolic processes of people with low thyroid, so when you have that present in high enough concentrations, the result is an antagonism to the function of thyroid hormone."*

Far from being an isolated problem, Shames says that recent data tags twenty million Americans being treated for thyroid problems, another thirteen million who ought to be treated if they would get a TSH (thyroid stimulating hormone) test, and another thirteen million who would show up normal on a TSH test but would test positive on another, more specific test. All in all, Shames believes that low thyroid conditions - many due to exposure to oestrogen-mimicking chemicals like PCBs and DDT in environment - are the mother of most modern health epidemics.

That's a lot of thyroid problems. Some estimate the number to be as high as one in ten. Shames says that 8 of 10 thyroid sufferers are women - often older women - like Dr. Gillespie. The same demographic the soy industry has set its targets on.

"If you're a normal person, and one in ten are not normal, the effect [of 50 mg of soy isoflavones] may be fairly insignificant, but even a normal person can have problems at levels greater than that," says Shames.

Dr. Gillespie says the daily amount to cause thyroid problems may be as low as 30 mg, or less than a serving of soymilk.

A number of soy proponents say the thyroid concerns are exaggerated and that if dietary iodine is sufficient, problems won't likely happen. Not so, says Shames: *"Iodine is a double-edged sword for people with thyroid problems, and for those people, more is going to increase their chance for an autoimmune reaction... throwing iodine at it is not going to be the protective solution."* Shames recommends limiting soy foods to a few times a week, preferably fermented or well cooked.

BIRTH CONTROL PILLS FOR BABIES?
Environmental toxicologist Mike Fitzpatrick, PhD says he doesn't have it out for soy. His original concern was for babies: *"They were getting more soy isoflavones, at least on a bodyweight basis, than anybody else,"* he notes. *"It wasn't so much that I knew what that would do, but that I didn't know what that would do."* Fitzpatrick, who is also webmaster of ... Soy Online Services (www.soyonline-service.co.nz), a website devoted to informing people about the potential problems with soy, stresses the potential dangers for the developing human body: *"Any person with any kind of understanding of environmental endocrine disruptors, compounds [like isoflavones] that are not in the body normally and can modify hormones and the way they work in the body, any expert will say that infants need to avoid these things like the plague."*

Fitzpatrick was quoted - and misquoted - worldwide a few years ago when he suggested that the isoflavones in soy formula were the equivalent of birth control pills: *"When I first did my review, I did compare the estrogenic equivalents of the contraceptive pill with how much soy infants and adults would be consuming,"* he says. *"It's at least the equivalent of one or two estrogen pills a day, on an estrogenic basis. I've been criticised that it's not the same form of estrogen, but in terms of estrogenicity, it's a crude but valid and alarming statistic."*

The typical response by industry experts has been to downplay the uniqueness of soy isoflavones, stating - accurately - that isoflavones of various kinds are prevalent in most fruits, vegetables, and legumes.

IS IT TIME TO TOSS OUT THE APPLE SAUCE?

"No, you're not going to do that because you get exposure from all kinds of things, but the exposure you get from soy is way, way higher," Fitzpatrick says. *"Soy formula is going to give babies a real whack, far in excess of what you might find in apples. Soy is a very rich source of isoflavones - that's how the industry markets its product. You don't see an apple extract to help women deal with menopause."*

You've got to wonder how the industry can market soy isoflavones as a form of estrogen replacement therapy for menopausal women (and a host of other health claims) and still claim that soy formula is safe for infants. And while the mechanism for biological activity is clearly defined, the industry keeps repeating the same tune: *"no credible evidence exists."*

But credible for whom? Says Fitzpatrick: *"We're not talking about little studies here but long-term effects on infants and adults, and that's what concerns me. It's very trite. They (the industry) give half-baked answers. What you really need is long-term studies."* Likewise, *"no credible evidence"* is not good enough for Dr. Naomi Baumslag, professor of paediatrics at Georgetown University Medical School. She joined a host of others in criticising a recent article in the *Journal of the American Medical Association (JAMA)*, purported to be the definitive study on soy formula safety.

"It was not an acceptable epidemiological study - you can take it to any decent epidemiologist and hear what they think about it, and they use it to say that soy is safe," says Baumslag. *"It's totally unsubstantiated."*

MANGANESE MADNESS

Besides the dangers of prematurity and other reproductive problems posed by isoflavones, Baumslag mentions the high levels of the mineral manganese (no, not magnesium) often found in soy formula. The problem of manganese is so serious that even one soy manufacturer put warning labels on its soymilk. The company's president, in a press release, states that *"there is mounting evidence of a correlation between manganese in soy milk (including soy-based infant formula) and neurotoxicity in small infants."* With manganese toxicity known for producing behavioural disorders, the press release even goes further stating, *"If research continues, showing that the current epidemic levels of ADHD in children, as well as impulsivity and violence among adolescents, are connected with the increase in soy-based infant formula use, our industry could suffer a serious setback by not dealing with the issue upfront."*

With all the potential problems with soy formula, Baumslag notes that formula is also missing key immunological factors only found in mother's milk, the lack of which could give a child a life sentence of chronic health problems. She links soy-pushing to corporate profits and the PR campaigns that they fund.

"There's been so much PR in regards to soy formula and I think you also have to ask yourself why it's so much cheaper for them to make, which means there's more profit. How come only 1% in the UK are on formula, where it's closer to 30% in the United States? I don't know why it's so important for them to push soy, they should push breast-feeding." Perhaps it's because breast milk for babies isn't as lucrative as milking the soybean for profits.

CAVEAT EMPTOR

As a former vegan - and big soy-eater - I'm disturbed by the vast array of modern, processed soy products that have come on the market in the last few years, without any recognition of potential pitfalls. Safe bet: If it hasn't been eaten safely for thousands of years, you probably shouldn't put it at the centre of your diet. We've been sold a bill of goods that says "*soy is good for you*", but it doesn't tell you what kind of soy or how much, or even definitively if soy really is what makes Asians so supposedly healthy.

It's well known that the Japanese also eat a very large amount of omega 3 fatty acids from fish each day - substances which have been clearly shown to have anti-cancer and anti-heart disease effects. So, is it the soy or is it the fish? As the industry spends millions and millions of dollars to find something that isoflavones are good for - some health claim to justify their unprecedented presence in the American diet - I have to ask: why are they trying so hard? Why is there such a push to push soy?

Soy isoflavones are clearly biologically active - they affect change in your body. It's no longer acceptable for the industry to see no bad, hear no bad, and speak no bad. Legitimate concerns need to be studied - and not studies funded by the industry, conducted by soy scientists.

In the meantime, I've located a wonderful, old miso company on the north coast. They age their miso for three years in wood barrels and sell it in glass jars. It's rich, earthy, and real. I enjoy a teaspoon in a glass of hot water a few times a week after dinner. It tastes lively and feels good. I no longer get the "*urge*" to eat soy "*dogs*" or soy "*burgers*," though I now suspect that urge didn't come from my own instinct, but from the lofty dictates of the soy experts.

But why wait years, while ignorant armies clash over this and that isoflavone and studies that say one thing or another? Perhaps the safest way to use soy, if you choose to use soy, is the way it's been used by Asians for thousands of years: fermented, in moderation, as a condiment. In short, colour me cautious.

OTHER FOOD COMBINATION IDEAS

BROWN RICE
1 cup brown long grain rice
1¼ cups of water
pinch of sea salt
freshly ground black pepper
paprika, to garnish

Rinse the rice thoroughly and drain well. Put the water in a non-stick saucepan and bring to the boil. Add the rice, stir well, reduce the heat, cover and simmer very gently for 30 minutes. Season well with the salt and lots of pepper and fluff up with a fork. Serve sprinkled with a fine dusting of paprika.[31]

BROCCOLI AND SESAME SEED NOODLES
8 oz whole-wheat tagliatelle
6 oz broccoli, cut into florets
3 tbsp sesame seeds
1 tbsp olive oil

Cook the tagliatelli, adding the broccoli in the last 4 minutes of cooking time. Drain and return to the saucepan. Dry-fry the sesame seeds in a non-stick frying pan until golden. Add the pasta with the oil, toss and serve.[32]

CHICK PEA STROGANOFF
1 onion
4 cups mushrooms
2 tbs butter
4 tbs water
¼ tsp ground nutmeg
*¼ tsp ground **apricot kernels***
1 tsp soy sauce
¼ tsp mustard powder

---

[31] Humphries, Carolyn, *7-Day Low Cholesterol Diet Plan,* op. cit.
[32] Ibid.

2 ½ cups **chickpeas**
2 tsp cider or wine vinegar
2 cups wholewheat noodles
¾ cup of plain yoghurt

Chop the onion and mushrooms. Melt the butter and sauté the vegetables until tender. Add the stock, seasonings, chickpeas and vinegar. Cover and simmer on a low heat for about 10 minutes. Add the yoghurt to the chickpea mixture over the lowest heat. Stir constantly, without bringing to the boil, until heated through. Serve over cooked noodles.[33]

VEGETARIAN LENTILS

1 ¼ cups wild rice
1 ¼ cups red **lentils**
3 ¼ cups warm water
½ cup olive oil
1 medium onion, peeled and chopped
¾ tsp fresh ginger, crushed
¾ tsp garlic, crushed or finely chopped
cinnamon stick
6 cloves
1 bay leaf
1 ¼ tsp ground coriander
½ tsp turmeric
¾ tsp granulated kelp (seaweed)

Wash the rice and lentils in cold water, then drain. Put both into a large bowl and cover with the warm water. Soak for 40 minutes then drain but reserve the water. Gently heat the oil in a large saucepan, add the onion and fry slowly for about three minutes, stirring often to prevent burning.

Add the ginger, garlic, cinnamon stick, cloves and bay leaf, fry for a minute. Add the rice and lentils, coriander turmeric and kelp. Stir over heat for 2 minutes, until rice and lentils are covered with oil.

---

[33] Leneman, Leah, op. cit.

Pour the reserved water into the rice mixture and bring to the boil. Reduce the heat and cover the pan with a lid. Simmer for 8 – 10 minutes without stirring, or until the water has been totally absorbed. Stir the rice and lentils together and serve at once.

LEEK PARCELS WITH PROVENCAL VEGETABLES

1 large leek, green part only, trimmed, cut in half and cut lengthways
1 aubergine, cut into 8 slices
1 courgette (zucchini), sliced
olive oil for brushing
½ tsp herbs de Provence
Sea salt and fresh ground black pepper
1 red pepper, cored, seeded, roasted and peeled
canned tomatoes, drained
3 tbsp ready-made pesto
2 garlic cloves, chopped
Carrot Julienne, to garnish

PESTO DRESSING
olive oil
3 tbsp white wine vinegar
1 tsp ready-made pesto

Blanche the leek for 1 minute. Drain and rinse. Separate the green layers to give 13 strips. Brush the aubergine and courgette slices with the oil and sprinkle with herbs de Provence and salt and pepper to taste. Cook under a hot grill for 5 minutes. Cut the pepper and tomato into chunks. Brush aubergine with pesto. Cut one of the strips of leek into 4 long strands and set aside. Take 3 strips of leek and place on top of one another in a star formation. Assemble the leek parcels.

Place a slice of aubergine where the strips of leek cross. Place a piece of red pepper on top, then a courgette, a little of the chopped garlic, a piece of tomato and finish with another slice of aubergine.

Fold the ends of the leek up over the filling so that they meet in the middle and enclose the vegetable filling.

Tie the parcel with one of the long strands of leek or with a length of string. Repeat with remaining leeks and vegetables.

Put the parcels on a baking tray and bake in a pre-heated oven at 180 C/350F/Gas Mark 4 for 10 minutes. Make the pesto dressing, whisk the oil, vinegar, and pesto. Spoon the dressing onto 4 serving plates, place a parcel on top, garnish and serve.[34]

CARAWAY CABBAGE

¼ pint of vegetable stock
1 lb green cabbage, finely chopped
1 tbsp caraway seeds
freshly ground black pepper

Put the stock in a saucepan and bring to the boil. Add the cabbage and stir well. Cover tightly and boil for five minutes, shaking the pan occasionally until the cabbage is still bright green and just tender. Season with caraway seeds and pepper and serve straight away.[35]

LENTIL BOLOGNAISE
(serves 4)

*4 oz **brown lentils***
½ green pepper
1 carrot
1 cup water
1 tsp dried oregano
1 tsp dried basil
1 stick celery
1 onion
1 clove garlic
1 pint tomato passata
1 bay leaf
black pepper

Wash the lentils well. Chop the onions, green pepper and celery finely. Dice the carrot and press the garlic cloves. Place all the

---

[34] Berry, Mary, op. cit.
[35] Humphries, Carolyn, *7-Day Low Cholesterol Diet Plan*, op. cit.

ingredients in a pan, bring to the boil and simmer, covered for 30 minutes, until lentils are soft. Great with salad.

KIDNEY BEAN AND WALNUT CHILLI

1 tsp sesame seed oil
1 medium onion, finely chopped
3 cloves garlic, crushed or finely chopped
2 bay leaves
1 tbsp mild chilli powder
1 tsp powdered cumin
½ tsp dried oregano
*½ cup lightly tossed **walnuts**, coarsely chopped*
*2 cups cooked drained **kidney beans***
bean cooking juices, soup stock, or combination to cover minced scallions or chives.

Sauté the onions in oil or water. Add the kelp to draw out their moisture, stir until tender. Add the garlic and spices. Add the nuts, beans and bean stock to barely cover. Bring to the boil, reduce heat and simmer for 2½ hours on low. Stir occasionally and add more liquid if the chilli needs to be moistened. The beans should be thick - almost as stiff as refried beans. Remove the lid and simmer to remove any excess juice if necessary.

For a vegetarian meal, serve with a grain dish and a green, leafy vegetable. Alternatively, serve this chilli with baked fish or chicken, salad or green vegetables and a grain. All of these side dishes increase the vitamin B6 content of this food. Serves 4-8.[36]

MIXED BEAN CHILLI

1 onion, chopped
1 red pepper, chopped
1 tbsp olive oil
1 tsp ground cumin
1 tsp dried oregano
½ tsp hot chilli powder
1 large can chopped tomatoes

---

[36] Heinerman John, op. cit.

*15 oz mixed **pulses**, drained*
shredded lettuce
chopped cucumber

Fry the onion and red pepper for 3 minutes. Add the cumin, oregano and chilli powder and stir for 1 minute. Add the chopped tomatoes and drained pulses. Cook, stirring for 10 minutes until the ingredients are covered in a rich sauce. Top with the lettuce and chopped cucumber.

KIDNEY BEAN RISOTTO

1 onion, chopped
2 tbsp olive oil
1 carrot, chopped
1 red pepper, diced
*4 oz frozen **peas***
3 oz button mushrooms, sliced
*1 cup **brown, long grain rice***
2 1/2 cups vegetable stock
1 tbsp soy sauce, organic
1 tbsp dried mixed herbs
1 tbsp tomato puree
freshly ground black pepper
1 small can sweetcorn
1 large can kidney beans (organic), rinsed and drained
2 tbsp pumpkin seeds

Fry the onion for 2 minutes. Add the carrot, celery, pepper, peas, mushrooms and rice and cook for 1 minute, stirring. Add the remaining ingredients except the sweetcorn, kidney beans and pumpkin seeds. Bring to the boil, reduce heat, cover and cook gently for about 30 minutes, stirring occasionally, until the rice is tender but nutty and has absorbed the liquid. Add the contents of the can of sweetcorn, the beans and the pumpkin seeds. Cover and cook for 5 minutes. Fork through and serve.[37]

---

[37] Humphries, Carolyn, *7-Day Low Cholesterol Diet Plan*, op. cit.

ROASTED VEGETABLES WITH
WHOLE SPICE SEEDS

3 parsnips
3 potatoes
3 carrots
3 sweet potatoes
60 ml/4 tbsp olive oil
8 shallots, peeled
2 garlic cloves, sliced
10 ml/2 tsp white mustard seeds
10 ml/2 tsp coriander seeds, lightly crushed
5 ml/1 tsp cumin seeds
2 bay leaves
sea salt and ground pepper

Pre-heat the oven to 190C/375F/Gas Mark 5. Bring a saucepan of lightly salted water to the boil. Cut the parsnips, potatoes, carrots and sweet potatoes into chunks. Add them to the pan and bring the water back to the boil. Steam for 2 minutes, then drain the vegetables.

Pour the olive oil into a large heavy roasting tin, and place over a moderate heat. Add the vegetables, shallots and garlic. Fry, tossing the vegetables over the heat until they are pale golden at the edges.

Add the mustard seeds, coriander seeds, cumin seeds and bay leaves. Cook for 1 minute, then season with sea salt and pepper. Transfer the roasting tin to the oven and roast for about 45 minutes, turning occasionally, until the vegetables are crisp and golden and cooked through.[38]

TRADITIONAL SALSAS
(Salsas are served cold as a garnish or a dip)

AVOCADO SALSA

Peel and stone 1 ripe avocado and cut the flesh into dice. Chop ½ onion and 4-6 ripe tomatoes and stir gently into the diced avocado. Then add 1 or 2 chopped jalapeno peppers and 1-2 tablespoons

---

[38] **Taylor, Beatrice H** *The Cancer Prevention Cookbook*, Lorenz Books, 1999

chopped fresh coriander, and season to taste with sea salt, lemon juice and olive oil.[39]

SALSA FRESCA

Chop some fairly mild green chillies, ripe plum tomatoes and red onion. Combine them in a bowl. Add a little chopped fresh coriander for flavour and crushed dried chillies. Finish the salsa with ground cumin, dried oregano, ground **apricot kernels**, sea salt, lemon juice and olive oil to taste.

PINEAPPLE AND SWEETCORN SALSA

Peel and core ½ fresh pineapple and cut the flesh into small dice. Add 1 small can of drained sweetcorn and ¼ tsp ground **apricot kernels** and season to taste with diced red onion, chopped fresh coriander, salt, lemon juice and olive oil. (*In instances where fruit is used in a recipe, 'neutral' salad material and condiments will not cause the fruit to spoil the mix.*)

RED ONION SALSA

Dice 1 large red onion and stir into 4-6 diced ripe plum tomatoes. Season with 1 or 2 chopped jalapeno peppers, 1-2 tablespoons chopped fresh coriander, ¼ teaspoon of ground **apricot kernels**. Add sea salt, lemon juice and olive oil to taste.

CHRISTMAS SALSA

Cut 1 large red pepper and 1 large green pepper into quarters. Remove the stem and core, cut the quarters into dice and combine with 2 diced ripe plum tomatoes. Season with 1 or 2 chopped jalapeno peppers and chopped fresh coriander, ¼ teaspoon of ground **apricot kernel**s, sea salt, lemon juice and olive oil.

MILLET CASSEROLE

2 onions
2 carrots
1 small cabbage
1 cup **millet**

---

[39] **Carrier, Robert** *New Great Dishes of the World*, MacMillan, 1997

1/3 cup vegetable oil
3¾ cups of boiling water
sea salt
¼ cup wholewheat flour
1 1/3 cups water
2 tbs soy sauce
½ cup breadcrumbs

Chop the onions, cut the carrots into slices and shred the cabbage. Sauté the millet in 2 tbsp of the oil until it is beginning to brown. Cover with the boiling water and salt. Simmer for 20 minutes. Sauté the vegetables in 2 tbsp of the oil until tender. In a separate saucepan, heat the remaining oil, add the flour and stir well. Slowly add the water, stir constantly to avoid lumps. Add the soy sauce and bring to the boil. Simmer for 2-3 minutes. In a greased baking dish, place alternate layers of millet, vegetables and sauce, ending with a layer of sauce. Sprinkle with breadcrumbs. Bake in oven 180C/350F/Gas Mark 4 for about 20 minutes until the top is lightly browned. [40]

TERIYAKI BROCCOLI
(serves 3)
3 or 4 thick broccoli stalks without florets
1 tbsp sesame or sunflower oil
1-2 cloves of garlic, minced
2 tbsp tamari
squeeze of fresh lemon juice (optional)

Use carrot-peeler to remove thick skin from outside of stalks. Cut stalks lengthwise in thin slices. In large skillet, heat oil. Add garlic, sautéing briefly. Add broccoli. Sauté 3-5 minutes over medium-high heat until tender. Toss in tamari and lemon. [41]

---

[40] Leneman Leah, op. cit.
[41] Diamond, Harvey, *Fit For Life*, op. cit. p. 217

OLIVE OIL BRAISED
MEDITERRANEAN VEGETABLES
(serves 4 as a main dish)

4 tbsp extra virgin olive oil
1 medium onion, finely chopped
2 celery stalks, finely chopped
1 medium carrot, finely chopped
4 garlic cloves, crushed
½ tsp crumbled, dried rosemary or 1 tsp finely chopped fresh
rosemary
½ crushed chilli flakes
medium aubergine, cut into ½ inch cubes
medium courgettes, cut into ½ inch cubes
2 red peppers cored, seeded and cut into ½ cubes
2 potatoes cut into ½ inch cubes
4 ripe, fresh tomatoes or tinned plum tomatoes, quartered
4 fluid oz (125 ml) filtered water
14 oz white beans, drained and rinsed
1 handful fresh basil, mint or parsley or a combination, chopped
sea salt and black pepper
additional extra virgin olive oil to serve

Heat the oil in a large pot. Add the onion, celery, carrot and garlic and cook over medium heat, stirring constantly until soft (usually 5 minutes). Add the rosemary, chilli flakes, aubergine, courgettes, peppers, potatoes, tomatoes and water. Turn the heat down low and cover. Cook gently, stirring occasionally until very soft, 30 minutes. Stir in the beans and cook until hot through, 5 minutes. Add the herbs, sea salt and pepper to taste. Serve hot in warmed bowls, drizzled with the olive oil.[42]

OLIVE OIL BRAISED WINTER VEGETABLES
(serves 4 as a main dish)

Follow directions to previous recipe, but replace aubergine, courgette and red pepper with 1½ lb squash, cut into chunks, 2 leeks, thickly sliced and 2 fennel bulbs, roughly chopped. Proceed as directed.

---

[42] **Elliott, Renee & Eric Treuille** *Organic Cookbook*, Dorling Kindersley, 2000

*To both these recipes **ground apricot kernels** can be added as a seasoning.

RED PEPPERS STEWED WITH POTATOES AND OLIVES
(serves 4 as a main dish)

4 tbsp extra virgin olive oil
1 onion finely, sliced
4 garlic cloves, finely sliced
¼ tsp crushed chilli flakes
3 red peppers, cored, seeded and cut into 2 inch long and 1 inch wide strips.
4 medium potatoes, cut into 2 inch chunks
14 oz tin Italian plum tomatoes, chopped
4 oz pitted black olives
1 handful fresh basil or parsley, chopped
sea salt and black pepper

Heat the oil in a heavy-based pot. Add the onion and cook, stirring frequently over medium heat until soft and just golden, for 5 minutes. Add the garlic, chilli flakes, pepper, potato, tomato and olives. Turn the heat to low and simmer gently, stirring occasionally until the potatoes are tender, for 30-40 minutes. Stir in the basil or parsley. Add salt and pepper to taste. Serve hot or at room temperature.[43]

CAULIFLOWER WITH NUTMEG

1 small cauliflower
1 bay leaf
freshly grated nutmeg
freshly milled black pepper

Wash the cauliflower upright in a pan with an inch of boiling, sea-salted water. Add bay leaf and grate generously with nutmeg. Cover the pan with lid and simmer for 8-10 minutes. Drain well. Season with pepper.

---

[43] Elliott, Renee & Eric Treuille, *Organic Cookbook*, op. cit.

ZUCCHINI WITH TOMATOES

8 small zucchini (courgettes)
1 tbsp olive oil
1 garlic clove, crushed
4oz tomatoes, skinned and chopped
sea salt and freshly milled black pepper

Wipe courgettes with damp cloth and cut into rounds about ¼ inch thick. Sauté in olive oil for about 10 minutes, turning occasionally. Add crushed garlic and chopped tomatoes and cook for a further 6 minutes. Season with salt and freshly ground black pepper.

BRUSSELS SPROUTS WITH CHESTNUTS AND APRICOT KERNELS

*8 oz **Brussels sprouts**, cleaned and trimmed*
*3-4 oz canned whole **chestnuts***
1 tsp raw butter
*3 g **ground apricot kernels***
Sea salt and freshly milled black pepper

Steam the Brussels for 5-6 minutes. Drain the chestnuts, cut them into halves and sauté in butter. Add the Brussels sprouts and apricot kernel dust to the chestnuts and cook for 1 minute. Season with the sea salt and pepper.

MIXED VEGETABLE CASSEROLE

1 aubergine
115 g/4oz/ ½ cup okra, cut in half lengthways
250 g/8 oz/2 cups frozen or fresh peas
250 g/8 oz/1½ cups green beans, cut into short pieces
2 onions, finely chopped
4 courgettes, cut into 1 cm/1/2 in pieces
500 g/1lb potatoes, diced into 2.5 cm/1 in pieces
1 red pepper, seeded and sliced
400 g chopped tomatoes
150 ml/¼ pt vegetable stock (must not include yeast)
60 ml/4 tbsp olive oil
75 ml/5 tbsp chopped fresh parsley
5 ml/1 tsp paprika

FOR TOPPING
3 fresh tomatoes
1 courgette, sliced

Pre-heat oven to 190 C/375 F/Gas Mark 5. Dice the aubergine into 2.5 cm/1 in pieces and place all vegetables into a large, ovenproof casserole dish. Add the canned tomatoes, vegetable stock, olive oil, chopped parsley and paprika, and combine well. Level the surface of the vegetables and arrange alternate slices of tomato and courgette on top.

Place lid on or cover the casserole with kitchen foil. Cook in the oven for approximately 1 hour. Casserole may be served hot or warm.

SPRING VEGETABLE STIR-FRY

*15 ml/1 tbsp groundnut or **apricot kernel oil***
5 ml/1 tsp toasted sesame oil
1 garlic clove, chopped
175 g/6 oz/1/3 cup asparagus tips
2.5 cm/ 1 inch piece of fresh root ginger, finely chopped
225 g/8 oz/1 cup baby carrots
350 g/12 oz/3 cups broccoli florets
2 spring onions, cut on the diagonal
175 g/6 oz/1½ cups spring greens, finely shredded

30 ml/2 tbsp light organic soy sauce
15 ml/1 tbsp sesame seeds, toasted
*3 g **apricot kernels**, ground*

Add the asparagus, ginger, carrots and broccoli and stir-fry for 4 minutes. Add the spring onions and spring greens, and stir-fry for a further 2 minutes. Pour over the organic soy sauce and cook for 1-2 minutes until the vegetables are just tender, adding a little water if the stir-fry appears too dry. Sprinkle the sesame seeds and ground apricot kernels on top to serve.[44]

TURKISH- STYLE NEW POTATO CASSEROLE
(serves 4)

60 ml/4 tbsp olive oil
1 large onion, chopped
2 medium aubergines, cut into small cubes
4 courgettes, cut into small chunks
1 green and 1 red or yellow pepper, seeded and chopped
115 g/4 oz/1 cup fresh or frozen peas
115 g/4 oz green beans
450 g/1 lb new potatoes, cubed
2.5 ml/½ tsp cinnamon
2.5ml/½ tsp paprika
4-5 tomatoes, skinned
400g/14 oz chopped tomatoes
15 g/½ oz chopped, fresh parsley
3-4 garlic cloves, crushed
350 ml/12 fl oz vegetable stock (without yeast)
freshly ground black pepper, black olives and fresh parsley to garnish

Heat the oven to 190 C/375 F/ Gas Mark 5. Heat 45 ml/3 tbsp of the oil in a heavy based pan then add the onions and fry until golden. Add the cubed aubergine to the pan, sauté for 3 minutes then add the courgettes, peppers, peas, beans and potatoes, together with the spices and freshly ground black pepper.

---

[44] Adapted from Taylor, Beatrice, *The Cancer Prevention Cookbook*, op. cit.

Continue to cook for about 3 minutes, stirring all the time. Transfer the vegetables to a shallow, ovenproof dish. Halve the fresh tomatoes and remove their seeds using a teaspoon. Chop and place in a bowl. Mix in the canned tomatoes, parsley and garlic and the remaining olive oil.

Pour the vegetable stock over the aubergine mixture, then spoon the prepared tomato mixture over the top. Cover with foil and bake for 35-45 minutes until the vegetables are tender. Serve hot, garnish with black olives and fresh parsley.

WALNUT STEAK

*500 g/2 cups **walnuts** (soaked 8 hours)*
250 g/8 oz/1 cup sunflower seeds (soaked 8 hours)
250 g/8oz/1 cup almonds (soaked 8 hours)
6 cloves garlic
1 tsp sea salt
medium size onion
2 tbsp fresh rosemary
250 g/8oz/1 cup red bell pepper
1 tbsp dried jalapeno pepper
1½ tsp cumin powder
500 g/1 lb/2 cups fresh tomatoes
250 g/8 oz/1 cup sun dried tomatoes (soaked 1 to 2 hours, then drained)
9 dates (soaked 1 to 2 hours)
6 fresh basil leaves or 1 tsp dried basil

Mix garlic, salt, onion, rosemary, red pepper, jalapeno pepper, cumin, tomatoes, dates and basil in food processor. Blend nuts in food processor. Continue blending until the texture is smooth.

Form into 4 to 5 oz (115 g) patties or one large loaf and dehydrate for 2 hours. Serve warm or make ahead of time, or refrigerate and serve cold. You can use as a dip or spread if you don't dehydrate.

MUSHROOMS A LA GRECQUE

filtered water
juice of ½ lemon

81

2 tbsp olive oil
sprig of thyme (or good pinch of dried thyme)
1 bay leaf
1-2 garlic cloves, crushed
1 tbsp tomato purée
sea salt and freshly milled pepper
8 oz small button mushrooms

Put all the ingredients except the mushrooms into a saucepan. Bring to the boil. Add washed but not peeled mushrooms and simmer gently for 5 minutes. Remove from heat and allow to cool. Refrigerate for about 4 hours until well chilled.

SIZZLING GARLIC GREENS
(serves 4 as a side dish)

2 tbsp extra virgin olive oil
2 garlic cloves, finely sliced
¼ tsp crushed chilli flakes
*10 oz – 1 lb of greens, e.g. broccoli, **spinach**, etc.*
2 tsp lemon juice
sea salt and black pepper

Heat the oil in a large frying pan. Add the garlic and chilli flakes and cook over medium high heat until the garlic is just golden for 1 minute. Add the greens and cook, stirring occasionally until wilted and tender but still bright green. Add the lemon juice and salt and pepper to taste. Serve hot.

WHICH GREENS?

Any greens work for this recipe but the cooking times will vary. Choose from:

*1 lb **spinach** or Swiss chard washed, stems finely chopped, leaves coarsely chopped. Cook for 5-8 minutes.*

1 lb cabbage, core cut out and discarded, leaves coarsely shredded. Steam for 15-20 minutes

1 lb green or purple sprouting broccoli, stems finely sliced, florets separated. Steam over boiling sea-salted, filtered water until the stems are just tender, 6-8 minutes. Add garlic and chilli flakes in pan as required. Cook for 5-7 minutes.

10 oz kale, coarsely chopped. Steam for 15-20 minutes.
10 oz spring greens, coarsely chopped. Steam for 15-20 minutes.

Health Note: *Vitamin-rich and fine-calcium-packed, dark leafy greens are super-charged with anti-carcinogenic antioxidants.*[45]

* ground **apricot kernels** may be added to any of the above as a seasoning.

ROASTED VEGETABLE RAGOUT

1 tbsp olive oil
3 parsnips, diced
1 fennel bulb
4 celery sticks, diced
1 onion, chopped roughly
3 large carrots, diced
1 pt herb stock
¼ pt white wine
4 oz quick-cooking tagliatelle, broken up roughly
8 tsp ready-made tomato salsa
sea salt and freshly ground black pepper

Pre-heat oven to 200 C/400 F/Gas Mark 6. Heat the oil on a hob in an oven-proof pan. Add the parsnips, fennel, celery, onion and carrots. Fry for 2 minutes. Transfer the pan to the oven and bake uncovered for 20-25 minutes. Remove the pan from the oven and place back on the hob. Pour in the stock and wine, season and bring to the boil. Simmer for 2 minutes then stir in the tagliatelle.

Cover the pan and cook for a further 4-5 minutes or until the pasta is cooked. Serve the ragout in individual bowls topped with 2 tsp each of fresh tomato salsa. Serve with a mixed salad and a sensible dressing if desired.[46]

---

[45] Elliott, Renée & Eric Treuille, op. cit.
[46] *Daily Mail*, "The Definitive Diet" series.

CANDIDIASIS
Candida albicans, yeasts, fungi, parasites, bacteria, etc.
Excerpted from *The ABC's of Disease*
by Phillip Day

Little critters are a fact of life with all organic life-forms. The human body is no exception. Our bowel, for instance, plays host to over three pounds' weight of up to 400 species of bacteria and other organisms that help break down food for nutrient absorption and create the necessary waste products to be eliminated from the body. These micro-organisms, in a properly healthy body, exist in harmony with one another inside the host. It's when we change our internal environment through diet and lifestyle choices that serious problems start.

Candida albicans, a usually benign and beneficial yeast, is one of the main trouble-makers. When fed a constant diet of its favourite totty, glucose, and housed in its ideal environment of acidic, oxygen-repelling, fermentation-rich tissues and ductal structures, it multiplies prolifically and feeds and grows, damaging healthy cells and producing toxins that compromise the body's own immune defences.

Parasites
All people, especially those with cancer, play host to one form of parasite or another. Parasites are life-forms that are uninvited lodgers in our acidic bodies who do not pay rent. They can range from tiny amoebae detectable only with a microscope to tapeworms many feet in length.

We inadvertently pick up parasites through our day-to-day activities and especially through eating undercooked or contaminated food. Try an experiment and put some cat food out in an isolated part of your yard for a few sunny days and then go back and examine it (don't let any pets interfere and keep away from grass and earth). You will invariably find it crawling with infestation.

Blood flukes can enter our systems through infected drinking water and take up residence in the bladder, intestines, liver, lungs, rectum and spleen, laying their eggs and breeding in humans for up to 20 years. Trichina worm larvae found in undercooked pork migrate from the intestines through the blood and lymphatic system, eventually lodging in muscles and ducts. Threadworm larvae enter skin from the soil and pass through the bloodstream to the lungs, sometimes causing pneumonia.

Eliminating parasites is effectively a three-phase program. Killing them, flushing them out and then supplementing our relieved bodies with healthy nutrients to maintain optimum health.

Fungi and yeasts

Fungi also inhabit our bodies. Canadian researcher Ron Gdanski describes them to us: *"There are about 500,000 fungal species on Earth. Biologically, they are closely related to both the plant and animal kingdoms.... Fungi are not plants because they lack the vascular tissues (phloem and xylem) that form true roots, stems and leaves of higher plants. Fungi also lack chlorophyll for photosynthesis and must therefore live as parasites. Their function on Earth is to break down dead and dying matter for renewal. **Fungi also attack living tissue and survive by producing toxins and enzymes to defeat the host's immune system.***"* [47]

Yeasts like *Candida* are single-cell fungi, which multiply prolifically when fed organically bound carbon, one essential element that characterises all dead and living matter. Fungi and yeasts are like the hyenas of the veld. They are scavengers. Abundant carbon compounds like sugars are their favourite. The more sugary foods we eat, the more these life-forms feast within us. Yeasts are well known to ferment sugar into alcohol in the absence of oxygen. Breweries depend on it! If we fail to exercise or eat oxygen-rich, organic fruits and vegetables, we are inviting the dangerous and unwelcome proliferation of fungi – by providing an oxygen-poor, fermentation-rich breeding ground in which they can boom. We literally become our own brewery to the delight of our squiggly little lodgers deep inside. *The Columbia Encyclopaedia* states:

---

[47] Gdanski, Ron, op. cit. p.29

"Their bodies [fungi] consist of slender, cottony filaments called hyphae; a mass of hyphae is called a mycelium. The mycelium carries on all the processes necessary for the life of the organism, including in most species, that of sexual reproduction."

The connection between parasites and cancer

Cancer is a healing process that has not terminated upon completion of its task.[48] *Candida* and other trouble-makers have a powerful ability to hurt our bodies, their thread-like mycelia penetrating and invading the walls of human cells to take root and feed. This damage initiates a healing process of these infected cells which can proceed uncontrolled into a cancer tumour. This cancer is fuelled further by the sugary diet of the patient which, in an acidic, anaerobic environment, produces alcohol waste products through fermentation, which in turn fuels the cancer further.

As fungi and yeasts, and their progeny – tumours – thrive, they secrete enzymes of their own to depress the immune system of the cells around them and rob them of their oxygen, thus maintaining their ideal fermentation environment, enabling them to invade and corrupt more cells.

Here we have the dynamic connection between parasites/yeasts/ fungi and cancer. Cancer occurs commonly in areas of the body hosting tubes, ducts and storage areas where sugars can become trapped and bereft of oxygen, for this is where the critters can feed most gluttonously. Blood clots, stagnant lymph fluids, injuries that won't heal and benign tumours are also prime spots where blood sugars collect and provide fodder for opportunistic parasites. These then thrive and damage cells, which trigger the healing process, which replicates these mutated cells into tumours, etc.

Killing overgrowths of *Candida* and other parasites is not the only task necessary for a full and complete remission from diseases like cancer, heart complaints, multiple sclerosis and AIDS. A reorganisation of your body into a well nourished, oxygen-rich, active

---

[48] Day, Phillip, *Cancer: Why We're Still Dying to Know the Truth*, op. cit.

and toxin-free environment is essential to ensure that you cut off the food supply to these insidious and selfish beasties, and boost immune function and cleansing to restore your body to its rightful health.

Candidiasis

Trouble caused by *Candida* is known as 'candidiasis' or 'the yeast syndrome'. The problems parasites, fungi and yeasts cause in the body are only now being understood and appreciated. Before, most doctors would not suspect this type of problem unless presented with the obvious symptoms of thrush, jock itch, athlete's foot or toenail fungal infections. But, like a leviathan, fungal problems have risen from obscurity within our consciousness to become a major health hazard today. What's caused it? Excess antibiotic intake and those sugary, yeasty, alcoholic lifestyles.

Symptoms of parasitic infection

Poor immune function, lack of sex drive, toe-nail fungus, chronic bloating and gas, rectal itching, mouth sores (white patches on the tongue or inside the cheeks), tingling, sexually transmitted diseases (STDs), numbness or burning sensations, chronic fatigue (ME), allergies, food sensitivities, chemical sensitivities, thrush, chronic vaginal yeast infections and discharges (usually thick, white), rashes and itching around male genitalia, bladder infections, intestinal cramps, cravings for sugar-rich foods and sweets, cravings for foods rich in yeast and carbohydrates.

Those suffering from candidiasis may have a history of use of antibiotics, prednisone or other cortisone-type drugs. They are bothered by tobacco smoke and perfumes. They can feel spacy or 'not quite there', variously suffering menstrual irregularities, endometriosis, spots in front of eyes, diarrhoea, constipation, chaotic bowel movements, muscle aches and prostatitis.

Associated complaints

Irritable bowel syndrome, eczema, psoriasis, depression, irritability, pre-menstrual syndrome (PMS), cancer, multiple sclerosis, heart disease, arthritis, osteoporosis, chronic fatigue syndrome (ME), leaky gut syndrome, esophageal reflux, lupus, gout, Crohn's disease, hyperactivity, infertility, herpes, chlamydia, Alzheimer's, scleroderma, Raynaud's disease, kidney stones, Cushing's disease.

Causes

Parasites, yeast, fungi and bacteria invariably proliferate in moist, warm zones, especially when beneficial gut flora, which usually control the uglies, are killed by prolonged exposure to any of the following:

- Antibiotics and other drugs
- Malnutrition
- Constant cooked food devoid of enzymes
- Constant acid ash food consumption
- Cigarette smoking
- Fluoridated water consumption
- Antacids
- Excess sugar and high glycaemic carbohydrate intake

The antibiotic assault

Steven Ransom in his *Wake up to Health in the 21st Century*, conducts a full-on assault against the wilful prescription of antibiotics, arguing that often they do more harm than good, especially to children, who tend to have them routinely prescribed for common ailments, such as middle ear infections (*otitis media*):

"During the first two years of their lives, American children will spend an astounding 90 days taking antibiotics. This may be causally related to the current increase in chronic respiratory diseases, such as wheezing and asthma, in young children. A research group from Boston reported recently that 32 percent of such children wheeze, 26 percent use bronchodilators, and 12 percent have asthma before the age of five." [49] [50]

---

[49] **Ransom, Steven** *Wake up to Health in the 21st Century*, Credence Publications, 2003

[50] "Time to Stop the Misuse of Antibiotics", *Mothering Magazine* online at http://www.mothering.com/10-0-0/html/10-4-0/10-4-healingear104.shtml

Michael Schmidt states in his book, *Beyond Antibiotics*:

"[Antibiotics] cause the destruction of normal bowel flora. Like pesticides, antibiotics kill good bugs along with the bad ones. Wide-spectrum antibiotics are notorious for this. The human intestine has a delicate ecology in which certain bugs help digest food, produce certain vitamins, and maintain a balance of organisms that prevents harmful bacteria and yeasts from multiplying. Wide-spectrum antibiotics derange the normal ecology of the intestine. This can cause parasitic infection, vitamin deficiencies, loss of minerals through diarrhoea, inflammation of the gut, mal-absorption syndromes and development of food allergies due to defects in intestinal function." [51]

Take action♥

Clinics can do a stool analysis in which *Candida* and other problems will be apparent if they are the cause of your problems. Measures adopted against *Candida*, fungi, yeasts and other parasites are designed to starve the parasites into submission. **THE ANTI-*CANDIDA* DIETARY REGIMEN** forms the backbone of this and should be adhered to strictly. Components below are designed to kill parasites and flush them from the system. The magnesium oxide bowel cleanse will take three truck-loads out in one go, but beneficial flora such as *Lactobacillus acidophilus/bifidum* need to be reinstated afterwards to keep the balance.

- **DIET: COMMENCE THE ANTI-*CANDIDA* DIETARY REGIMEN**
- **DIET:** AVOID ALL SUGAR AND YEAST
- **DIET:** Avoid all products that readily break down into glucose or have a yeast component: e.g. bread, pasta, pastries, sweets, pies, alcohol, beers and some fruits and vegetables (see diet above)
- **DIET:** Drink at least four pints of clean, still mineral water a day (not out of plastic bottles and please avoid distilled water)

---

[51] **Schmidt, Michael** *Beyond Antibiotics*, North Atlantic Books, 1992

- **PREVENTION:** Don't smoke and avoid second-hand smoke
- **PREVENTION:** Avoid behavioural and dietary problems that have caused the condition
- **DETOXIFICATION:** Conduct a two-week bowel cleanse with magnesium oxide
- **DETOXIFICATION:** Cancer patients should also consider colon hydrotherapy for extra internal cleanliness
- **RESTORING NUTRIENT BALANCE: COMMENCE THE BASIC SUPPLEMENT PROGRAM**, including:
- **ANTI-*CANDIDA*/FUNGAL SUPPLEMENTATION**
- A priobiotic supplement to install beneficial flora
- Vitamin C complex (ascorbates plus bioflavonoids), 5 g per day. This amounts to one heaped teaspoon of C-complex powder. Take a half teaspoon in a bland juice, such as pear, every morning and another half teaspoon at night
- Vitamin A emulsion, as directed
- 1 tbsp of ground flaxseed (linseed) meal or oil daily
- **BOOSTING IMMUNITY:** Astragalus and echinacea (herbs), two capsules, three times a day
- **BOOSTING IMMUNITY:** Indulge in regular and vigorous exercise (unless health problems prevent this) to exercise and pump the lymphatic system, rid the body of waste products and draw oxygen into the body
- **BOOSTING IMMUNITY:** Get plenty of rest!
- **TIP:** Be consistent!
- **TIP:** Do not fall prey to sugar cravings. Who really wants to splurge and feed inside you? Starve 'em.

Herxheimer's reaction

During the parasite-killing process, the body may become clogged with catabolic debris, dead beasties and their resultant toxaemia, including ammonia. You may feel ill as your symptoms apparently worsen. This is known as Herxheimer's reaction, after the venerable German dermatologist of the same name. It is temporary and will be experienced in proportion to the vehemence with which you apply your attack strategies. Symptoms may be alleviated by commencing the anti-*Candida* diet a full two weeks prior to starting on the anti-fungal/yeast supplements.

Maintenance – The open road ahead

Once clear of the problem(s), avoid the minefields to prevent re-infestation. Remember: what you eat determines the condition of your body's immune system, and poor immunity is written on the gravestone of many a promising lad and lass. Solving the fungal/parasite problem in the body can lead to tremendous health benefits, not to mention advances in finding the answers to many of the vexing diseases which still afflict us.

MAINTENANCE RECIPES

The purpose of the following section is to provide recipes that will help with an ongoing regimen of 80% alkali/20% acid ash foods (see ash charts at end of book). Ensure that a good percentage of the diet comprises raw, living, whole foods (see previous section for ideas). The key in this section is to have fun rather than rigidly follow 'food fascism'. The point to bear in mind while preparing or eating food is to limit the intake of protein to the body's usual requirements (20-40 g a day). Excess protein consumption and overeating, especially to the degree we see today, are unnecessary and dangerous to health.

MILLET BREAD
(makes 4 loaves)

*500 g **millet flour***
500 g strong wholemeal bread flour
500 g strong white flour (or use wholemeal instead)
2 x 7 g sachets dried yeast
2 tbsp honey
4 tsp sea salt
approx 2 pints water
approx 5 tbsp sunflower oil or olive oil

Sheryl McMillan: Helen's recipe states to use the normal method for making bread. For convenience I have written such a procedure below, but you may already be used to baking bread and have your own variation, in which case it is probably best if you do it the way you normally would first.

Note about flour and water; Different flours and different climates will vary the amount of water needed and this is something that cannot be predicted 100%, so you may want to start with slightly less water and add as needed until the dough reaches the right consistency.

Combine the yeast with a couple of ounces of warm water in a glass or small bowl. Stir in 1 tsp honey and set aside. In a few minutes a foam should be forming on the top. This indicates that the yeast is good. If nothing happens use a new batch of yeast and try again.

In a bowl or saucepan, pour approx 2 pints hand-hot water and mix in the honey and salt until they dissolve.

Sift the flour into a large mixing bowl and form a well in the centre. Add the yeast and oil and gradually add in the water and honey/salt mixture, stirring until all the ingredients are added and mix to a soft dough. If the dough is too sticky, add some flour, and if it is too dry, add a tiny bit of water until it becomes soft and pliable, but not wet.

On a lightly floured surface knead for about 10 minutes and then form into a ball, cover and set aside in a warm place for about an hour (may take longer if the room temp is colder). The dough should rise to about twice its original size. Then gently punch down and knead again for about 5 - 10 minutes. Form into loaves and let stand covered for another 45 minutes or until well risen.

Place in lightly oiled baking tins or 'free form' on a baking sheet and bake for about 10 minutes at 190C/375F/Gas Mark 5, then lower heat to 180C and cook for another 20-30 minutes. Baking times will vary depending on size of loaves and individual ovens.[52]

SPICY MILLET BREAD
(makes 1 loaf)

3½ oz **millet**
6 oz **buckwheat flour**
2 tsp sea salt
1 tsp raw honey
1 tsp dried chilli flakes (optional)
¼ oz sachet of easy-blend dried **yeast**
12 fluid oz warm water
2 tbsp butter
1 onion, roughly chopped
1 tbsp cumin seeds
1 tsp ground tumeric

Bring 7 fl oz water to the boil, add the millet, cover and simmer gently for 20 minutes until the grains are soft and the water is absorbed. Remove from the heat and leave to cool until just warm. Mix

---

[52] Clifford, Helen E. Edit and baking method by Sheryl McMillan

together the flour, salt, honey, (chilli flakes if using) and yeast in a large bowl. Stir in the cooked millet then add the warm water and mix to form a soft dough.

Turn out onto a floured work surface and knead for 10 minutes until smooth and elastic. Place in an oiled bowl and cover with an oiled, clear film or a dish/tea towel. Melt the butter in a heavy-based frying pan and fry the onions for 10 minutes until softened, stirring occasionally. Add the cumin and turmeric and fry for 5 to 8 minutes longer, stirring constantly until the cumin seeds begin to pop. Set aside.

Knock back the dough by pressing down with your knuckles to deflate the dough. Shape it into a round. Spoon the onion mixture into the middle of the dough bringing the sides over the filling to make a parcel. Seal the parcel well. Place the loaf on an oiled baking sheet, seam side down. Cover and leave in a warm place for 45 minutes until doubled in bulk.

Meanwhile, pre-heat the oven to 220C/425F/Gas Mark 7. Bake the bread for 30 minutes until golden. Check the bread is fully cooked by tapping on its underside – it should sound hollow. Leave to cool on a wire rack.

EZEKIEL'S BREAD

*4 pkgs **yeast***
1 cup warm water
½ - ¾ cup honey
8 cups whole wheat flour
*5 cups **barley** flour*
*1½ cup **millet** flour*
1/4 cup rye flour
*1 cup **lentils**, cooked and mashed*
4-5 tbsp olive oil
4 cups warm water
1 tbsp sea salt

Dissolve yeast in 1 cup warm water and 1 tbsp honey. Set aside 10 min. Combine the next 5 ingredients. Blend lentils, oil, remaining honey and a small amount of water in a blender. Place in a large mixing bowl with remaining water. Stir in two cups of (mixed) flour. Add the yeast mixture. Stir in salt and remaining flour. Place on floured bread board and knead until smooth. Put in oiled bowl. Let rise until double in bulk (about 1½ hours). Knead again, cut dough and shape into 4 large loaves. Place in greased pans. Let rise about 45-60 min. Bake at 375F for 45 min. to 1 hour.[53]

CHICKPEA PANCAKES
(The pancakes may be made in advance and reheated)

1 egg
175 ml water
2 tsp raw honey
3 tbsp olive oil
*80 g fine **chickpea flour***
a pinch of sea salt

Beat the egg together with the milk/water, honey and 3 tbsp of the olive oil. Sieve the chickpea flour into another bowl with the salt, and gradually mix in the egg mixture until totally smooth. Strain through a fine sieve. Leave to rest for 30 minutes at room temperature.

---

[53] http://lifemakes.hypermart.net/archive/September.html

To make the pancakes, you can either do individual ones in a small non-stick pan, or smaller versions by pouring small spoonfuls of the mixture into a larger pan, four or five at a time.

Lightly coat the pan with the olive oil and heat. Pour in a small ladleful of the batter and rotate the pan to make a thin pancake. Fry for 30-40 seconds, then turn over with a spatula and fry the other side for the same length of time.[54] Toppings that would go on your pancakes:

DRIED APRICOTS OR FIGS WITH LEMON OR HONEY
200 g dried apricots or figs
*½ tsp ground **apricot kernels***
grated rind and juice of 1 unwaxed scrubbed lemon
2 tsp runny honey

Bring the honey and lemon rind and juice to simmer point. Add the apricots and the ground apricot kernels, bring back to boil, simmer for 2-5 minutes. Serve warm or cold.

SULTANAS OR RAISINS IN APPLE JUICE WITH A TOUCH OF GINGER
200 g sultanas or raisins or both mixed
200 ml apple juice
1 tsp grated fresh ginger

The above toppings can be sprinkled with 1 tsp ground apricot kernels. Bring the apple juice and ginger to the boil, add the fruit, bring back to boil, remove from heat and cover. Leave for 5 minutes. Serve either warm or cold.

SUNFLOWER SEED MUFFINS
¾ cup filberts (or any nuts), ground
¾ cup sunflower seeds, (ground)
¼ Celtic salt (or sea salt)
2 egg yolks (organic)
1 tbsp oil
2 tbsp vegetable glycerin (found in some health food stores)

---

[54] **Blanc, Raymond** *Blanc Vite*, Headline Books, 2000

¾ *cup water*
1 tsp vanilla
2 egg whites, beaten

Pre-heat oven to 190C/375F/Gas Mark 5. In a bowl, combine nut meal, sunflower seed meal and salt. In another bowl, beat egg yolks, then add oil, glycerine and water. Combine wet and dry mixtures. Fold in beaten egg whites. Bake in oiled mini muffin tins for 15-20 minutes. Yields 18 mini-muffins. They may be frosted with egg white protein powder, vegetable glycerin, butter, vanilla and a little water and cinnamon to taste. [55]

SESAME SEED COOKIES
(makes about 12 cookies)

1 egg (organic)
¼ cup sesame flour
½ tsp vanilla extract
¼ tsp salt
*¼ cup **cashew** butter*
¼ cup sesame seeds, plus more as needed
¼ tsp baking powder
1 tsp oil

Mix all the ingredients together. Roll each ball in additional sesame seeds until covered. Flatten slightly on an oiled baking/cookie sheet. Bake for 12 minutes. [56]

DATE AND WALNUT LOAF

2 cups of wholemeal self-raising flour
2 cups white self-raising flour
2 tbsp olive oil spread
3 tbsp honey (clear)
*½ cup **walnuts**, chopped*
1½ cups of skimmed milk
1 tsp bicarbonate of soda

---

[55] Mercola, Joseph, *The Mercola Cookbook*, op. cit.
[56] Ibid.

Mix the two flours together in a large bowl. Rub in the spread. Stir in the honey, dates and nuts. Mix a little of the milk with the bicarbonate of soda and add to the bowl with enough of the remaining milk to form a soft dough. Turn into a non-stick, 2 lb baking tin, the base lined with non-stick baking parchment. Bake in a pre-heated oven at 190C/375F/Gas Mark 5 for about an hour. Cool then turn out onto a wire rack, remove the paper and leave to cool. Serve sliced with an olive oil spread.[57]

PERFECT CAULIFLOWER SOUP

1 large cauliflower, cored and cut into florets
1 medium onion, finely chopped
6-8 spring onions
1 clove of garlic, crushed
1 tsp curry powder
2 tbsp groundnut oil
200 ml coconut milk
sea salt and pepper to taste

Heat the groundnut oil and add the spring onions and garlic and cook gently until soft. Add the cauliflower and cover with water, cook over a medium heat until tender (about 20 minutes). Drain.

Liquidise in a blender or food processor with coconut milk until smooth. Season to taste and add a pinch of nutmeg. Sprinkle with 1 tsp coriander seeds and some finely chopped fresh coriander. Reheat gently.

TOASTED ALMOND & WATERCRESS SOUP
(serves 4)

3 bunches **watercress**
500 ml home-made stock
50 g flaked almonds
1 tsp ground **apricot kernels**
450 g bio yoghurt

---

[57] Humphries, Carolyn, *7-Day Low Cholesterol Diet Plan,* op. cit.

Wash watercress and shake off excess moisture. Chop roughly. Place in saucepan with cold stock and bring to the boil. Simmer gently for 8 minutes, leave to cool. Strain, reserving the stock.

Toast almonds slowly either under grill or in griddle pan until golden brown, reserving a few for garnish. Grind the almonds to a fine powder together with the apricot kernels. Liquidise watercress and the powdered nuts and process again. Add the yoghurt and incorporate quickly. Finally, add the hot watercress-flavoured stock and give final blend. Season well to taste. Leave to cool, cover and chill. Serve in individual bowls garnished with a few toasted almonds and a sprig of watercress.

MORE SUBSTANTIAL SOUPS WITH PULSES

A word on pulses. Cooked properly they should not give any digestive problems at all. Follow these hints:

- Weigh the required amount of beans
- Check them over, discarding any that are damaged or marked
- Rinse thoroughly in a sieve

Soak overnight using 4 measures of water to 1 measure of beans. After soaking rinse the beans in several changes of fresh water. Place in a large pan and cover so that the water is about 10 cm above the level of the beans. Add 1 tbsp cider vinegar. Bring to a fast boil and remove completely any scum that forms on the top. Drain and rinse the beans, cover again with fresh water and bring to the boil. Turn down the heat so that the beans are just bubbling. Keep the water topped up with boiling water from a kettle, so that the beans remain covered.

Continue cooking in this way until the beans are easily broken with the point of a knife. Cooking times vary with the type of bean, so check with your own recipes or the guidance on the product packet, but constantly check as you go along. Herbs added to the boiling liquid will also aid digestion, but do not add seasoning until the end of cooking as this will harden the skins.

TOM KHA GAI
THAI CHICKEN SOUP

2 tsp **macadamia oil**
1 tbsp fresh chopped lemon grass
3 tsp grated fresh ginger
1 clove garlic, crushed
3 green Thai chillies, chopped finely
4 kaffir lime leaves, sliced thinly
¼ tsp ground turmeric
3 ¼ cups light coconut milk
3 cups chicken stock
2 cups water
1 tbsp fish sauce
4 cups shredded chicken
3 green onions
¼ cup lime juice
2 tbsp chopped coriander
fresh mint
bean sprouts

Heat oil in a large saucepan. Add lemon grass, ginger, garlic, chilli, lime leaves and turmeric, stirring for 2 minutes until fragrant. Stir in the coconut milk, stock water and sauce, bring to the boil. Add the chicken and reduce the heat. Simmer, uncovered for 10 minutes. Just before serving, stir in the onion, juice and coriander. Top with fresh mint and bean sprouts. [58]

---

[58] *The Australian Women's Weekly Cookbook*, "Meals in Minutes".

WHITE BEAN SOUP

3 large spoons of white beans
1 large onion, peeled and chopped
2 cloves garlic, peeled and crushed
1 stalk celery
1 sprig each of parsley, thyme and rosemary
1 bay leaf
2 litres stock, vegetable or chicken
4 tbsp extra virgin olive oil
juice ½ lemon
sea salt and freshly ground pepper

Soak the beans overnight in twice their volume of water. Next day heat 2 tbsp oil in a large saucepan and soften the onion for 5-10 minutes without letting it brown. Add the garlic and cook for 1 minute. Add the drained beans, celery, herbs, bay leaf and pepper. Pour in the stock and bring to a simmer. Cover and continue to simmer gently for 1½ hours, stirring from time to time. Check whether the beans are tender. If not, continue to cook for a further 15-30 minutes. When the beans are cooked, season with salt and liquidise. When ready to serve, re-heat the soup gently add the lemon juice and 2 tbsp olive oil. Check the seasoning before serving.

SPICED TURNIPS WITH SPINACH, TOMATOES AND COURGETTES

500 g/1 lb plum, or other well flavoured tomatoes
60 ml/4 tbsp olive oil
2 onions, sliced
500 g/1 lb baby turnips, peeled
3 baby courgettes, cut in half lengthways
500 g/1 lb fresh, young spinach with stalks removed
60 ml/4 tbsp chopped fresh coriander
5 ml/1 tsp paprika
freshly ground black pepper

Remove skin from the tomatoes by covering them with boiling water and allowing them to steep for three minutes. Pour away the water and cover the tomatoes with cold water and allow to steep for 5 minutes. Peel away loosened skin and chop into medium sized chunks.

Heat the olive oil in a large frying pan and fry the onion slices until they are golden brown. Add the baby turnips, tomatoes and paprika and cook until the tomatoes become pulpy. Add the courgettes and cover with a lid. Continue to cook until the baby turnips are soft.

Stir in the chopped coriander, the prepared spinach and a little ground, black pepper. Cooking for a further 2-3 minutes until the spinach has wilted. Add more ground black pepper to taste. Serve this stew warm or cold.

RED PEPPER CREAM
(a delicious summer soup)

4 red peppers
4 ripe beef tomatoes
2 tbsp extra virgin olive oil
2 onions
3 cloves garlic
1 tbsp **buckwheat flour**
½ tsp chilli flakes or a dried chilli, seeded and finely chopped
raw honey to taste
850 ml vegetable stock

Skin the peppers by placing them under a very hot grill until the skin is seared on all sides, then place in a polythene bag for 5 minutes after which the skins should slip off easily. Cut in half and remove seeds, then slice the peppers.

In a large, heavy pan, heat the oil and fry the onions gently until transparent for 5-8 minutes. Add the garlic and cook for one more minute. Stir in the buckwheat flour, add the sliced peppers (reserving a few slices for decoration), tomatoes, chilli flakes, raw honey and stock.

Season well and simmer for 30 minutes. Remove from heat, allow to cool, remove a few slices of peppers, then liquidise the soup. Chill, then serve in bowls. Decorate with a slice or two of peppers.

This soup can also be served hot. Heat the soup very gently being careful not to allow it to boil. Serve in bowls.

AVOACADO CHILLED SOUP

avocados
vegetable stock
juice of a lemon or lime
1 chilli, de-seeded and chopped

Puree the avocado with vegetable stock. Flavour with the lemon or lime juice and chilli. Garnish with natural yoghurt and diced avocado.

PURE INDULGENCE! OVEN ROASTED CHIPS

900 g potatoes (Desiree are best)
*1 dessert sp **apricot kernel oil***
sea salt

Pre-heat oven to 230C. Leaving on the peel, wash and dry the potatoes. Slice in quarters lengthways to produce wedges about 5 cm thick. Place in a bowl with the oil and salt until all the potatoes are well covered in the oil. Roast in the hottest part of the oven for about 30 minutes or until crisp & golden brown. Sprinkle with a little more salt and serve straight away.

CREAM CHEESE SAUCE

Cream cheese is a useful addition to a food-combining diet, making a starch cheese sauce possible.

2 tbsp unsalted butter
*1½ oz **buckwheat flour***
8 oz cream cheese
1 pint spring water

Melt the unsalted butter and stir in the flour to form a roux. Remove pan from heat and mix in the cream cheese. Gradually stir in the water to form a smooth mixture, then bring gently to the boil, stirring continuously until the mixture thickens. Season to taste. (Some powdered mustard may be added if a stronger flavour is required).

ROAST TOMATOES
(serves 4)

8 plum or other well-flavoured tomatoes, cut in half
4 tbsp extra virgin olive oil
1 clove garlic, crushed
14 basil leaves
sea salt and freshly ground black pepper

Pre-heat oven to 190C/375F/Gas Mark 5. Heat 1 tbsp oil and the garlic in an oven roasting dish. Add the tomatoes, cut side down, and sauté for a few minutes until coloured.

Add half the basil leaves and the remaining olive oil. Transfer the dish to the oven and cook for 5-10 minutes depending on the size of the tomatoes. Transfer all but two of the tomatoes to serving dish and keep warm. Mash the remaining tomatoes in the oil over a gentle heat. Season to taste. Sieve or liquidise together with the oil. Pour over the baked tomato. Decorate with the remaining basil leaves and serve.

THAI CHICKEN IN LETTUCE LEAF CUPS

8 large iceberg lettuce leaves
1 tbsp dark soy sauce
1 tbsp sesame oil
1 tbsp lime juice
1 large courgette, grated

1 medium carrot, grated
2 green onions, sliced
1 medium red capsicum, sliced thinly
4 cups shredded chicken
1 tbsp fresh mint, chopped
2 tbsp coriander, chopped
2 tbsp chilli sauce

Trim the lettuce leaf edges with scissors. Place leaves in a large bowl of iced water, refrigerate. Meanwhile, combine soy sauce, oil and juice in a bowl. Add the courgette (zucchini), onion, capsicum, chicken, mint and half of the coriander, toss gently. Dry the lettuce, divide leaves among serving plates. Top with chicken mixture, drizzle with combined sauce and remaining coriander. [59]

BUCKWHEAT WITH LEMON AND HERBS

Buckwheat is as quick to prepare as couscous and **bulgar wheat**. This dish makes a great accompaniment to all kinds of vegetable dishes, roasted or stir-fried. Feta cheese or goats cheese or **cashew nuts** can be added for a more substantial dish.

9 oz untoasted **buckwheat,** *preferably organic*
1 tbsp olive oil
long strands of lemon zest
juice of 1 lemon
4 heaped tbsp flat-leaf parsley, chopped
4 heaped tbsp chives, chopped
6 salad onions, cut into shreds

Rinse the buckwheat in a sieve, then place in a dry saucepan and cook over a moderate heat for about 5 minutes, stirring it from time to time, until more golden. Pour 1 pint boiling water into the saucepan. Cover and leave for 15 minutes away from the heat.

---

[59] *Women's Weekly Cookbook*, op. cit.

Using a fork, stir in the olive oil, lemon zest and juice, parsley, chives and salad onions into the buckwheat. Season with salt and black pepper.[60]

BRAISED STUFFED ONIONS

4 large onions
1 bay leaf
fresh thyme
2 large cloves of garlic, peeled and finely chopped
150 g brown rice
50 ml extra virgin olive oil
1 bunch fresh parsley, finely chopped
tomato sauce, left un-strained

Start with the tomato sauce, made with:
400 g tomatoes, de-seeded and chopped
100 ml extra virgin olive oil
1 small onion
2 cloves garlic, peeled and finely chopped
4 tbsp brown wholemeal crumbs

Heat the olive oil in a pan. Add the chopped onions and cook until transparent. Add the chopped tomatoes and garlic, cover, bring to the boil and simmer 8-10 minutes. Cool and liquidise. If a smoother sauce is required, strain through a sieve.

Bring sufficient water to cover the onions to the boil. Add the bay leaf, thyme and garlic. Add the onions, making sure the water covers them, and bring back to the boil. Simmer gently for about an hour until the onions are soft. Remove carefully and drain on kitchen paper. Reserve the onion water.

Meanwhile, make the stuffing. Boil the rice in plenty of salted water until cooked. Strain thoroughly and transfer to a bowl. Add the oil and chopped parsley. Stir together. Season to taste.

---

[60] **Elliot, Rose** *Fast, Fresh, and Fabulous*, BBC, 2003

106

Carefully remove the centres of the onions, leaving an outer shell of two or three layers. Chop the onion centres and add to the stuffing. Carefully fill the centres of the onions with the stuffing. Top with the crumbs. Pour the tomato sauce, dilute with a little of the onion water in a heatproof dish. Place the onions on top. Heat through in a hot oven for about 10 minutes and finish off under a hot grill to glaze the tops. Sprinkle with the chopped parsley.

RICE AND SEAWEED SALAD
(serves 6)

225 g (8 oz) white long grain rice
1 tbsp sunflower oil
1 tbsp sesame oil
1 medium courgette, thinly sliced
1 orange pepper, de-seeded and thinly sliced
1 bunch spring onions, trimmed and shredded
1 inch piece of fresh root ginger, peeled and cut into thin strips
2 tbsp sesame seeds
55 g packet of crispy seaweed

FOR THE DRESSING
3 tbsp soy sauce
2 tbsp extra virgin olive oil
2 tbsp clear honey

Bring a large pan of lightly salted water to the boil and cook the rice for 10 minutes until just cooked. Drain and set aside. Meanwhile, heat both the oils in a large wok or frying pan and cook the courgette and orange pepper for 5 minutes until golden and cooked through.

Add the spring onions, ginger and sesame seeds and cook for a further 2 minutes. Add the drained rice and toss together well over the heat. Add the crispy seaweed and toss together again. Pour all the dressing ingredients into a small pan and heat, stirring until well blended.

Transfer the rice and seaweed salad to a large serving dish and drizzle over the warm dressing to serve. [61]

---

[61] *Woman And Home*, June 2001

A POPEYE SPECIAL

½ lb fresh **spinach** leaves
watercress
1 tbsp lemon juice
3 tbsp olive oil
sea salt
1 clove of garlic
ground black pepper
1 hard – boiled egg, cut into wedges
1 medium tomato, cut into wedges
½ red onion, sliced into rings

Dry the spinach, then tear into bite-sized pieces. Sprinkle the salt into a wooden bowl and rub the garlic clove around the bowl. Add the lemon juice and olive oil and refrigerate the bowl for 1 hour. When ready to serve, add the spinach and watercress and sprinkle with pepper. Garnish with egg tomato and onion rings. Toss and serve.[62]

KITCHRI
(serves 4)

3 tbsp olive oil
1 finely chopped Spanish onion
4 garlic cloves, finely chopped
½ tsp ground turmeric
½ tsp ground ginger
½ tsp curry powder
1 tsp cumin seeds
1 pinch of chilli powder
1 potato, cubed
2 tomatoes, quartered
8 oz **mung beans**, soaked overnight
8 oz long grain **brown rice**
15 fl oz milk (preferably goat's milk)
Freshly ground salt and black pepper
1-2 tbsp lemon juice

---

[62] Adapted from Mercola, Joseph, *The Mercola Cookbook*, op. cit.

Heat the oil in a flameproof casserole dish. Add the chopped onion and garlic and cool for ten minutes, stirring until soft but not browned. Add the ground turmeric and ginger, the curry powder, cumin seeds and chilli powder and fry for a further 3-4 minutes, stirring occasionally.

Add the cubed potato, tomato quarters, drained mung beans and brown rice to the mixture. Fry gently for five minutes then stir in the milk and 15 fl oz water. Season with freshly ground black pepper. Bring to the boil, then cover and simmer gently for 40/45 minutes, until the rice and beans are cooked. Stir occasionally.

Turn off the heat and leave to stand covered for 15 minutes, or until all the liquid has been absorbed. Season with salt and lemon juice. Stir the mixture with a fork and serve immediately on a warmed plate.[63]

CAESAR SALAD
(serves 4)

4-6 heads baby lettuce
2 hard-boiled eggs, quartered
6 tbsp extra virgin olive oil
1 clove garlic, crushed
1 tsp Dijon mustard
¼ tsp sea salt and freshly ground pepper

SERVE WITH CROUTONS
1 slice wholegrain bread
2 tsp butter
1 clove garlic

Cut bread into cubes, melt the butter in a small heavy frying pan, swirl the garlic clove around to flavour the butter and then discard the garlic. Sauté the bread cubes turning frequently until they are golden and crisp. Drain on kitchen paper.

Mix the garlic and oil in the salad bowl and add lemon juice and seasoning. Add the salad leaves and croutons and toss thoroughly.

---

[63] **Carrier, Robert** *Making the Most of Vegetables*, Marshall Cavendish House, 1985

SPROUTING FOR HEALTH!
(some words of wisdom from cook Barbara Robinson)

Seeds and certain grains are latent powerhouses of nutritional goodness and life energy. Add water to germinate them, let them grow for a few days in your kitchen and you will harvest delicious, inexpensive fresh foods of quite phenomenal, health-enhancing value.

The vitamin content of seeds increases dramatically when they germinate. For instance, the Vitamin C content in some seeds multiplies five times within 3 days of germination. Sprouted seeds and grains also appear to have anti-cancer properties, which is why they form an important part of the gentle, natural methods of treating the disease.

When you sprout a seed, enzymes, which have been dormant, spring into action, breaking down stored starch into simple, natural sugars, splitting long-chain proteins into amino acids and converting saturated fats into free fatty acids. What this means is that the process of sprouting turns these seeds into foods, which are very easily assimilated by your body when you eat them. Sprouts are, in effect, pre-digested and as such have many times the nutritional efficiency of the seeds from which they have grown. They also provide more nutrients ounce-for-ounce than any natural food known.

Another attractive thing about sprouts is their price. The basic seeds and grains are cheap and readily available in supermarkets and health-food stores - **chickpeas**, **brown lentils**, **mung beans**, wheat grains, and so forth. Since you sprout them yourself with nothing but clean spring water, they become an easy source of organically grown fresh vegetables, and you don't even need a garden! Sprouted vegetables provide a fresh, unpolluted nutrient source and are ready to eat in a minute by popping them into salads or sandwiches.

With the rising cost of food and the falling nutritional value in the average diet, sprouted vegetables are the cheapest form of natural food around. (One researcher actually calculated that by eating sprouted vegetables alone you could live on less than 20p per person per day! Of course, no one would suggest that you should live on sprouts alone.) Sprouts are an ideal addition to the table of every family, particularly if the budget is tight.

110

Children love to grow them themselves and because they grow so quickly, the average sprout is ready for the table in about three days.

HOW TO SPROUT

The easiest way to sprout seeds and grains is to buy an inexpensive sprouter from your local health store. (They will soon order one if there are none in stock). All you need to do is sprinkle the seeds on each layer of the sprouter (they usually have three or four tiers) and water twice a day – it's as simple as that!

SEEDS TO SPROUT

ALFALFA - (complete protein) Vitamins A, B, C, D, E, F, and K. rich in iron. Alkaline.

FENUGREEK - These have a curry flavour. Rich in iron, Vitamin A and protein. Good for ridding the body of toxins.

RADISH - The hot flavour is great for dressings or mixed with other sprouts. Good for clearing mucus.

BEANSPROUT SALAD WITH FETA CHEESE
(serves 2 as a main course)

A mixture of:
alfalfa
sprouted **lentils**
sprouted **mung beans**
chickpeas
green pepper, seeded and finely chopped
small onion, thinly sliced
tomatoes diced
some freshly chopped herbs of your choice
6 oz feta cheese
black olives

DRESSING

1 clove of garlic, chopped finely
1 tbsp chopped fresh basil
1 tbsp lemon juice
1 tbsp virgin olive oil
black pepper

Mix the sprouts with the salad ingredients and chopped herbs. Mix and arrange on individual plates. Top with feta cheese and olives. Mix together the dressing ingredients in a screw-top jar by shaking them. Pour the dressing over the salad and serve immediately.

SHERYL'S CUSTOMISABLE CURRY SAUCE

This sauce is a very versatile curry and can be used to make many different dishes by adding your favourite vegetables. Cooking time - at least an hour.

sunflower oil for frying
1 large onion, chopped very fine in a food processor or blender
5 cloves garlic, crushed
1 1/2 inch piece root ginger, peeled and thinly sliced
hot green chillies, to taste
3/4 tsp turmeric powder
3/4 tsp ground cumin
3/4 tsp ground coriander seed
7 tablespoons plain passata (smooth, thick, sieved tomatoes in liquid, may be called tomato purée but is NOT tomato paste)
vegetables of your choice (peas, carrots, aubergine, cauliflower, potatoes, squash, mushrooms, etc.)
coconut milk (optional)

Most of these ingredients should be easy to find either at your local grocery store, or most certainly at a good Indian grocer. One distinction that is not always clear is that there is a difference between the coriander (cilantro) powder that you commonly see, the green coriander leaves and the coriander seeds. You need the actual seeds and these will most likely not be ground already. I usually just use a mortar and pestle as the quantity is small. Crushed seeds are much more aromatic and lively.

One note regarding cooking. This dish is best when cooked slowly for a long time, but do not let the spices burn, or it will create a bitter taste. Spices often open up more when lightly roasted but they cannot be allowed to go too long on a high heat.

Heat the oil in a heavy pan then add the chopped onion and stir for a few minutes on a high heat (but do not let anything burn or brown).

Add the ginger, garlic and green chilli. Stir for 30 seconds then lower the heat (just above simmer). Cook uncovered for 15 minutes on low, stirring from time to time making sure nothing browns or burns. Add the turmeric, cumin and coriander and cook, still very gently, for about 5 minutes. Then add the passata and about 5-6 oz water and stir thoroughly.

At this point you can add vegetables if you want, keeping in mind how long it usually takes to cook the specific vegetable, i.e: if using carrots, potato or aubergine. Add various coarsely crushed nuts (**cashews** are quite nice, as are many others - use about a tablespoon or so). If you like the flavour of coconut, you may add about a tablespoon or so of dried coconut milk powder (OR a comparable sized chunk of coconut cream, OR approx two tablespoons of coconut milk, whichever is available). This is optional. At this stage you could also add a few teaspoons of ground **apricot kernels**.

Simmer uncovered for about 25-30 minutes (more if you want) stirring occasionally. The curry is generally served hot with rice and Naan.

GADO GADO
(serves 4)

5 tbsp sesame seed oil
1 lb white cabbage, shredded
4 oz cauliflower florets
3 oz green beans, cut into 1 ½ inch lengths
*6 oz **bean sprouts***
4 oz salted peanuts
*15 **apricot kernels***
3-4 tbsp lemon juice
1 garlic clove, finely chopped
1 shallot, finely chopped

Heat the sesame oil in a wok or deep frying pan, add the shredded cabbage, cauliflower florets, green beans and bean sprouts and cook over a high heat, stirring for 3-4 minutes until soft but still crisp. Remove the vegetables from the pan and arrange on a plate. Allow to cool.

Meanwhile heat 3 tbsp of the sesame seed oil in a small saucepan, add the salted peanuts and kernels and fry for 5-6 minutes over high heat until golden, stirring constantly. Drain and dry thoroughly on absorbent paper. Put them in a blender with 3 tbsp of lemon juice and blend to a puree.

Add the remaining sesame oil to the saucepan and sauté the finely chopped garlic clove and the shallot for 5 minutes, or until softened. Add the peanut sauce and add more lemon juice if necessary, mixing well. Put the warmed sauce in a small bowl, place this on the serving dish of salad and serve.

MUSHROOM PATE EN CROUTE

2 large onions, chopped
2 tbsp olive oil
2 garlic cloves, chopped
9 oz chestnut mushrooms, sliced roughly
8 oz **cashews**, powdered
10 **apricot kernels**, powdered
8 oz ground **bitter almonds** or regular almonds
8 oz soft wholemeal breadcrumbs
2 tbsp soy sauce
2 tbsp lemon juice
2 tsp dried tarragon
1 tsp yeast extract
1 lb 2 oz puff pastry
beaten egg, for brushing

Pre-heat oven to 200C/400F/Gas Mark 6. Fry the onions in the olive oil in a large saucepan for 7 minutes, until tender, then add the garlic and mushrooms and cook for a further 5 minutes, or until the mushrooms are tender. Tip the mixture into a food processor and blend to a puree.

Put the ground cashew nuts, apricot kernels and almonds into a bowl with the breadcrumbs, the mushroom puree, soy sauce, lemon juice, tarragon and yeast extract, and mix well. It will be quite stiff. Season well with salt and pepper.

Roll the puff pastry out on a lightly floured board to make a square about 15 inches in size. Transfer the pastry to a baking sheet and add the mushroom mixture in the centre, forming it into a loaf shape.

Make diagonal cuts in the pastry about ½ in apart on each side of the mushroom mixture, then fold these up over the mushroom pate to make a kind of plait effect. Tuck in the ends neatly, trim off any extra bits and brush with beaten egg.

Bake for 40 minutes, or until the pastry is puffed and golden brown. Great with cranberry sauce or horseradish sauce.[64]

---

[64] Elliot, Rose, op. cit.

MEATING A MAIN PROBLEM
by Phillip Day

Excessive meat consumption is a leading cause of ills today for several reasons. One, meat consumption (indeed any animal protein consumption) creates acidosis in the body on a cumulative basis, which the body has to counter, using buffering methods to alkalise the acid prior to expelling though the kidneys. This usually involves the depletion of alkalising minerals, such as sodium, calcium and magnesium, which have to escort the protein acids out of the body, 'sacrificing' themselves in the process.

Eating small amounts of organic meat however will not usually cause a problem with acidosis, provided that enough vegetables and alkali ash foods are consumed in the diet as well. Your blood needs to remain rigidly between pH 7.35-7.45, a slight alkali. Any variance above or below this would be life-threatening within hours.

The answer, as previously stated, is to consume a maintenance diet, which is 80% alkali ash foods and 20% acid ash foods. The charts showing these components are at the back of this book.

ARE HUMANS CARNIVORES?
Answer: No, they are omnivores who are physiologically adapted to consume flesh foods in moderation. Small amounts of organic flesh foods (including fish) for optimum nutrient intakes, especially folic acid (B9) and cyanocobalamin (B12), are ideal.

WHY HUMANS ARE NOT CARNIVORES...
- A carnivore's teeth are long, sharp and pointed for tearing and biting. Humans have flat molars for grinding and crushing
- A carnivore's saliva is acid to digest animal proteins. Human saliva is alkaline for carbohydrates
- A carnivore's saliva does not contain ptyalin for breaking down starch. Human saliva contains ptyalin
- A carnivore's stomach is a simple round sack that secretes 10 times more hydrochloric acid than a non-carnivore to digest meat. Human stomachs are oblong, convoluted and have a duodenum for vegetation

- A carnivore's intestines are three times the length of its trunk for expelling animal proteins quickly before they rot. Human intestines are twelve times the length of our trunks for extracting nutrients from vegetation over a period of time
- A carnivore's liver can expel 10-15 times more uric acid from meat consumption than a non-carnivore. Uric acid is toxic to humans
- Humans do not have the enzyme uricase to break down uric acid. Carnivores do
- A carnivore does not sweat through the skin and has no pores. We sweat through the skin and have pores
- A carnivore's urine is acid. Ours is alkaline
- A carnivore's tongue is rough. Ours is smooth
- Our fingers are designed to pluck apples out of a tree, not to tear animals apart.

THE DANGERS OF EXCESSIVE MEAT CONSUMPTION

- Excessive meat digestion consumes pancreatic enzymes, which are vital for arresting healing processes in the body. Low levels of pancreatic enzymes trypsin and chymotrypsin, for example, can leave us vulnerable to non-terminated healing processes which go on to form cancers.
- Meat is almost always combined with carbohydrates in our diets to produce putrefaction in the body. Animals in the wild instinctively do not combine proteins and carbs.
- Meat products can take up to 70 hours to pass through the alimentary tract. In the elderly, intestinal transit time (ITT) can take up to two weeks.
- Animal proteins require bile acids to digest them. Bile acids in the colon are carcinogenic in humans.
- Animal proteins cannot be used by humans directly. They have to be broken down into their constituent amino acids and then reconstructed into human proteins.
- Meat when cooked loses any amino acid benefit and produces toxic acidic metabolites, such as uric acid. If we were to eat meat for its nutritive value, we would eat it raw and unadulterated.

- Carnivores don't eat other carnivores unless in an emergency. They almost always consume plant and vegetation eaters and go for the contents of their stomachs first for the nutrients.
- Meat for strength? The silverback gorilla is three times the size of a human and thirty times as strong. It is vegetarian.
- Meat contains high saturated fats, almost no carbohydrate content, no fibre and is an extremely inefficient protein source.
- Chronic consumption of animal products is being blamed for causing heart disease, colon cancer, obesity, diverticulosis and arthritis.
- Excessive meat consumption is also being blamed for early sexual development in our children.
- Commercially raised meat contains many chemical contaminants common to milk. Excessive meat-eaters show higher levels of estrogen than low- or non-meat-eaters.[65]

CONCLUSION

Cut way down on meats. Ensure those you do eat are hormone- and pesticide-free (organic).

Cold, deep-caught fish are an ideal source of essential fatty acids and other vital nutrients. Ensure where possible that the fish you choose have not run the risk of being contaminated in rivers or off-shore areas with pesticides and other chemical residues. Again, consume fish according to the alkali/acid ash food chart at the back of this book.

---

[65] All points sourced in Day, Phillip *Health Wars*, op. cit.

ORIENTAL SOLE

700 g fillets lemon sole or plaice, skinned
6 cm root ginger, finely sliced
1 tbsp soy sauce
1 tbsp sesame seeds
*1 tsp **apricot kernels**, finely ground*
2 cloves garlic, finely chopped
2 spring onions, finely chopped including the green parts
1 dessert sp sesame oil
*1 dessert sp **groundnut oil***
juice 1 lemon

Heat oven to 200C. Heat a heavy frying pan over medium heat. When it is hot, toast the sesame seeds for 1-2 minutes until golden brown. Shake the pan constantly. Place seeds in a bowl, together with the apricot kernels.

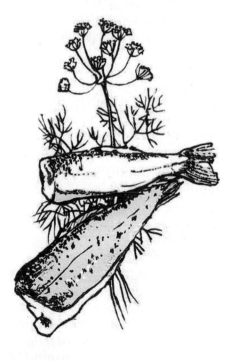

Add the oils to the pan and over medium heat fry the garlic and ginger until just golden. Add these to the nuts together with any oil left in the frying pan. Mix in the lemon juice, soy sauce and spring onions. Season fish and spread the nut mixture over the surface. Place on a greased baking tray and cook in centre shelf oven at 200C. Decorate plates with green salad leaves and serve with a side salad.

DEVILLED TURKEY STIR-FRY

3 tbsp olive oil
½ cup of almonds, blanched
*2 tbsp ground **apricot kernels***
4 sticks of celery, thinly sliced on the diagonal
6 oz organic carrots, thinly sliced on the diagonal
500 g turkey/chicken breast, cut into strips
2 tbsp curry powder
1 tsp mustard powder
½ tsp paprika
1 tbsp corn flour
1 tbsp Worcestershire sauce
8 fl oz orange juice
bamboo sprouts
***watercress**, chopped*

Heat the oil in a large frying pan or wok and fry the almonds until golden. Remove from the pan with a slotted spoon. Add the vegetables and cook over a high heat for 3 minutes, stirring all the time. Stir in the turkey and spices and stir fry for a further 5 minutes. Put the corn flour, Worcestershire sauce and orange juice in a jug, and mix together. Pour the mixture into the pan and simmer for 2 minutes. Season with salt to taste. Sprinkle with the almonds and apricot kernels. Serve immediately on a bed of bamboo sprouts and chopped watercress.[66]

ORIENTAL DUCK WITH ORANGES

3 oranges
1 duck
1 tbsp butter
1¼ tbsp sesame seed oil
1¼ cups light chicken stock
2/3 cup Tsingtoa or Sapporo (Chinese or Japanese beer)
2½ tbsp red currant jelly
sea salt and fresh ground black pepper
1¼ tsps arrowroot
1¼ tbsp cold water

---

[66] *Tesco Recipe Collection*, June 1996, p. 11

Using a potato peeler, carefully pare the rind thinly off two of the oranges. Cut the rind into very large fine shreds using a sharp knife. Put the shredded orange rind into a small bowl and cover with boiling water. Set aside. Cut away the peel and the pith from the remaining orange and slice into thin rounds. Set aside also.

Wash the duck inside and out and pat thoroughly dry. Put the butter and the oil in a wok and heat. Add the duck and fry, turning frequently until brown. Remove from the wok and cool down for about 10 minutes. Cut away the leg and wing ends, then cut the duck in half lengthways. Now cut each half into 1-inch strips.

Remove the fat from the wok then return the duck to the wok. Add the stock, Chinese or Japanese beer and red currant jelly, squeezed orange juice and the well-drained strips of rind. Bring to the boil, season to taste. Reduce the heat, cover the wok and simmer gently for another 20 minutes until well cooked.

Skim away any surface fat and thicken the sauce by mixing the arrowroot with the water and stirring them back into the wok. Bring to the boil and simmer for another 7 minutes, or until the sauce is fairly thick. Arrange the duck on plates and garnish with orange slices and fresh watercress.[67]

STIR-FRY CHICKEN AND ALMONDS

1 cup whole **almonds**, (bitter if possible)
1 tsp **apricot kernels**
1 tbsp **macadamia** (or peanut) oil
chicken breasts, sliced thinly
1 red onion, chopped coarsely
1 small leek, sliced
2 garlic cloves, crushed
2 tbsp hoisin sauce
green beans, halved
2 sticks celery, sliced thinly
1 tbsp soy sauce
1 tbsp plum sauce

---

[67] Heinerman John, op. cit.

Heat wok. Stir-fry almonds and apricot kernels until lightly browned, remove from wok. Heat half of the oil in same wok; stir-fry chicken until brown. Heat remaining oil in wok, fry onion, leek and garlic until fragrant. Add Hoisin sauce, beans and celery; stir-fry until beans are just tender. Return chicken to wok with remaining sauces; stir-fry until heated through. Toss almonds through chicken mixture.[68]

HONEY CHILLI CHICKEN SALAD

organic chicken breast fillets, sliced thinly
¼ cup honey
4 red Thai chillies, seeded and sliced
1 tbsp fresh ginger, grated
asparagus, trimmed
*2 tbsp **macadamia oil***
4 green onions, sliced
1 medium green capsicum, sliced
1 medium carrot, sliced thinly
1 Chinese cabbage, finely shredded
1/3 cup limejuice

Combine the chicken, honey, chilli and ginger in a bowl. Cut asparagus spears in half, lightly steam until tender, rinse immediately under cold water, drain. Heat half the oil in a large wok or frying pan, stir-fry the chicken until browned and cooked through. Place chicken and asparagus in a bowl with the onion, capsicums, carrot, cabbage, juice and remaining oil, toss gently.[69]

CHICKEN AND BEAN MADRAS

*1 ½ cups **brown wholegrain rice***
*1 tbsp **macadamia oil***
1 large white onion, sliced thinly
chicken thigh fillets, sliced thinly
¼ cup madras curry paste
green beans, chopped coarsely
½ cup chicken stock
1 tbsp tomato paste

---

[68] *Woman's Weekly Cookbook*, op. cit.
[69] Diabetes UK, *Diabetes Cookbook*, op. cit.

Cook the rice. Heat the oil in a wok or frying pan, stir-fry the onion and chicken until browned. Place curry paste in another wok, stir-fry until fragrant. Return the chicken mixture to the wok with beans, stock and tomato paste. Stir-fry until the sauce thickens slightly and chicken is cooked through. Serve rice with chicken.[70]

QUICK FISH AND PRAWN CURRY
(serves 4)
In a blender mix until smooth:

½ unwaxed lemon peel, grated with juice of 1 lemon
2 cloves garlic, crushed
2 tsp curry powder
35 g unsalted peanuts

Then you will need:

500 g uncooked medium prawns, shelled & de-veined, but leaving on the heads and tails
800 g boneless white fish fillet, such as haddock, cod, chopped into bite sizes
1-2 tbsp extra virgin olive oil
3 spring onions sliced, including some of the green
60 ml water

Heat a large frying pan with 1 tbsp olive oil, cook prawns & fish separately in batches until just tender, adding more oil if needed. Remove the fish from the pan and keep warm. In the same pan add the onions and cook for 1 minute then add the curry mixture and water

---

[70] *Women's Weekly Cookbook*, op. cit.

stirring gently. When blended adjust the seasoning and add the prawns and fish and warm through. Serve with a favourite salad.[71]

CRISPY SEA BASS
(serves 6)

1 sea bass, about 1.5 kg, cleaned and de-scaled
1 kg leeks, trimmed, washed and thinly sliced
2 shallots, peeled and finely chopped
1 fennel bulb, trimmed and finely sliced
1 tbsp sunflower oil
sea salt and freshly ground pepper
1 tbsp fennel seeds
*2 tsp finely ground **apricot kernels***
finely grated peel of 1 unwaxed or scrubbed orange
finely grated peel of ½ lemon

Pre-heat oven to 220C. Heat the oil and a little butter in a large sauté pan. Add the leeks, shallots and fennel, season and cover. Cook over a low heat, stirring occasionally for about 30 minutes, or until soft. Leave to cool.

Mix the fennel seeds, apricot kernels, grated orange and lemon peel with 1 tbsp olive oil. Spread inside the cavity of the fish. Lightly oil a gratin dish and spread the leeks on the base. Place the fish on top. Season and brush with oil, cover with foil and cook for 20 minutes. Remove foil and continue cooking for a further 10 minutes until the skin is crisp and the fish cooked through. Serve with lemon wedges and a crisp endive, chicory and walnut salad.

SHERYL'S FAST SUSHI

For some people the word 'Sushi' means something exotic and strange, involving raw fish. In reality the word 'sushi' can be used to describe any dish made with the special variety of rice and cooked with a certain blend of Japanese vinegar. For those who are turned off by the word 'sushi', think of it as a new and interesting rice dish and forget about the raw fish, we won't be using any if that's not for you.

---

[71] *Waitrose* Magazine, Waitrose Stores, UK

Japanese sushi rice
roasted seaweed sheets (sushinori)
wasabi paste
Japanese soy sauce
raw honey
Japanese rice wine vinegar
various vegetables in small amounts (cucumber, carrot, etc.)

EQUIPMENT
Bamboo shushi rolling mat
cutting board
sharp knife

About ingredients: The rice is a short-grain Japanese rice and it will sometimes say 'sushi rice' on the package. The roasted seaweed sheets used in this recipe are 8x7 inches in size, and you will usually see them in packages of 10.

First you must cook the rice as you would normal white rice. The amount is dependant on how many rolls you want, but a general guideline is that a reasonable portion of rice you would normally serve one person will make two rolls. You will probably have a little rice left over and it's not an exact science anyway.

So, begin by adding your portion of rice to a saucepan with a lid. Add just slightly more water than rice, cover and bring to the boil. As soon as the water boils, reduce the heat to a very low simmer and allow to cook for about 10 to 15 minutes. If you are used to cooking rice a certain way, you may do this rice the same way. Sometimes the directions say to rinse the rice first, but I have had no problems skipping that step and it still worked fine.

While the rice is cooking, pour approx 1/4 tablespoon of the Japanese rice vinegar in a small bowl or glass. Add about 1/4 tablespoon of honey and stir until the honey is dissolved (keep in mind this quantity is for one person, about two rolls).

When the rice is thoroughly cooked, turn off the heat and uncover so the steam escapes and the rice begins to cool. Add the vinegar and honey mixture and gently fold into the rice, taking care not to 'mush' the rice in the process. If you used the right amount of water, the rice should not be soggy but should be sticky and fluffy (we want it sticky).

Lay a sheet of the roasted seaweed on the sushi rolling mat. The sheets I use are almost square but are slightly oblong. The longest side of the sheet should go in the direction of the length of the roll as opposed to wrapping around it, since you will have plenty of height to wrap with.

Spoon out a portion of the rice and place it in the centre and towards your end of the seaweed sheet and begin flattening the rice into a thin layer. Continue this process until you have a layer of rice approx ¼ inch deep and extending all the way across the sheet about 3½ inches wide. We want the rice all the way to the edge nearest and all the way to both ends. At this point there should be a couple inches of bare seaweed sheet on the far side facing away from you. This is something you will get a feel for after you make a few.

For a basic cucumber roll, cut a strip from the cucumber lengthwise keeping the outside skin and forming a wedge approx ¼ inch wide and ¾ inch deep. Trim off the seed part on the inside edge so that you have an almost square strip of cucumber about ¼ inch square with the skin on one side.

Lay the cucumber strip across the middle of the rice on your seaweed sheet. If it doesn't go all the way across, use another bit to make up the difference, letting it stick out a bit at each end.

Now roll the seaweed starting from the near side (where the rice is at the edge, this side should be nearest you while the extra seaweed should be facing away). It should roll around with the cucumber in the middle and both edges of the rice area should now touch each other. There will be some extra seaweed and you don't want to leave it on or it will be too tough, so trim this extra inch or so off.

You should now have a roll about 8 inches long and about 1¼ inches in diameter and the seaweed should be joined so that it stays together. This is really not difficult and you'll quickly get the feel of it. Use the remaining rice to make as many rolls as you want.

Once the roll is complete, slice it in half in the centre and then slice each of the halves into three pieces so you have six pieces just over an inch long each.

To serve, put a little wasabi in a small dish (like a saucer or other small dish approx 4 or 5 inches in diamcter) and pour in enough soy sauce to form a pool about 1/8 inch deep. Mix the wasabi in the soy sauce until some of it is dissolved. (In my experience there is a range of strength and some wasabi is very potent, so don't over do it, you can always add more or smear a dab on the roll if you want). Then take a slice and let it sit for a couple seconds in the soy sauce/wasabi dish and then eat it immediately.

There are many variations in the fillings for sushi. Among them are crab leg, avocado, thin strips of carrot, various smoked fish, spinach and many, many more. This is a great dish to experiment with and try different combinations.

Professional sushi chefs generally do them in combinations that have contrasting colours and flavours, but this is something you can customise to create your own unique sushi dishes if you want.

SHERYL'S CHINESE-STYLE NOODLES

Here is a very quick and easy dish that can be used as a side dish or a main course if you are not very hungry and just want something light and easy. The cooking time is approximately 20 minutes.

Chinese dried noodles
onion, chopped (regular and/or salad (spring) onions)
*choice of vegetables (**bamboo shoots**, green pepper,*
***water chestnuts**, **bean sprouts**, olives, tomato, etc.)*
hoisin sauce
root ginger
shoashing (Chinese rice wine)
sunflower oil for cooking
hot green pepper (optional)
sea salt/pepper
*crushed **apricot kernels** (optional)*

This dish can be made in almost any quantity, and the ratio of ingredients is not terribly critical, so any amounts listed are for one serving and you can multiply that for a larger quantity.

About the noodles: I do not use egg noodles. The appropriate noodle is a fine to extra fine dried noodle, which is made almost entirely of wheat flour and water - this is the authentic Chinese ingredient for this dish. I have had good results with the noodles from Winner Foods Ltd with a green label that says 'Earthbrand' and I like the 'extra fine' ones. You may have something different in your area but just be aware that the choice of noodles makes a big difference.

For the noodles: In a medium (or large if making more) saucepan, bring some water to a boil. I use about the same amount of water I would for pasta. Add the amount of noodles you want, keeping in mind that they will expand from their dried state. It's usually not critical when you add them and you can put them in before the water boils and get on with the stir-fry. They don't take long to cook, probably just a few minutes once the water boils, so keep an eye on them while frying the other ingredients. When they become soft (but still 'al dente'), turn off the heat and drain off the water and return the noodles to the pan (there is no need to rinse them).

For the stir-fry: Take a frying pan or wok and heat over a medium flame for about 30 seconds. Pour in a little sunflower oil (just enough to coat the bottom of the pan for stir-frying), and heat over a medium flame. You should not need a lot of oil as long as your pan or wok is in good condition and not scarred or scratched. When the oil is beginning to heat up, add either chopped regular onion (approx 1/4 of a medium onion for one person) and/or add the white part only of about two salad onions chopped into small slices.

Add approx 1/4 inch of root ginger, chopped finely (this can be varied depending on how much you like ginger). If you want the dish a little spicy and hot, add some chopped green hot peppers at this point. I have found a variety that is not terribly hot, but adds a nice 'kick' to the dish. You can use your own judgement on this depending on what is available in your area and how hot you like it.

When the onions are starting to soften and look transparent, add your choice of vegetables. Do not let the onions brown. If they start to brown, either the heat is too high or you are letting them cook too long.

This dish is really intended to be mainly noodles, so I don't add many vegetables, but this is subject to interpretation depending on what you like. I generally add approx one tablespoon (or a conservative handful) of bamboo shoots and this is one of the distinctive flavours of Chinese cooking. You can then add a bit of chopped green pepper, chopped water chestnuts, chopped tomato or even chopped black olives. Some of these items would not technically be 'authentic' to a Chinese dish, but can be lovely all the same.

You can also add **spinach** if you like, and I usually use about a large handful for one person. The uncooked leaves will seem to be too much, but once they wilt in the heat they settle nicely into the dish. You could also add bean sprouts, but be careful not to cook them too long or they will become soggy and lose their crispness.

At this stage, add the green part of the salad onions, if you are using them, chopped into approx 1/4 inch slices. Pour in approx 1/2 tablespoon Shaoshing and stir the onions and vegetables around to coat them.

At this point the noodles should be done and the water drained off so they are back in the pan and dry. Pour the contents of the frying pan into the pan with the noodles and then add approx 1½ teaspoons of Hoisin sauce and approx 2 teaspoons of crushed apricot kernels (if using). Stir all the ingredients lightly until the noodles are pretty much coated and brown-tinted from the Hoisin sauce. Add a bit of sea salt to taste and a touch of black pepper if you like. (You can use soy sauce but it is not really required, and if you do, it may well be salty enough to negate adding more salt).

Serve immediately in an appropriate sized bowl.

CRISPY RAINBOW TROUT WITH
CREAMED CELERIAC
(serves 4)

2 small rainbow trout, filleted
250 g peeled & chopped celeriac
3 potatoes, peeled and chopped
2 tsp sea salt flakes
2 tsp freshly ground black pepper
*2 tbsp **juniper berries**, coarsely chopped*
*2 tsp **apricot kernels**, finely ground*
2-3 tbsp olive oil

Place the chopped celeriac and potatoes in a pan and just cover with almond milk (made with 100 g almonds, blanched and skinned, blended at high speed for 2-3 minutes with 300 ml cold water. This should then be strained through a fine sieve).

Simmer the celeriac & potatoes until both are soft. Strain, reserving a little of the hot milk. Add 1 tbsp olive oil and sea salt to taste and mash until smooth and creamy. Keep warm whilst preparing the fish. Mix 1 tsp sea salt flakes with the chopped juniper, ground pepper and apricot kernels. Coat the trout with this mixture. Heat a frying pan and add a little oil. When hot, add the fish, skin-side down and cook for about 4 minutes, until the skin is crisp. Turn carefully and cook on the other side until tender. Serve on a mound of creamed celeriac and with a salad as above.[72]

BAKED PLAICE WITH PARMESAN CRUMBS

(serves 2)

2 large plaice fillets, skin on
4 heaped tbsp fine fresh white breadcrumbs
*2 tsp ground **apricot kernels***
6 tbsp finely grated Parmesan cheese
4 tbsp melted raw butter
2 tbsp extra virgin olive oil

Lay the fish skin-side down in an ovenproof dish. Mix the breadcrumbs, apricot kernels, cheese, melted butter and oil and grind over a little salt and black pepper. Spread the seasoned crumbs loosely over the fish, then bake for twenty minutes in an oven pre-heated to 220C/Gas Mark 7.[73]

NUT STUFFED TROUT WITH SUN-DRIED TOMATOES

2 filleted trout (1¼ lb)
*½ cup of mixed unsalted **cashews, pine nuts, apricot kernels** and **walnuts***
olive oil
1 small onion, finely chopped
2 tbsp grated fresh root ginger
4 tomatoes, chopped
4 sun-dried tomatoes, chopped
2 tbsp chopped fresh tarragon
salt and freshly ground black pepper
salad leaves, to garnish.

Pre-heat oven to 190C/375F/Gas Mark 5. Put the nuts in a shallow tray and place in the oven for 3-4 minutes until golden, shaking the tin occasionally. Chop roughly. Heat a small amount of oil in a frying pan and fry the onion for 3-4 minutes until soft and golden. Stir in the

---

[72] *Waitrose* Magazine (recipe adapted).
[73] **Slater, Nigel** *Real Food*, Fourth Estate, 1998

ginger and cook for another minute and spoon into a mixing bowl. Stir in the tomatoes, sun-dried tomatoes, toasted nuts and tarragon, and season with salt and pepper.

Place the two trout onto oiled foil and spoon the stuffing into the filleted cavities. Bring the foil round to encircle each fish and add a sprig of tarragon and a little olive oil to each. Fold the foil over to secure and place the fish parcels in a large roasting tin. Cook for 20-25 minutes until the fish is just tender. Cut into thick slices and serve with salad leaves.

TROUT IN FOIL

1 medium sized trout, gutted and cleaned
¼ cup olive oil
½ shallot or small onion, thinly sliced
1 tsp sea salt
1 tbsp lemon juice, (lime, grapefruit or a combination)
ground black pepper to taste

Heat oven to 200C/400F/Gas Mark 6. Oil a sheet of kitchen foil large enough to envelope the trout when it is laid on its side. Brush the inside of the trout with olive oil and place 3 or 4 onion rings inside the fish.

GRILLED SALMON WITH PAK CHOI
(serves 4)

2 oz pak choi
1 shallot, peeled and sliced
7 oz plump salmon fillets
1 tbsp walnut oil
2 tbsp olive oil

DRESSING:
1 red chilli, deseeded and chopped
½ oz fresh root ginger, peeled and chopped
1 oz fructose
juice of 1 lime
2 fl oz olive oil
½ tsp sesame seeds

handful of roughly chopped coriander
salt and freshly ground black pepper
walnuts

Put the chilli and ginger in a pestle and mortar and grind to a paste. Add the fructose. Add the lime juice, olive oil, sesame seeds and coriander. Season to taste. Slice the pak choi and mix with the shallot.

Heat the griddle pan. Brush the salmon fillets lightly with walnut oil, season, then grill until cooked. Heat the olive oil in a frying pan and cook the pak choi and shallot until the pak choi wilts.

Divide the pak choi between four warmed plates. Place a salmon fillet on each and drizzle with dressing.

NUT ROAST
(This mixture can be used for a number of popular dishes)

8 oz mixed nuts (ground almonds and hazelnuts) plus finely chopped walnuts
2 medium sized onions
1 tbsp virgin olive oil
*3 oz whole-wheat breadcrumbs or cooked **millet***
1 clove garlic
1 tsp dried mixed herbs
2 level tsps yeast extract or 2 tbsp mild curry powder
8 oz fresh tomatoes, skinned and chopped
4 oz chopped mushrooms (optional)
1 egg, beaten
*finely ground **apricot kernels***
sea salt and freshly milled black pepper

Pre-heat oven to 190C/375F or Gas Mark 5. Large oven-proof deep dish or loaf tin. Gently fry onions in a little oil until they are softened – about 10 minutes. Meanwhile mix the nuts, breadcrumbs or cooked millet together in a large bowl. Add the garlic, herbs, yeast extract or mild curry powder then stir in the onions, mushrooms (optional) and tomatoes. Mix thoroughly and season.

Now add the beaten egg to bind the mixture together. Finally, pack the prepared mixture into the dish and bake for 30 to 40 minutes until golden and set. Sprinkle with finely ground apricot kernels and serve hot with tomato sauce or brown onion gravy; serve cold with salad and millet, couscous or rice.[74]

COTTAGE PIE
(a vegetarian version of Shepherd's pie)

Make up as for Nut Roast, but add sufficient vegetable stock to give a loose mixture. Spoon into an oven-proof dish and top with boiled potatoes mashed with a little milk, butter, flaked almonds and a little ground apricot kernels.

Season to taste. Bake in the oven at 200C, 400F or Gas Mark 6 for 20-30 minutes until the potato is crisp and golden.[75]

BURGERS

Make as for Nut Roast but, when cold, shape into burgers. Coat with a mixture of finely ground apricot kernels and/or wholemeal flour and fry in shallow oil for 3-5 minutes each side until golden brown. Serve hot with sliced onion and a wholemeal bap or with vegetables and gravy. Alternatively, the burgers can be baked in a pre-heated oven at 180C/365F/Gas Mark 5 for 30 minutes. [76]

NUT AND SAUSAGE MASH

Make Nut Roast as above, omitting mushrooms. When cold, mould into sausage shapes, dip into flour mixed with a little finely ground apricot kernels and place into refrigerator an hour before cooking. When ready to cook, place on a greased baking tray and cook in a pre-heated oven at 180C/365F/Gas Mark 5 for 30 minutes. Serve with mashed potatoes, onion gravy and fresh vegetables. [77]

---

[74] Robinson, Barbara
[75] Ibid.
[76] Ibid.
[77] Ibid.

STUFFED MARROW RINGS,
MUSHROOMS, TOMATOES, ETC.

FOR MARROW RINGS: Cut marrow into 2-inch slices and place on a greased roasting tin. Fill centres with the cooked Roast Nut filling and cover with foil. Bake in a pre-heated oven 200C, 400F or Gas Mark 6 until marrow is tender (approximately 40 minutes). Serve with tomato and basil sauce and top with watercress.

Note: A nice variation of this is to place a heaped tsp of cream cheese with herbs on top of the Nut Roast before covering with foil.

FOR MUSHROOMS: Select one large open mushroom per person. Chop the stalk and mix with the cooked, Nut Roast mixture then fill each mushroom. Cover with a teaspoon of cream cheese and herbs if preferred, cover with foil and bake at above temperatures until the mushrooms are tender (approx 20 minutes, depending on size and thickness). Serve with tomato sauce poured over the top and garnish with watercress. (Recipe for tomato sauce below).

FOR TOMATOES: Choose one large tomato per person. Cut off the top and carefully scoop out the seeds, making a hollow inside. Stuff with the Cooked Nut Roast mixture and replace the tops. Place on a greased roasting tin and cover with foil. Serve with a cheese and chive sauce poured over the top. Garnish with parsley.

FOR STUFFED GREEN PEPPERS: Cut peppers lengthways and remove seeds and stalks. Cook the peppers in boiling water for 5 minutes. Drain. Stuff with Nut Roast mixture and pack into a shallow ovenproof dish. Bake on the middle shelf of a pre-heated oven at 190C, 375F, Gas Mark 5 for about 30 minutes. Serve with tomato sauce (recipe below).

FOR BUCKWHEAT SPAGHETTI BOLOGNESE: Cook the spaghetti according to instructions. Add tomato sauce to Nut Roast mixture and pour over spaghetti. (As an alternative, use chopped, fresh oregano, marjoram or coriander instead of the basil, if you wish). Sprinkle with parmesan cheese and serve.

TOMATO SAUCE
(makes 1 pint)

1 medium sized onion
12 oz tomatoes
1 oz butter
½ pint (300 ml) of vegetable stock or water
1 crushed garlic clove
1 tbsp tomato paste
chopped fresh basil leaves or ½ tsp dried basil
salt and pepper to taste

Chop the onion and tomatoes. Melt the butter in a large saucepan and fry the onion gently until transparent. Add the remaining ingredients (except the fresh basil) and then bring to the boil. Simmer uncovered for 20 minutes until reduced. Add chopped fresh basil and liquidize, if necessary, to get a smooth sauce. Some ground **apricot kernels** can be added at this stage to the sauce. [78]

TOASTED "NUTSTEAK" AND ONION SANDWICHES

Slice leftover, cold Nut Roast and chop some onions. Spread some soft butter thinly on both sides of each slice of wholemeal bread (preferably **spelt** bread). Spread one side of one slice of bread with yeast extract, top with the Nut Roast mixture and onion, top with another slice of bread and cook under medium grill until crisp on top. Serve with horseradish sauce if liked and a mixed salad garnish. For a really tasty addition to the salad garnish, add some sprouted fenugreek seeds plus some chopped beetroot mixed with creamed horseradish.

LENTIL AND WATERCRESS PATTIES

1 large onion, peeled and finely chopped
1 garlic clove, peeled and crushed
3 tbsp olive oil
*½ lb (225 g) split red **lentils**, washed and drained*
1 pint vegetable or chicken stock
2 tbsp tomato puree

---

[78] Ibid.

2 oz **cashew nuts**
2 oz chopped **apricot kernels**
1 bunch organic fresh **watercress**, *finely chopped*
1 tbsp fresh mint
chopped fresh coriander or any other fresh herb, such as oregano
marjoram
buckwheat flour, *for dusting*
sea salt and freshly ground pepper

Fry the onion and garlic in the oil for 2 minutes. Add the lentils and stir. Pour on the stock and add the chopped herbs. Bring to the boil. Lower the heat and cover the pan and allow to simmer for 40 minutes. The lentils should be soft and have absorbed the stock. Beat the lentils with a wooden spoon and beat in the tomato puree, cashew nuts, apricot kernels, watercress and mint. Add salt and pepper.

Divide the mixture into 12 and mould into flat 'burger' shapes. Toss them in the flour to coat thoroughly. Fry the patties in hot oil over moderate heat for approximately 5 minutes on each side or until they are crisp. As this is a starch meal these patties would be very good served cold with a salad. They can also be served in a wholemeal bap.

MILK – MASS HUMAN FOOD?
(or commercial whitewash?)
by Phillip Day

Another food that creates confusion is cow's milk. My position on this issue, based on the research Credence has done, is that milk creates problems for some and not for others. Physiologically, humans are designed to feed from their mother's milk, but following weaning, the humans in many cases lose the enzymes required to break down milk proteins, rendering them 'lactose intolerant'. It is a fact that millions of people today can't consume milk or milk products because these make them ill.

There are other problems caused by EXCESSIVE milk consumption, which are listed below. Once again, small amounts of milk and milk products, for those who can consume them, are OK. Milk however must NOT be viewed as an essential human food past infanthood. It is NOT an ideal source of calcium or human protein, and often creates more problems than it is worth with acidosis, which the body then has to combat. Many of the problems surrounding milk also stem from the chemical residues found within commercially farmed animals. If milk is to be consumed, it should be chemical- and pesticide-free.

So why do we drink cow's milk? Why don't we drink lion's milk to make us braver, or rat's milk to make us slyer or cat's milk so we can scratch up the furniture? The question is not as silly as it sounds. We drink cow's milk because that is culturally what we have always done. Also we can catch cows easily and they are docile when milked. You're not likely to have the same success if your penchant is for polar bear milk – and you probably won't live to get the Queen's telegram either.

No, we drink cow's milk because it is readily available and we have been conned into believing we cannot get by without it. And then along comes the breakfast cereal industry and hooks us on sucrose, gluten and milk, all mixed up together with some raisins sprinkled on the top for good measure. This then is our breakfast 'health food'. What is the difference between my getting out of the car and suckling a cow in the field to your evident horror, and Sainsbury's and Walmart obtaining it for me, packaging it and sticking it on their supermarket shelves for me to grab on the way to the till? The answer? Marketing. We'll drink it if it is provided for us. If it isn't, we won't go suckle the cow. Figure out the logic of that one when you've got a minute.

- Cow's milk is designed to make baby cows into big cows.
- Humans are the only mammals which are weaned off our mother's milk only to spend the rest of our lives stuck under the udders of a cow.
- Milk is often viewed by many as a more exciting alternative to fresh, clean water.
- Renin and lactase, the two enzymes responsible for breaking down milk in the human body, are usually gone from the human body by the time we are 3 years old. People who retain these enzymes do not have a problem with digesting milk. Then again, many do have problems (lactose intolerance). With these...
- Milk creates digestion problems because these humans cannot assimilate it efficiently.
- Milk can contain traces of the drugs fed to cattle to increase milk yield and the weight of the animal for slaughter: Bovine Growth Hormone (BGH), antibiotics, steroids, estradiol, insecticides, pesticides.
- Milk contains blood and (white) pus cells from the cow.
- Cow's milk has higher levels of protein for the development of big bones.

- Milk is deficient in essential fatty acids, such as linoleic acid, required for neurological development (cows are not noted for their mental gymnastics).
- Cow's milk contains coarse calcium that cannot be absorbed properly by humans.
- Pasteurisation kills enzymes and damages amino acids in milk.
- Milk creates acidic toxicity in the body.
- Milk is one of the most mucus-forming substances on the planet.
- Excessive milk consumption has been linked to Type 1 diabetes, heart disease, cancer, asthma and ear infections in children.

Conclusion: Go easy on the white stuff. Use according to the acid/alkali ash chart at the back of this book.

BEEF STROGANOFF

2lbs organic top sirloin steak
4 tbsp olive oil
*½ cup **buckwheat flour***
1 cup yogurt or sour cream
1 clove of garlic
1 tsp sea salt
freshly ground pepper, to taste
½ lb mushrooms, sliced

Mix the flour, salt and pepper together and coat the meat. Heat the oil and add the meat a few strips at a time. Try not to let the meat touch as this will prevent the meat from browning. Turn the meat, being careful not to overcook. Brown the mushrooms for a minute and place on top of the meat. Add the garlic and yoghurt to the pan, stirring and mixing with the juices. Do not boil. Salt to taste and spoon over the meat. Serve immediately.[79]

SUNFLOWER AND POPPY SEED CRACKERS
(makes approximately 15 crackers)

4 oz ground sunflower seeds
2 tsp poppy seeds
1 oz melted, unsalted butter
*4 oz ground **cashew nuts***
1 tsp baking powder
a little milk (2-3 tbsp)
extra ground sunflower seeds, for rolling out

Pre-heat oven to 190C/375F/Gas Mark 5. Combine the sunflower seeds, ground cashew nuts, poppy seeds and baking powder together in a bowl. Mix in the unsalted butter then add the milk and stir the mixture. Bring mixture together with hands to form a firm but moist dough. Roll out thinly on a surface sprinkled with some of the extra ground sunflower seeds. If the mixture sticks, top with some more sunflower seeds.

---

[79] **De Spain, June** *The Little Cyanide Cookbook*, American Media, CA USA, 1999

Cut into rounds with a 2-inch pastry cutter and lift carefully with a palette knife onto a greased baking sheet. Bake 10 to 15 minutes or until brown and firm in texture. Leave to cool and harden on the sheet for a few minutes then transfer to a cooling rack to cool completely.

MORROCCAN CHICKEN STEW WITH SAFFRON AND APRICOT
(serves 4)

2 oz butter
2 onions, finely chopped
4 garlic cloves, crushed
pinch of saffron threads
1 tbsp turmeric
1 ½ tsp ground cumin
1 ½ tsp ground coriander
1 ½ tsp paprika
1 tsp black pepper
¼ tsp cayenne
8 chicken thighs, skinned
juice of one lemon
8 fluid oz of chicken stock or water
4 oz dried apricots
*14 oz tin **chickpeas**, drained*
sea salt

Melt the butter in a heavy-based pan over a medium low heat. Add the onions, garlic, saffron, turmeric, cumin, coriander, paprika, pepper and cayenne. Cook, stirring occasionally, until the onions are very soft, 10 minutes.

Add the chicken, lemon juice, stock, dried apricots, and chickpeas and bring just to simmering point. Cook gently until the chicken is tender and opaque throughout, with no trace of pink at the bone, 30-40 minutes. Add salt to taste.

Arrange the chicken pieces on warmed plates and spoon over the sauce. Scatter with add-ons if using. Serve hot, with buttered couscous or warm flatbread.[80]

MOROCCAN CHICKEN STEW ADD-ONS

Add a final flourish of colour, texture and flavour to this sweetly spiced stew with 1 handful of coriander, parsley or mint leaves and 2 tbsp flaked almonds.

*It is possible to add ground **apricot kernels** as well.

LAYERED VEGETABLE TERRINE

3 red peppers, halved
1 lb potatoes
*4 oz **spinach** leaves, trimmed*
1 tbsp butter
pinch grated nutmeg
*grated **apricot kernels***
4 oz cheddar cheese, grated
1 courgette, sliced lengthways and blanched
salt and pepper

Pre-heat oven to 180C/350F/Gas Mark 4. Place the peppers in tin and roast them with the cores in place for 30-45 minutes until charred. Remove from the oven. Place in a plastic bag to cool. Peel the potatoes and boil in plenty of salted water for 10-15 minutes until tender.

Blanch the spinach for a few seconds in boiling water. Drain and pat dry on kitchen paper. Line the base of the sides of a 2 lb baking tin, making sure the leaves overlap slightly. Slice the potatoes thinly and

---

[80] Elliott, Renee Elliott & Eric Treuille, *Organic Cookbook*, op. cit.

143

lay one-third of the potatoes over the base, dot with a little butter and season with salt pepper nutmeg and apricot kernels. Sprinkle with a little cheese.

Arrange three of the peeled pepper halves on top with the remaining peppers and a little more cheese, seasoning as you go. Lay the final layer of potato on top and scatter over any remaining cheese. Fold the spinach leaves over. Cover with foil.

Place the loaf tin in a roasting tin and pour boiling water around the outside, making sure the water comes halfway up the sides of the tin. Bake for 45 minutes to 1 hour and turn the loaf out. Serve sliced.[81]

SPAGHETTI WITH TUSCAN HERBS
(serves 4)

1 lb spaghetti
a little warm olive oil, if desired
freshly grated Parmesan cheese

To cook the pasta, bring a large saucepan of salted water to the boil, add the spaghetti and cook for 7-11 minutes until 'al dente' (just tender, but not overcooked).

FOR THE SAUCE
4 tbsp olive oil
2 cloves garlic, finely chopped
8 anchovy fillets in oil, drained and chopped
2 tbsp passata or 2 tbsp of tomato puree
2-3 tbsp finely chopped fresh flat-leaf parsley
1 tbsp each finely chopped fresh thyme, rosemary and marjoram
crushed dried chillies

TO PREPARE SAUCE: Heat the olive oil in a small saucepan. Sauté the finely chopped garlic gently until it begins to change colour. Strain the olive oil into a frying pan (reserving the garlic), then add the chopped anchovies and cook over the lowest possible heat, stirring until they have dissolved into a smooth paste. Stir in the passata or tomato puree and continue to cook for one minute. Then add the finely

---

[81] Carrier, Robert, *New Great Dishes of the World*, op. cit.

chopped fresh herbs and stir over a low heat for a few minutes. Add the reserved garlic and remove the pan from the heat.

TO SERVE: Drain the spaghetti thoroughly in a colander and pile it in a deep, heated serving dish. Pour the sauce over, toss well and season with some crushed dried chillies. Add a little salt and warm olive oil too, if desired. Serve at once, with an accompanying bowl of fresh Parmesan.

VANILLA VERMOUTH MARINATED SALMON
1 vanilla pod, slit
1 tbsp lemon juice
225 ml vermouth
3 shallots, peeled and sliced into thin rounds
6 x 180-200g salmon fillets, skin on
groundnut oil
sea salt
black pepper
400 g green beans
75 g unsalted butter

Open the vanilla pod with a knife to remove the seeds. Select a shallow container that will hold the salmon fillets. Blend the seeds with the vermouth and lemon juice. Add the shallots, and chop up and add the vanilla pod. Place the salmon fillets in the marinade, cover and chill for several hours, turning them halfway through.

Just before grilling the salmon, bring a large pan of water to the boil. Transfer the fillets to a plate. Discard the pieces of vanilla pod in the marinade and pour it into a small saucepan. Bring to the boil and simmer until reduced to a couple of tbsp.

Brush the salmon fillets with oil and season them. Grill skin-side for 6-7 minutes and 3-4 minutes flesh-side or until they feel firm to the touch. At the same time add the green beans to the boiling water bring back to a simmer and cook for 3-5 minutes, then drain them. Re-heat the marinade, season and whisk the butter. Serve the salmon on warm plates. Place a pile of green beans to the side and spoon the sauce over them.[82]

ALMOND STEAK

1½ lbs organic beef
4 tbsp almonds raw, freshly ground in a blender
*1 tsp **apricot kernels**, ground*
1 tbsp olive oil
sea salt, to taste
¼ cup of brandy
*4 tbsp **watercress**, chopped*

Press the almonds into the steak one hour before cooking. Leave to stand at room temperature. Heat the oil in a frying pan, add the steak. Season to taste with salt, place on a warm plate. Sprinkle with the chopped watercress. Add the kernels to the juices in the skillet. Add the brandy and flame. Heat until slightly thickened. Spoon over steak and serve.[83]

CHERRY TOMATO & GOATS' CHEESE BROCHETTES
(serves 6)

24 large cherry tomatoes
250 g goats' cheese, cut into 1-2 cm cubes
12 spring onions, trimmed and cut into 5 cm lengths
extra virgin olive oil
sea salt and black pepper

BASIL OIL
25g basil leaves
6 tbsp extra virgin olive oil
a squeeze lemon juice
sea salt

Use the slenderest barbecue skewers you can find (if using wooden ones, soak them in water for half an hour first). Make the basil oil by

---

[82] *YOU* Magazine, *The Mail on Sunday*, 8th July 2001
[83] de Spain, June, *The Little Cyanide Cookbook*, op. cit.

bringing a small pan of water to the boil. Add the basil leaves, then immediately drain them into a sieve. Liquidise them with the olive oil, lemon juice and a little salt.

For the skewers, thread 3 cherry tomatoes and 2 pieces each of goat's cheese and spring onion onto 12 x 18 cm skewers, starting and ending with cherry tomatoes. Set these aside - they can be prepared well in advance of eating.

Brush the brochettes all over with olive oil, season them and barbecue for 2-4 minutes each side until lightly golden. Drizzle with basil oil if wished.

INDOORS: Heat a double-ridged grill over a medium low heat and cook the brochettes for 4-5 minutes each side until lightly golden.[84]

CHICKEN WITH LEMONS AND OLIVES
(serves 4)

½ tsp ground cinnamon
½ tsp ground turmeric
3- 3½ lb chicken (free range or organic)
2 tbsp olive oil
1 large onion, thinly sliced
2 inch piece fresh root ginger, grated
2 ½ cups chicken stock
2 preserved or fresh lemon or limes, cut into wedges
3 oz pitted brown olives
1 tbsp clear honey
4 tbsp chopped, fresh coriander
salt and freshly ground pepper
coriander sprigs, to garnish

Pre-heat oven to 190C/375F/Gas Mark 5. Mix the ground cinnamon and turmeric in a bowl with a little salt and pepper and rub all over the chicken skin to give an even coating. Heat the oil in a large sauté pan and fry the chicken on all sides until it turns golden.[85]

---

[84] 'YOU' Magazine, *The Mail on Sunday*, 8th July, 2001
[85] Taylor, Beatrice H, *The Cancer Prevention Cookbook*, op. cit.

Transfer the chicken to an ovenproof dish. Add the sliced onion to the pan and fry for 3 minutes. Stir in the grated ginger and stock and bring just to the boil. Pour over the chicken, cover with a lid and bake in the oven for 30 minutes.

Remove the chicken from the oven, add lemons or limes and brown olives and drizzle with the honey. Bake, uncovered, for a further 45 minutes until the chicken is tender. Stir in the chopped coriander and season to taste. Garnish with coriander sprigs and serve at once.

HERB ROASTED CHICKEN WITH SPICY CORN SALSA

4 lb organic chicken
handful of fresh herbs, such as parsley, basil and tarragon
2 tbsp olive oil

SPICY CORN SALSA

3 corn cobs
1 tbsp olive oil
1 red chilli, de-seeded and finely chopped
2 tbsp chopped fresh coriander
juice of one lime

Pre-heat oven to 190C/375F/Gas Mark 5. Sit the chicken on a board. Using your fingers, gently loosen the skin from the flesh at the neck end of the bird to about halfway up the breast. Stuff the pocket between the skin and the flesh with the fresh herbs. Tuck the flap of the skin back underneath and sit the chicken in a roasting tin. Drizzle with oil, season with freshly ground salt and black pepper and roast for 1½ hours or until cooked through.

Meanwhile, make the salsa. Heat a griddle pan until hot. Remove the husks and any fibres from the corn and brush the cobs with a little olive oil. Place on the pan and cook for 5 minutes, turning frequently, until tender and slightly charred. Remove from the pan and set aside until cool enough to handle.

Holding a cob up right on a chopping board, strip off the corn with a sharp knife and transfer to a bowl. Repeat with the other two cobs. Stir in the rest of the olive oil, chilli, coriander and lime juice. Season with salt and pepper. Serve with the roast chicken and lots of crusty bread.[86]

LAMB CURRY

2½ lb boned lamb, cubed
1 tbsp olive oil
1 small finely chopped onion
1 tbsp curry powder
pinch of basil, thyme, rosemary, sage
1 clove of garlic, chopped
1 tsp sea salt
fresh ground black pepper
1½ cups stock or water
1 tsp grated organic lemon peel
*½ cup of **mung bean sprouts***
2½ tsp arrowroot

Brown the lamb and onions in the oil. Add the remaining ingredients, except the arrowroot. Simmer, covered for about 2 hours. When the lamb is tender, remove it to a warm plate. Stir the arrowroot

---

[86] *Woman and Home*, August 2001

into the juices in the pan. Stir until sauce has thickened. Pour over lamb.[87]

LENTIL AND MUSHROOM MADRAS
(serves 4)

8 oz brown **lentils**
1 large onion, thinly sliced
1 tbsp olive
1 tbsp Madras curry powder
6 oz button mushrooms, halved
2 large carrots, grated
2 tbsp Mango chutney
2 tbsp chopped coriander
pinch of sea salt
1¼ cups vegetable stock
1 bay leaf
1 tsp garam masala
sliced cucumber and a few sprigs of coriander
Brown rice, to serve

Soak the lentils in cold water for several hours. Drain and place in a saucepan. Cover with water, bring to the boil and boil for about 45 minutes until really tender. Drain. Fry the onion for 3 minutes. Stir in the curry powder, mushrooms and carrots and continue cooking for about a minute, stirring.

Add all the remaining ingredients except the garam masala, and stir in the cooked lentils. Simmer for about 30 minutes, until the mixture is thick and well flavoured, stirring occasionally. Discard the bay leaf and stir in the garam masala. Taste and re-season, if necessary. Serve garnished with sliced cucumber and sprigs of coriander on a bed of brown rice.

---

[87] de Spain, June, *The Little Cyanide Cookbook*, op. cit.

AN FDA TOXICOLOGIST ON VITAMIN B17

"Because of its unique molecular structure, this compound releases cyanide only at the cancer site, thus destroying cancer cells while nourishing non-cancer tissue. Those populations in the world which eat these vitamin-rich foods simply do not get cancer – and they live to be much older than those who subsist on a typical modern diet.

Cyanide in minute quantities and in the proper food forms, instead of being poisonous, actually is an essential component of normal body chemistry. Vitamin B12, for instance, contains cyanide in the form of cyanocobalamin.

Vitamin B17 (also known as Laetrile or amygdalin) gradually has been replaced in the menus of modern man with foods which have been sweetened, processed, refined and synthesised. During this same time span, the cancer rate has been climbing steadily upward."

June de Spain, author of "The Little Cyanide Cookbook"

ALMOND WILD RICE

¾ cup wild rice
*2 oz **frozen peas***
3 tbsp flaked almonds
*ground **apricot kernels***
2 tbsp currants
freshly ground black pepper

Cook the rice, adding the peas in the last 5 minutes of cooking time. Drain thoroughly. Meanwhile dry-fry the almonds and apricot kernels in a non-stick frying pan until golden, stirring all the time to prevent burning. Remove from the pan as soon as they are brown. Add the rice with the currants and season well with pepper. Toss to serve.

RICE AND BEANS WITH AVOCADO SALSA

*1½ oz dried, or 3 oz canned **kidney beans**, rinsed and drained*
4 tomatoes, halved and seeded
2 garlic cloves, chopped
1 onion sliced
3 tbsp olive oil
8 oz long grain brown rice, rinsed
1 pint vegetable stock
2 carrots, diced
3 oz green beans
salt and freshly ground black pepper
4 wheat tortillas and soured cream, to serve

FOR THE AVOCADO SALSA:
1 avocado
juice of 1 lime
1 small red onion, diced
1 small red chilli, seeded and chopped
1 small red onion, diced
1 tbsp chopped fresh coriander

If using dried kidney beans, soak overnight in cold water. Drain and rinse well. Place in a saucepan with enough water to cover and bring to the boil. Boil rapidly for 10 minutes, then simmer for about 40 minutes until tender. Drain and set aside.

Heat the grill. Place the tomatoes, garlic and onion on a baking tray. Toss in 1 tbsp of the olive oil and grill for 10 minutes or until softened, turning once. Set aside to cool.

Heat the remaining oil in a saucepan, add the rice and cook for 2 minutes, stirring, until light golden. Puree the cooled tomatoes and onions in a food processor or blender, then add the mixture to the rice and cook for a further 2 minutes, stirring frequently. Pour in the stock, then cover and cook gently for 20 minutes, stirring occasionally.

Reserve 2 tbsp of the kidney beans for the salsa. Add the rest to the rice mixture with the carrots and green beans and cook for 15 minutes until the vegetables are tender. Season well with salt and pepper. Remove the pan from the heat and leave to stand, covered, for 15 minutes.

SALSA: To make the avocado salsa, cut the avocado in half and remove the stone. Peel and dice the flesh, then toss in the lime juice. Add the onion, chilli, coriander and reserved kidney beans then season with salt. To serve, spoon the hot rice and beans on to the tortillas. Hand round the salsa and soured cream.[88]

FRUITY COUSCOUS
(serves 6)

9 oz couscous
4 tbsp extra virgin olive oil
pinch of saffron
1½ pints hot vegetable stock
400 g can **chickpeas***, drained and rinsed*
4 oz apricots, roughly chopped
4 level tbsp roughly chopped coriander
juice of 1 lemon

---

[88] Taylor, Beatrice H, *The Cancer Prevention Cookbook*, op. cit.

Put the couscous in a bowl, add 1 tbsp oil and the saffron and mix well. Add the stock, cover and soak for 20 minutes. Use a fork to fluff up the couscous, then add the chickpeas, apricot pieces and coriander.

Mix together the remaining oil and the lemon juice and season. Pour dressing over couscous and toss together. [89]

TACOS

Question: How to make tacos without a carbohydrate shell?
Answer: Use Romaine lettuce leaves as a shell instead!

Romaine lettuce leaves
Ground round or turkey (organic)
Grated cheese (optional)
Tomato chunks
Picante sauce
Chopped peppers, onions and olives

Stay away from taco mixes - they usually contain sugar, etc. Read labels carefully!

CALVES LIVER WITH RAW CASHEWS

1 lb calves liver, sliced thinly
5 tbsp olive oil
6 tbsp garlic wine vinegar
*1 tbsp **sorghum cane syrup***
1 tsp sea salt
*1 cup ground **cashews,** raw*
½ cup grated Parmesan cheese

Brown the liver in the oil. Add the vinegar and syrup and cook through. Mix salt and cheese. Sprinkle over the liver and place under the grill for a few minutes to brown. Sprinkle on the cashews. Serve immediately.[90]

---

[89] *Good Housekeeping*, April 2001
[90] de Spain, June, *The Little Cyanide Cookbook*, op. cit.

FARFALLE WITH TUNA
(serves 6)

2 tbsp olive oil
1 small onion, finely chopped
1 garlic clove, finely chopped
14 oz can of chopped Italian plum tomatoes
3 tbsp dry white wine
8-10 pitted black olives, cut into rings
2 tsp fresh, chopped oregano or 1 tsp dried oregano with a little extra for garnishing
14 oz dried farfalle
6 oz can tuna in olive oil
salt and freshly ground black pepper

Heat the olive oil in a medium skillet or saucepan. Add the onion and garlic and fry gently for about 5 minutes until the onion is soft and lightly coloured. Add the plum tomatoes to the pan and bring to boil then add the white wine and simmer for a minute or so. Stir in the olives and oregano with salt and pepper to taste. Cover and cook for 20-25 minutes stirring from time to time.

Meanwhile, cook the pasta in a large saucepan of salted, boiling water according to the instructions on the packet. Drain the canned tuna and flake it with a fork. Add the tuna to the sauce with 4 tbsp of the water used for cooking the pasta. Taste and adjust the seasoning.

Drain the cooked pasta well and tip it into a large, warmed bowl. Pour the tuna sauce over the top and toss to mix. Serve immediately, garnished with sprigs of oregano.[91]

MERCIMEK CORBASL (CREAMY LENTIL SOUP)
(serves 3-4)

*1 cup **red lentils***
1½ medium onions
1 tbsp olive oil
7 cups water or vegetable stock

---

[91] Taylor, Beatrice H, *The Cancer Prevention Cookbook*, op. cit.

juice of 1 lemon
sea salt and pepper to taste

This light, delicious soup can be served hot or cold. Rinse the lentils and remove any pebbles. Chop onions in eighths and sauté them in the oil in a large soup pot for 5-10 minutes. Add the water and the lentils. Bring to a boil, then cover and simmer until the onions have almost dissolved, approximately 25 minutes.

Either puree soup in a blender or mash as much as will go through a sieve with a wooden spoon, and save. Discard whatever is left in the sieve. Return mixture to pot and boil for five minutes, adding water if the soup is too thick. Remove from heat. Add the lemon juice and season to taste. Serve immediately. [92]

TURLU - MIXED VEGETABLE STEW
(serves 4)
Enjoy this hearty Turkish stew!
1 onion, finely chopped
2 tsps olive oil
2 tomatoes, coarsely chopped
3 medium potatoes, chopped into 1-inch cubes
water or vegetable broth
1 small head cauliflower, chopped
2 zucchini (courgettes)
1 ordinary or 2 Japanese eggplant
1 pinch curry powder
sea salt and pepper to taste

In a large pot, sauté onions in oil until soft. Add the tomatoes. Add the potatoes and enough water (or broth) to cover. Bring to a boil. Add the cauliflower. Halve the zucchini lengthwise and chop into inch-long pieces. Do the same with the eggplant. Add these when the potatoes are almost tender. Simmer until the eggplant is done but still firm. Add curry powder and salt and pepper to taste. Serve over rice.[93]

---

[92] Blackington, Tatiana
[93] Ibid.

TURNIPS ANNA
(serves 4)

3 tbsp unsalted butter
4 turnips (about 1 lb)
1 shallot, peeled and very thinly sliced
sea salt and freshly ground black pepper to taste

Pre-heat oven to 425F. Melt the butter in a skillet or a frying pan and sauté the turnips just until coated in butter and partially cooked, 3 minutes. In an 18-inch-round cake-pan/tin (preferably non-stick), arrange a layer of overlapping turnip slices. Sprinkle with some of the shallot, and salt and pepper. Repeat with the remaining ingredients, ending with a layer of turnips. Bake until crisp and golden, about 30 minutes.[94]

PATLICAN SALATASL - COLD EGGPLANT SALAD
(serves 4)

2 pounds Japanese eggplant
1 tbsp olive oil (optional)
1 small onion, finely chopped
1 small bunch parsley
2 medium tomatoes, finely chopped
juice of 1 lemon
sea salt and pepper to taste

If you can't find Japanese eggplants, buy one large or two small ordinary eggplants. Make sure they are long and thin rather than short and round.

Roast eggplants on an open flame until the skin turns brownish black and the eggplant is soft, or barbecue. (If using the large ordinary eggplant, and they are not tender enough, slice in half, coat with olive oil and broil 5-10 minutes.) Let them cool. Split and scoop out the insides into a bowl.

---

[94] Mercola, Joseph, *The Mercola Cookbook*, op. cit.

Put in a food processor with the onion and puree. Chop the parsley and the tomatoes fine. Combine all the ingredients in a bowl and mix. Serve cold with bread.[95]

KABAK DOLMASL - STUFFED ZUCCHINI
(serves 8)

2 tsps olive oil
1 medium onion, chopped
3 tbsps **pine nuts**
1½ tomatoes, chopped
¾ cup white rice, uncooked
1 cup vegetable stock
1 small bunch dill, finely chopped
several mint leaves, chopped
3 tbsps currants
4 large zucchini (courgettes)
sea salt and pepper to taste

Pre-heat oven to 350F. Sauté the onion in the oil, add the pine nuts and sauté until they turn golden brown. Add the tomatoes. Add rice and stock. Cook covered on a low heat until the rice is almost done (about 15 minutes). Add the dill, mint, and the currants.

Halve the zucchini and steam them until slightly tender, no more than 5 minutes. Scoop out the middles, chop, and add to the rice mixture. Add salt and pepper to taste. Fill the zucchini with the rice mixture and place in a casserole dish. Pour a half-cup of water in the dish, cover, and bake for 15 minutes at 350F. [96]

BULGUR PILAV
(serves 6)

2 cups dried **chickpeas**
2 cups coarse-grained bulgur
2 tsps sunflower or other oil
1 tomato, chopped
2 medium potatoes, chopped

---

[95] Blackington, Tatiana
[96] Ibid.

*3 1/2 cups vegetable broth (or use **chickpea stock**)*
1 green pepper, chopped

Soak chickpeas overnight. Cook until tender - about an hour. Wash the bulgur. Sauté the tomato in the oil, then add the potatoes. Add the chickpeas and the liquid. Once it comes to a boil, add the bulgur and the green peppers. Cover and simmer for about 15 minutes on a low heat. It helps to put a clean, damp dishcloth between the lid and the pan while it's cooking. Turn off heat and let stand for 15 minutes before serving. [97]

ASURE
(serves 10)

This dessert is made at the same time each year to commemorate a number of important events in Islam. The dish supposedly originated on the day that the great flood subsided and Noah and his family were able to go on land again. They collected all the food they had left - mostly dried fruits and nuts - and cooked it in one big pot. Tradition dictates that the dish be shared with at least seven poor neighbours.

1 cup wheat berries (available in healthfood stores)
*¾ cup **walnuts***

[97] Ibid.

½ cup hazelnuts
*½ cup **chickpeas***
7 dried figs
10 dried apricots
½ cup raisins
¼ cup rose water (optional - available in health food stores, often in the vitamin section, or in Indian markets)
cinnamon to taste

In separate bowls, soak the wheat berries, nuts and chickpeas for at least eight hours. Rub the chickpeas to loosen as many skins as possible and discard the skins and the water. Cook chickpeas in fresh water until tender. Drain the wheat and cook covered in about eight cups fresh water until tender.

Meanwhile, soak the dried fruit in a little warm water for about 15 minutes, drain and chop. Drain the nuts, rubbing them to remove the hazelnut skins, and chop. Once the wheat berries are cooked, drain off any excess water and reserve. Puree in a food processor.

Combine the wheat berries, fruits, nuts, raisins and the liquid in a large soup pot and simmer uncovered, stirring frequently, for 15 minutes or until mixture becomes more gooey than soupy. Add water if necessary during cooking. Mix in the optional rose water and sprinkle with cinnamon when done. Serve hot or cold. [98]

BROCCOLI AND PASTA

*organic broccoli garden rotini (the screw-shaped pasta, that includes **spinach**, carrot, **beet**, and plain)*
a shot or two of Pace mild salsa
1 small bunch of fresh cilantro (coriander), chopped
2 slices of red onion, chopped fine

Pan broil the broccoli (chopped in florettes and peel the stem and chop) so that it turns a dark green and stays crisp. Cook the rotini until it is 'al dente'. Mix in the broccoli, the salsa, chopped cilantro and the

---

[98] Ibid.

chopped red onion. The idea is to enhance the flavours in the commercial salsa by adding more of them from fresher sources.[99]

CHICKEES AT THE BEACH

*1 cup of cooked **millet**, (use as little water as possible for cooking.*
Do not overcook.)
*1 cup **chickpeas**, cooked*
1 organic lemon, squeezed for juice
pinch of cayenne
1 small onion, finely diced
1 small pepper, diced
2 large tomatoes, chopped
4 tbsp vegetable oil
1 cup chopped mint
1 clove garlic, chopped
1 tbsp chopped chives
½ tsp cinnamon

Toss ingredients and chill. Serve on a bed of ***watercress***.[100]

KERNEL DUST

7 g pumpkin seeds
7 g sesame seeds
7 g sunflower seeds
*14 g **flax seeds***
*7 g **apricot kernels***

Grind ingredients together in a coffee grinder. Store in an air-tight jar. Use as spice or seasoning. 1½ - 2 tbsp a day is a convenient way to generate intakes of Vitamin B17, essential fatty acids and other vitamins and minerals. Ideal for hyperactive kids!

PENNE PRIMAVERA

(serves 6)

8 oz pasta penne, uncooked
½ cup red onion, peeled and sliced
2 garlic cloves, minced

---

[99] Bozinovich, Lu
[100] de Spain, June, *The Little Cyanide Cookbook*, op. cit.

1 red bell pepper, seeded and sliced
1 cp sugar snap peas
¾ lb asparagus, cut in 2-inch pieces
1 med zucchini (courgette) squash, cut into matchsticks
1 med yellow squash, cut into matchsticks
4 plum tomatoes, cored and chopped
2 cups **fava beans**, fresh or canned
¼ tsp sea salt
¼ tsp black pepper
1 tbsp arrowroot
1½ cup vegetable stock
2 tbsp basil, fresh, chopped
1/4 tsp red pepper flakes

Cook the pasta in a large pot of boiling water until just tender, about 11 minutes. Drain and set aside to add to the vegetables later. In a large, high-sided skillet, sauté the onions in water. Add the garlic and cook for 1 minute.

Toss in the peppers and peas, and cook for 2 to 3 minutes. Now add the asparagus, zucchini, summer squash, tomatoes, fava beans, salt and pepper. Treat this like a stir-fry, tossing lightly and cooking the vegetables but keeping them crunchy, about 5 minutes. Remove the skillet from the heat.

Mix the arrowroot with the vegetable stock to make a slurry. Stir in the arrowroot slurry, return to the heat, and bring to a boil over medium-high heat, stirring constantly. Add the cooked pasta, basil, and red pepper flakes, and toss gently to mix well.

To serve: Dish the pasta into large bowls. Serve with a lightly dressed green salad and hearty Italian bread.

Notes: If you cannot find fava beans, just leave them out. **Kidney beans** might be good and would be a great colour with this dish. I always use the powdered vegetable broth (salt-free) that I get in bulk at the natural food store. Vegetable boullion cubes are all right, but they're quite high in sodium.[101]

---

[101] Busby, Marjorie, mgbusb@med.unc.edu

SPAGHETTI

1 lb spaghetti, uncooked, whole wheat
6 large or 10 medium tomatoes, diced
1 large or 2 medium onion(s), chopped
1 cp fresh parsley, chopped (no stems)
1 pepper red hot (red jalapeno), chopped
3-4 cloves of garlic
1/2 lb chopped mushrooms
black pepper
sage
basil
oregano

Using a large sauce-pan, first crush and sauté the garlic in ½ cup of water. After the garlic starts to turn clear, add the chopped onion(s). Now add the remaining items, bringing to a medium heat and let cook. Stir frequently initially until it starts to cook down, then reduce heat to low. If the sauce is soupy, leave off the lid, if it's too thick, add water (a little goes a long way). Let simmer for 45 minutes, longer if you need to thicken it up. The spaghetti will cook in about 15 minutes once put in boiling water. Once the sauce is thick, start the spaghetti noodles. Add black pepper, sage, basil and oregano to taste.[102]

ASPARAGUS RISOTTO

2oz butter
2 shallots, diced
2 garlic cloves, crushed
8oz Arborio rice
17 fl oz stock
2 tbsp mascarpone
3 oz Parmesan finely grated, plus shavings to garnish
2 tbsp freshly chopped parsley
14 oz asparagus spears, blanched and halved

Melt butter in a pan and sauté shallots and garlic until soft. Stir in the rice, add the stock and bring to boil. Simmer for 12 minutes or until rice is cooked. Add mascarpone, half the Parmesan and half the parsley

---

[102] Weatherly, Debbie

to the pan. Season then stir in the asparagus, remaining parsley and cheese. Spoon onto plates, garnish and serve.[103]

[103] *Good Housekeeping*, Sainsbury's and Carlton, June 2001

THE SWEETEST POISON?

The Lethality of Sweeteners
by Phillip Day
*"Let us go to the ignorant savage,
consider his way of eating, and be wise."*
– Harvard Professor Ernest Hooten[104]

When it comes to identifying the most common poison we willingly use against ourselves, an amazing feat resulting in millions of deaths worldwide every year, there really is no contest. The perpetrator is as unlikely a candidate as any you might wish to name, and its unmasking is probably all the more horrifying because this substance has burrowed its way into our civilisation like a parasite, draped in the false colours of comfort and familiarity. It has an entire industry behind it as usual, hell-bent on marketing the stuff any way it can. It's whiter than heroin, sweeter than your fiancée, more soluble than the National Debt, and more pernicious than nicotine because, like a true demon, this little beauty comes in a million disguises and always dresses like a friend.

We grew up being brainwashed with all the sayings: " Sugar and spice and all things nice." "Sweetheart", "Sugar-plum" – all painting the white stuff in a great and cuddly light. But seeing as we are in the mood for some truth, let's take a hard look at the 's' word, and also its partners-in-crime, the 'sweeteners' aspartame and saccharin. Are you nervous about shattering some highly refined illusions?

Dr William Coda Martin was the first publicly to label sucrose a poison. Martin's definition came about after he determined the classical definition of a poison was *"...any substance applied to the body, which causes or may cause disease."* [105] So what is sucrose? Obviously the first task we must carry out is identifying exactly what sugar is. Once again, we have to do our homework and pre-empt the vocabulary – so let's define our terms. There are a number of 'sugars' around. Here are the main ones:

---

[104] **Hooten, Ernest A** *Apes, Men and Morons*, Putnam, New York: 1937
[105] **Martin, William Coda** *When is a Food a Food – and When a Poison?* Michigan Organic News, March 1957, p.3

Glucose – found with other sugars, but occurs naturally in fruits and vegetables. A number of core foods we consume are converted by our body into glucose, or blood sugar as it is sometimes called, which is the form in which this highly efficient energy source is made available to our life-systems. Glucose is always present in our bloodstream and is a key material in the metabolic functions of all plants and animals.

Dextrose - known as 'corn sugar', is manufactured from starches.
Fructose - natural sugar found in fruits.
Lactose – milk sugar
Maltose – malt sugar
Sucrose – refined sugar manufactured from sugar cane and beet.

The last, sucrose, is the white stuff that goes into the tea, coffee, soft drinks and sodas, and shows up in everything from tomato ketchup to Twinkies. There are few manufactured or processed foods today that do not contain sucrose, aspartame or saccharin. Sugar's prevalence for 300 years has made the sweet-hearts in the sugar industry wealthy beyond most people's imaginations. Naturally, the sugar barons are willing to do or say just about anything to keep their products bathed in the safe and neighbourly light that has resulted in us scarfing the stuff down by the bushel-load without so much as a 'by-your-leave'. So let's firstly take a look at sugars, and see what the problems are.

Refined sugar, or sucrose, is manufactured from cane and beet extract, which has had its salts, fibres, enzymes, proteins, vitamins and minerals removed to leave a white, crystalline substance devoid of any nutritional content, only offering empty calories. Sucrose is labelled 'a carbohydrate', that most generic of terms which describes a compound comprising carbon coupled with hydrogen and oxygen. Of course, to label sugar 'a carbohydrate' gives manufacturers wide licence to lump this most popular of commodities in with other 'carbohydrates', refined or otherwise, which all show up on food packaging as... you guessed it, 'carbohydrates'! Thus the real content of sucrose in a product may be effectively concealed without technical fraud being perpetrated. In reality the different sugars listed above are composed of different chemical structures, which affect the body in radically different ways. Yet the well-meaning, 'think-no-evil' public has once again been snowed by a single word into accepting that one sugar is just about the same as another. Nothing could be further from the truth.

Sugars contained in natural, whole foods are easily metabolised by the body. Nature has ensured that fructose, for instance, obtained when we consume fruits, has the necessary vitamins and minerals accompanying it to allow this type of simple monosaccharide sugar to enter the bloodstream and become directly metabolised by our bodies for energy. Vitamins and minerals, which accompany fructose, are essential for these complete assimilation and conversion processes to occur.

The problems with sucrose begin with the rapidity with which it is hydrolysed into glucose and fructose after consumption. Fructose, as previously mentioned, is metabolised directly to produce energy. Abrupt intakes of glucose into the bloodstream however provoke a massive secretion of insulin, the hormone responsible for regulating blood sugar levels and storing fat. The result of excess insulin secretion is a sudden drop in blood sugar, which, as I discuss in *The Mind Game*, can bring on mood changes and behavioural upsets.

Now we have low blood sugar and get that wobbly sensation. What are we craving? Sugar! So, in go the doughnuts, Twinkies, Ding-Dongs and Bear Claws; up go the blood sugar levels again, out squirts all that insulin to regulate the glucose, and down come those blood sugar levels with a thump once more. This spiky, chaotic pattern of blood sugar in the body will eventually cause our cells to become resistant to all that insulin, resulting in the condition of type 2 diabetes.

Sucrose is a great oxidiser in the body, proliferating oxidation elements, or free-radicals, which constantly seek to stabilise themselves by robbing our healthy cells of available electrons. This action in turn degrades the cell and the cell dies.[106]

A recent study conducted at the University of Buffalo involved 14 healthy men and women fasting for 12 hours before being given a drink containing 75 grams of glucose, approximately equivalent to the sugar content of two cans of soda. Six control patients were given a water and

---

[106] Martin, William Coda, op. cit.

saccharin solution. Researchers collected blood samples from all the study subjects prior to the commencement of the trial and then at one, two and three hours after consuming the beverages. The purpose of the trial was not to highlight any irregularities with saccharin, but to demonstrate the oxidation capabilities of sugar. The results were as follows:

> Free-radical generation in the subjects who consumed the sugar water increased markedly at one hour and more than doubled at two hours.
> There was no change in free-radical generation in the control participants.
> In those who had consumed the sugar water, levels of alpha-tocopherol (Vitamin E), a powerful antioxidant, had dropped by 4% by the second hour and remained depressed at hour three.[107]

Researcher Dr Joseph Mercola remarks on these test results:

"Another reason to avoid sugar is to slow down the aging process. If you want to stay looking young, it is very important to limit sugar to the smallest amount possible. It is the most significant factor that accelerates aging. It is a negative fountain of youth. It does this by attaching itself to proteins in the body forming new sugar-protein substances called advanced glycation end-products (AGE). The higher the AGE levels, the faster you are aging. As this study points out, sugar also increases oxidation elements in the body (free radicals) which also accelerate the aging process." [108]

Advanced Glycation End-Products (AGEs) are readily seen as hard yellow-brown compounds that are, as Dr Mercola states, the results of blood sugar bonding with proteins in the body's tissue. This process is the precursor to degenerative disease, and may manifest itself initially as indicators associated with accelerated aging, such as premature wrinkles and grey hair.[109] We are oxidising and pre-aging our bodies

---

[107] *Journal of Clinical Endocrinology and Metabolism*, August 2000
[108] **Mercola, Joseph** *Sugar Creates Free Radicals and Reduces Vitamin E Levels*, 27th August 2000, www.mercola.com/2000/aug/27/sugar_free_radicals.htm
[109] **Lee and Cerami** *Annals of the New York Academy of Science*, "The Role of Glycation in Aging", #663, pp.6370; also **D G Dyer et al** *Journal of Clinical*

towards an early death with sucrose as surely as the pick-up rusts its way to the scrap-heap if we leave it out in the yard throughout the winter. *Scientific American* puts it this way: *"After years of bread, noodles and cake, human tissues inevitably become rigid and yellow with pigmented AGE deposits."* [110]

All refined sugars are parasitic. They have no accompanying vitamins and minerals of their own, and no nutritive value. They leach valuable minerals from the body when the latter frantically attempts to do something about them.[111] Sucrose can cause copper deficiency, which reduces the elasticity of veins and arteries, leading to aneurism and stroke.[112] We sophisticated Westerners do not detoxify our bodies and take out the garbage, which means that the build-up of sucrose metabolites and partially detoxified sugars continues to accumulate as fat, faithfully stored by all that insulin, rendering a toxic, acid siege within us.[113] The body must then, as the onslaught continues, dig deeper to marshal more minerals, such as calcium, to rectify the acid/alkali imbalance this sugar bombardment is causing. More calcium is taken from our bones and teeth, resulting in an increased risk of osteoporosis.[114]

Excess glucose is initially stored in the liver in the form of glycogen. As more sugar is stuffed into our sagging bodies daily, the liver swells like a balloon to accommodate it[115], waiting in vain for the garbage truck to take it out of the body (detoxification/elimination). The truck almost never arrives because we do not detoxify our bodies

---

Investigation, "Accumulation of Maillard Reaction Products in Skin Collagen in Diabetes and Aging", Vol. 91, #6, June 1993, pp.421-422

[110] *Scientific American*, July 2000, p.16

[111] **Couizy, Keen, Gershwin and Mareschi** *Progressive Food and Nutrition Science*, "Nutritional Implications of the Interaction Between Minerals", No. 17, 1933, pp.65-87

[112] **M Fields et al** *Journal of Clinical Nutrition*, "Effect of Copper Deficiency on Metabolism and Mortality in Rats Fed Sucrose or Starch Diets", #113, 1983, pp.1335-1345

[113] **Dufty, W** *Sugar Blues*, Warner Books, New York: 1975

[114] **Appleton, Nancy** *Lick the Sugar Habit*, Avery Publishing Group, NY: 1989, pp.36-38

[115] **Goulart, F S** *American Fitness*, "Are You Sugar Smart?" March-April 1991, pp.34-38

(sugar has also been linked constipation[116]). Finally, reaching its limit, the liver has had enough and pours the glucose back into the bloodstream in the form of fatty acids, which are then taken to storage bins in the inactive areas of the body, namely the belly, thighs, hips, breasts and the backs of our upper arms (triceps area).

But still the sugar keeps a-comin': "Another doughnut, Officer?" "Thank you, ma'am. Don't mind if I do..." Once the inactive storage areas are filled to capacity, the body begins distributing all this stored energy, in the form of fat, into the active organs, such as the heart and kidneys.[117] These fats accumulate as rapidly as the sucrose continues to pour in, impairing the functioning of vital organs, causing hormonal imbalance[118], creating lethargy, abnormal blood pressure as the circulatory and lymph systems are invaded, depleting vital Vitamin C reserves, threatening the cardiovascular system.[119] An overabundance of white cells occurs, leading to the slowing down of tissue formation. The system is nearing collapse at this point, and still the sugar keeps a-coming... "Do you want the one with extra icing, Officer?" (Naughty giggle). "Only if you insist, young lady..."

How about the cellulite, varicose veins and the rotten teeth?[120] [121] How about the kids bouncing off the walls with mineral depletion, ADD and ADHD because sucrose robs minerals, impairs brain function, resulting in increased emotional instability, concentration difficulties, hyperactivity and violence in the classroom[122] [123], ending up

[116] Ibid.
[117] **Yudkin, Kang and Bruckdorfer** *British Journal of Medicine*, "Effects of High Dietary Sugar", #281, 1980, p.1396
[118] **Yudkin, J** *Nutrition and Health*, "Metabolic Changes Induced by Sugar in Relation to Coronary Heart Disease and Diabetes", Vol. 5, #1-2, 1987: pp.5-8
[119] **Pamplona, Bellmunt, Portero and Prat** *Medical Hypotheses,* "Mechanisms of Glycation in Atherogenesis", #40, 1990, pp.174-181
[120] **Cleave and Campbell** *Diabetes, Coronary Thrombosis and the Saccharine Disease*, John Wright and Sons, Bristol, UK: 1960
[121] **Glinsman, Irausquin and Youngmee** "Evaluation of Health Aspects of Sugars Contained in Carbohydrate Sweeteners", Report from FDA's Sugar Task Force, Center for Food Safety and Applied Nutrition, Washington DC: 1986, p.39
[122] **Schauss, Alexander** *Diet, Crime and Delinquency*, Parker House, Berkeley, CA: 1981
[123] **Goldman, J et al** "Behavioral Effects of Sucrose on Preschool Children", *Journal of Abnormal Child Psychology*, #14, 1986. pp.565-577

no doubt with black eyes, detention, lousy grades... and conceivably a school shooting or two...[124]

Glutamic acid, the key to proper brain function, is derived from a diet rich in unrefined plant dietary. Glutamic acid is broken down by B vitamins into compounds that regulate stop and go functions in the brain. B vitamins however are manufactured by symbiotic bacteria inhabiting our intestines. As the sucrose bombing continues, these bacteria are killed by the toxic sugar metabolites, resulting in a severe depletion of our B-vitamin production. This in turn impairs brain function. The results in adults can traverse the awesome spectrum from sleepiness and the inability to calculate or remember, through to dizziness[125], heightened PMS symptoms[126] and possibly finishing with those famous murderous impulses, resulting in your lawyer's "Twinkie Defence".[127]

And so, as the human becomes the sugar equivalent of the Frankenstein monster, pancreatic function may become inhibited by excess sucrose, resulting in the impairment of enzymes such as trypsin and chymotrypsin, vital for arresting healing processes and preventing cancer growths.[128] Sugar may lead to cancer of the breast, ovaries, prostate and rectum.[129] It has been implicated in colon cancer, with an increased risk in women[130], and is a risk factor in biliary tract cancer.[131]

---

[124] *Journal of Abnormal Psychology*, #85, 1985

[125] *Journal of Advanced Medicine*, 1994 7(1): pp.51-58

[126] *The Edell Health Letter*, September 1991; 10:7(1)

[127] *"On 27 November 1978, Dan White, a former San Francisco city supervisor who had recently resigned his position, entered San Francisco's city hall by climbing through a basement window and then shot and killed both mayor George Moscone and supervisor Harvey Milk. After White's subsequent trial for the murders, a new term entered the American lexicon: "Twinkie defense." This phrase came to represent the efforts of criminals to avoid responsibility for their actions by claiming that some external force beyond their control had caused them to act the way they had, and it arose from the successful defense mounted by White's legal team that White's eating of Twinkies and other sugar-laden junk foods had diminished his mental capacity."* www.snopes.com/errata/twinkie.htm Author's note: The facts reveal that White's defence team argued that their client's junk-food diet was *evidence* of his depression, *not the cause of it*, as the papers subsequently reported.

[128] **Appleton, Nancy** *Healthy Bones*, Avery Publishing Group, NY: 1991

[129] *Health Express*, "Sugar and Prostate Cancer", October 1982, p.41

[130] **Bostick, Potter, Kushi, et al** "Sugar, Meat and Fat Intake, and Non-Dietary Risk Factors for Colon Cancer Incidence in Iowa Women", *Cancer Causes and Controls* #5,

Sugar can cause appendicitis[132], increase the risk of Crohn's Disease and ulcerative colitis[133], and can exacerbate the symptoms of multiple sclerosis.[134] Excess sugar consumption has also been linked to Parkinson's and Alzheimer's Diseases.[135] Complete removal of sugar from the diet has seen stunning recoveries from cancer, diabetes and heart illnesses.

Sucrose and massive insulin secretions have long been known to cause type 2 diabetes .[136] This condition usually occurs in adults, who have had years of food abuse to render their cells insulin-resistant. Type 2 can be controlled with a combination of diet and exercise. People with the condition not only lose their sensitivity to insulin, which regulates the build-up of blood sugar[137], but this repeated overload of insulin and glucose can lead to an increase in systolic blood pressure[138], fainting and coma.

Excessive consumption of refined, high-glycaemic carbohydrates, including items like white bread, white flour, pastries, white rice, breakfast cereals, as well as alcohol drinks, especially wine and beer, will all yield excessive sugars into the bloodstream with the predictable, aforementioned insulin effects.

1994, pp.38-52

[131] **Moerman, Clara et al** "Dietary Sugar Intake in the Etiology of Biliary Tract Cancer", *International Journal of Epidemiology*, Vol. 22, #2, 1993, pp.207-214

[132] **Cleave, T** *The Saccharine Disease*, Keats Publishing, New Canaan, CT: 1974, p.125

[133] **Cleave, T** *Sweet and Dangerous,* Bantam Books, New York: 1974, pp.28-43; also **Persson, B G et al** "Diet and Inflammatory Bowel Disease", *Epidemiology*, Vol. 3, #1, January 1992, pp. 47-51

[134] **Erlander, S** *The Disease to End Disease*, "The Cause and Cure of Multiple Sclerosis", No. 3, 3rd March 1979, pp.59-63

[135] **Yudkin, J**, *Sweet and Dangerous*, Bantam Books, NY: 1974, p.141

[136] **Jenkins and Jenkins** *Diabetes Care*, "Nutrition Principles and Diabetes. A Role for Lente Carbohydrate?" Dept. of Nutritional Sciences, University of Toronto, Ont, Canada: Nov, 1995 18(11)pp/1491-8; also *Federal Protocol*, "Sucrose Induces Diabetes in Cats", Vol 6, #97, 1974

[137] **Beck-Nelson, Pederson and Schwarz** *Diabetes*, "Effects of Diet on the Cellular Insulin Binding and the Insulin Sensitivity in Young Healthy Subjects", #15, 1978, pp.289-296

[138] **Hodges and Rebello** *Annals of Internal Medicine*, "Carbohydrates and Blood Pressure", #98, 1983, pp.838-841

Another problem is physical and emotional stress. This triggers what is known as Fight or Flight Syndrome. When we become agitated, stressed or physically threatened, the body prepares for combat or flight by generating powerful shots of adrenalin. This provokes the releasing of stored glucose into the bloodstream for energy to fuel explosive physical action. This in turn causes a surge of insulin to regulate blood sugar levels. Notice how, in previous eras, the Fight/Flight response would resolve itself *with explosive physical action* (either Fight or Flight!), which in turn would burn up the sugars.

What about today? When we are stressed with money, relationships, hardships or work pressures, or simply getting our kicks watching the FA Cup or playing video games, this Fight/Flight response still occurs and may endure for days or weeks. Consequently, the amount of insulin produced by the pancreas in today's stressful sugar-laden environment is substantially higher. This excess energy does not tend to discharge itself through physical action. The results of this insulin response also can be diabetes.

Dr Joseph Mercola clarifies type 2 diabetes:

"The overall concept of insulin for Type 2 diabetes is absurd and makes absolutely no sense if one understands the way the body is designed to work. However, since nearly all traditional physicians don't comprehend basic human physiology with respect to diet and health, it is not surprising that they could come up with the prescription for disaster of giving someone who is already overloaded with insulin more of what caused the problem.

The main reason most adult onset (type 2) diabetics have diabetes is that they have too much insulin. This is usually a result of having too many grains. The solution in nearly all of these individuals is to consume a proper low grain [gluten] diet and to exercise one hour per day." [139]

Those with type 2 diabetes would do well to change their diets to incorporate high-fibre vegetables, pulses, legumes and nuts, avoiding

---

[139] Mercola, J, www.mercola.com, op. cit.

traditional western processed foods (processed meats and dairy products), especially the high-glycaemic carbohydrates, such as grain products, bread, pasta, pastries, alcohol (beer and wine) and excessive amounts of potatoes, all of which yield glucose as they break down. Water only should be drunk – 4 pints or two litres a day. Small amounts of low-glycaemic fruits, such as pears and apples are OK, along with their seeds.

Sucrose addiction affects the vast majority of people today... and it IS an addiction. It must be shucked off *immediately*. Suffice to say for now that cutting out all forms of refined sugar, sugar foods, sugar products such as chocolate, candies, jelly beans, Twinkies and a million other products is *de rigeur* for a long and healthy future life. And don't think you can gallop away towards the hot and ready alternatives either. Let's burst those two pink and blue bubbles while we're hot to trot and burning with vision.

SACCHARIN (THE PINK)
Saccharin has long been a traditional alternative for those on diets and those aware of the damage done to both teeth and general health by a chronic consumption of sugar. But saccharin itself, far from being the panacea for those addicted to the taste concepts of sucrose, has been dogged from the outset with its own health concerns.

Saccharin is a synthetic, white crystalline powder, which, in its pure state, is over 500 times as sweet as sugar cane. In its commercial state, it is 350 times as sweet, meaning of course that you need 350 times less of the stuff to approximate the same level of sweetness usually provided by commercial sucrose. Saccharin's compound is $C_6H_4CONHSO_2$, declaring itself to be, once again, that most deceitful of terms - a 'carbohydrate'. Yet it has no nutritive value and is not digested by the body. Dr Elizabeth M Whelan explains some of the problems saccharin has experienced:

"Saccharin, which has been in use as an alternative to sugar since the early 20th century, officially assumed the 'carcinogen' title in March 1977, when a rodent study in Canada produced an excess of bladder tumours in the male animals. This finding immediately triggered the threat of the so-called "Delaney Clause", a Congressionally mandated provision that requires the Food & Drug

Administration to ban – literally 'at the drop of a rat' – any synthetic food chemical shown to cause cancer when ingested by laboratory animals.

When millions of weight-conscious Americans got the word that their only available low-calorie sweetener was going to be banned (cyclamates had been banned in 1970 for similar reasons), they were outraged – and immediately bought up almost every little pink packet in the land. Congress responded to this outrage by protecting saccharin from the Delaney Clause and allowing it back on the market with a health-warning label. Saccharin's reputation was further tarnished however when the US National Toxicology Program, referring again to the Canadian rat study, elected to put saccharin on its 'cancer-causing" list – formally declaring it an "anticipated human carcinogen."[140]

Evidence indicates that saccharin is a weak carcinogen in animals. Its potential for tumour mischief in humans however remains the subject of some heated debate. In May 2000, the upbeat United States National Institute for Environmental Health Services removed saccharin from its list of suspected carcinogens. Three years earlier though, a board of independent experts, which included the Center for Science in the Public Interest and the California Department of Health, had voted to err on the side of caution to keep saccharin 'a suspected carcinogen'.

The food industry has expended considerable resources attempting to get saccharin off the hook. Consumers appeared to have their own ideas. The food giants were encouraged by the many citizens who came forward to complain that every alternative to sugar was being systematically victimised as a carcinogen, as had been the case with cyclamate and aspartame. America's Food & Drug Administration, usually quick to follow its own policy of applying the Delaney Clause and banning even suspected carcinogens from public use, relented in the face of public pressure, but mandated that saccharin should carry a warning label.

---

[140] **Whelan, Elizabeth M** *The Sweet and the Sour News about Saccharin*, American Council on Science and Health, 17th May 2000

Dr Samuel Cohen, a pathologist at the University of Nebraska, is probably America's foremost authority on saccharin and its chemical ramifications. In answer to the investigative panel's queries on how exactly saccharin causes cancer, Cohen replied that when the sodium form of saccharin combines with rat urine, it creates crystal-like stones in the bladder of the creature. These stones in turn damaged the organs of the animal, leading to the potential for cancer.[141] Cohen however cast doubt on saccharin's danger to humans when he explained the significant differences between rat and human urine and how they would chemically react with the crystalline sweetener.

ASPARTAME (THE BLUE)

Today saccharin remains as controversial as ever, and the debate over whether or not it represents a cancer hazard to the public continues to rage. And yet, people who have turned to another alternative to saccharin and sugar over the past 20 years, have become equally dismayed at a parallel fur-fight over aspartame, decked out in the garb of a light blue sachet, which began adorning restaurant and diners the world over under the brand names Nutrasweet, Equal, Spoonful and Equal-Measure.

Aspartame was discovered by accident in 1965 by James Schlatter, a chemist working for G D Serle Company, who was testing anti-ulcer compounds for his employers. Aspartame's original approval as a sweetener for public consumption was blocked by neuroscientist Dr John W Olney and consumer attorney James Turner in August 1974 over concerns about both aspartame's safety and G D Serle's research practices. However, aspartame duly received its approval for dry goods in 1981 and its go-ahead as a sweetener for carbonated beverages was granted in 1983, despite growing concerns over its neurological effects.[142] In 1985, G D Serle was purchased by pharmaceutical giant

---

[141] Cohen's testimony is interesting as it dovetails with John Beard's findings that cancer is a healing process (survival response) that has not terminated. These healing processes are understood to be caused by damage done to the body by carcinogens. Therefore, a carcinogen can be deemed to be any material that causes cellular damage to the body, initiating a healing process carried out by stem-cell trophoblast.

[142] Two FDA scientists, Jacqueline Verrett and Adrian Gross, reviewed data from three studies which highlighted alleged irregularities in G D Serle's research procedures. The two government scientists declared that the irregularities they had uncovered were serious enough to warrant an immediate halt to aspartame's approval for use. *Food Magazine*, "Artificial Sweetener Suspicions", Vol. 1, No.9, April/June 1990.

Monsanto, and Serle Pharmaceuticals and The NutraSweet Company were created as separate corporate identities.

According to researcher Alex Constantine in his essay entitled "Sweet Poison", aspartame may account for up to 75% of the adverse food reactions reported to the US FDA, due primarily to its reported ability to affect neurological processes in humans. Dr Olney found that an excess of aspartate and glutamate, two chemicals used by the body as neurotransmitters to transmit information between brain neurons, could kill neurons in the brain by allowing too much calcium to collect in the neuron cells to neutralise acid. This neurological damage led Olney to label aspartate and glutamate 'excitotoxins', in that they, according to Olney, 'excite' or stimulate the neural cells to death.[143]

Side-effects laid at the door of aspartame include multiple sclerosis, Alzheimer's disease, ALS, memory loss, hormonal problems, hearing loss, epilepsy, Parkinson's disease, AIDS dementia, brain lesions and neuroendocrine disorders. Risks to infants, children and pregnant women from aspartame were also underscored by the Federation of American Societies for Experimental Biology, a research body that traditionally follows FDA policy and adopts a softly-softly approach to chemical problems. The Federation declared: *"It is prudent to avoid the use of dietary supplements of L-glutamic acid by pregnant women, infants and children. The existence of evidence for potential endocrine responses... would also suggest a neuroendocrine link and that... L-glutamic acid should be avoided by women of childbearing age and individuals with affective disorders."* [144]

Phenylalanine: The amino acid L-phenylalanine, used by the brain, comprises 50% of aspartame. People suffering from the genetic disorder phenylketonuria (PKU) cannot metabolise phenylalanine and so an excess of this amino acid builds up in parts of the brain, leading to a decrease of serotonin levels, bringing on emotional disorders and depression.

Methanol: Also known as wood alcohol, the poison methanol is a 10% ingredient of aspartame, which is created when aspartame is

---

[143] *The Guardian*, London, UK, 20th July, 1990
[144] *Food Magazine*, op. cit.

heated above 86°F (30°C) in, for example, the preparation of processed foods. Methanol oxidises in the body to produce formic acid and the deadly neurotoxin, formaldehyde, also used as a prime ingredient in many vaccinations. Methanol is considered by America's Environmental Protection Agency (EPA) as *"...a cumulative poison, due to the low rate of excretion once it is absorbed. In the body, methanol is oxidised to formaldehyde and formic acid; both of these metabolites are toxic."*[145]

A one-litre carbonated beverage, sweetened with aspartame, contains around 56 mg of methanol. Heavy consumers of soft drinks sweetened with aspartame can ingest up to 250 mg of methanol daily, especially in the summer, amounting to 32 times the EPA warning limit.

Dr Woodrow C Monte, Director of the Food Science and Nutritional Laboratory at Arizona State University, was concerned that human response to methanol was probably much higher than with animals, due to humans lacking key enzymes that assist in the detoxification of methanol in other creatures. Monte stated: *"There are no human or mammalian studies to evaluate the possible mutagenic, teratogenic, or carcinogenic effects of chronic administration of methyl alcohol."* [146]

Monte's concern about aspartame was so great that he petitioned the FDA through the courts to address these issues. Monte requested that the FDA *"...slow down on this soft drink issue long enough to answer some of the important questions. It's not fair that you are leaving the full burden of proof on the few of us who are concerned and have such limited resources. You must remember that you are the American public's last defense. Once you allow usage* [of aspartame], *there is literally nothing I or my colleagues can do to reverse the course. Aspartame will then join saccharin, the sulfiting agents, and God knows how many other questionable compounds enjoined to insult the human constitution with government approval."*[147]

---

[145] *Extraordinary Science*, Vol. 7, No.1, Jan/Feb/Mar 1995, p.39
[146] *The Guardian*, "Laboratory Animals Back from the Dead in Faulty Safety Tests", April/June 1990
[147] Ibid.

Ironically, shortly after Dr Monte's impassioned plea, Arthur Hull Hayes, Jr., the Commissioner of the Food & Drug Administration, approved the use of aspartame in carbonated beverages. Shortly after, he left the FDA to take up a position with G D Serle's public relations company.[148] In 1993, the FDA further approved aspartame as a food ingredient in numerous process foods that would always be heated above 86°F, as part of their preparation.

Dr Joseph Mercola is no lover of aspartame. The well-known nutrition and health researcher itemises another catalogue of woes that have come to punctuate aspartame's hopeless legacy as a food additive:

"In 1991, the National Institutes of Health listed 167 symptoms and reasons to avoid the use of aspartame, but today it is a multi-million dollar business that contributes to the degeneration of the human population, as well as the deliberate suppression of overall intelligence, short-term memory[149] and the added contribution as a carcinogenic environmental co-factor.

The FDA and Centers for Disease Control continue to receive a stream of complaints from the population about aspartame. It is the only chemical warfare weapon available in mass quantities on the grocery shelf and promoted in the media. It has also been indicated that women with an intolerance for phenylalanine, one of the components of aspartame, may give birth to infants with as much as a 15% drop in intelligence level if they habitually consume products containing this dangerous substance." [150]

SUMMARY
Once again, world populations have been seduced into the habitual consumption of products, whose apparent benefits have been sold to us by some of the slickest marketers on the corporate payroll. And so you, the reader, have a choice to make. If it is your desire to continue consuming sugar, aspartame or saccharin, then this chapter has gone

---

[148] Ibid.

[149] The FDA instigated hearings in 1985 on aspartame at the request of Senator Metzenbaum, when a sample case was heard, in which a woman's memory suffered almost complete collapse until she ceased taking aspartame-laced products.

[150] Mercola, Joseph, op. cit. See also: **Steinman, D** *Diet for a Poisoned Planet*, University of California study, p.190

some way to discussing the very real concerns that scientists and researchers have with these products.

The watchword for *Health Wars* and the longevity it espouses must be to halt the influx of toxins into the body, expel those already there, and ensure a continued and prolonged life using whole foods that are clean, uncontaminated and nutritious, which provide the ideal, slightly alkali internal environment which the body craves. In my opinion, sugar, saccharin and aspartame have no place in a healthy body or a healthy world. It's going to mean restructuring our diets and desires to wean ourselves off the 'taste monster' and back to the food our bodies desire most. Sucrose, as mentioned, is an addiction. So, for that matter, is the desire to have sweeteners of any kind in food which does not naturally contain them in a form the body can break down and metabolise. In the final analysis, your body just wants to ask one question about what you feed it. "Can I use this material to build cells to replenish my systems?"

Sucrose, saccharin and aspartame are incompatible with this process and have been shown to work against the body. Thus, these materials are incompatible with life.

SUITABLE FOR DIABETICS

These recipes have been devised to be low in fat, salt and sugar. Whatever type of diabetes a person has, choosing the right foods and changing eating habits can help to control and normalise blood glucose levels, especially cholesterol and triglycerides. Eat regular meals containing 80% unrefined, high-water-content plant dietary. Start the day with low-glycaemic fruit, such as a pear or apple, then have a balanced meal at noon and then later on in the day. Try to avoid *fried* fish or pastry; rather look at exciting vegetable dishes and the salad possibilities. Regular exercise for type 2 diabetics is also a must!

COURGETTE AND PEA SOUP WITH MINT PESTO

1 tsp butter
1 onion, chopped
1 clove garlic, crushed
2 large courgettes (zucchini), grated
*8 oz **peas**, defrosted if frozen*
1 pint vegetable stock
sea salt and fresh ground black pepper

PESTO:
8 tbsp chopped fresh mint
1 garlic clove
*3 tbsp **walnuts,** toasted*
2 tbsp olive oil
sea salt and black pepper

Heat the oil in a large saucepan. Add the onion, garlic and courgettes and fry gently for 3-4 minutes until soft. Add the peas and stock to the pan, bring to the boil, reduce heat and simmer for 5 minutes. Season. Place pesto ingredients in a blender and mix. Keep texture slightly rough. Serve the soup hot or chilled, with a spoonful of mint pesto on top.[151]

---

[151] **Diabetes UK** *Diabetes Cookbook*, Dorling Kindersley, 2000

WHITE BEAN SOUP

*13 oz **butter beans***
1½ pints vegetable stock
2 tbsp butter
3 cloves of garlic, sliced
6 tomatoes, finely chopped
2 tbsp chopped fresh sage
sea salt and fresh ground black pepper

Put the beans and stock in a saucepan, bring to the boil, reduce heat, cover and simmer for 10 minutes. Take out about a third of the beans from the saucepan and set aside. Transfer the remaining beans and the cooking liquid to a food processor or blender and process into a smooth puree. Return the bean puree and the whole beans to the pan.

Heat the butter in a saucepan, add the garlic, and fry gently until golden. Add the tomatoes and sage, cover the pan, and simmer for 5 minutes. Stir the tomato mixture into the bean mixture and heat through. Season to taste.[152]

CHINESE CHICKEN NOODLES

1 tsp sesame oil
1 boned and skinned chicken breast, sliced
1 bunch spring onions, sliced
3½ oz mange tout, halved
1 red chilli chopped finely
2 tbsp dark soy sauce
8 oz egg-thread noodles
2 tbsp chopped fresh coriander

Heat the oil, add the chicken pieces and stir-fry for 2-3 minutes. Add the spring onions, mange tout, and chilli, continue to stir-fry for 2 minutes. Stir in the soy sauce.

Cook the noodles. Drop them into a saucepan of boiling water, reduce heat, and simmer for 3-4 minutes. Drain. Toss the noodles,

---

[152] Ibid.

chicken mixture and coriander, turn into a warmed serving bowl and serve immediately. [153]

TOMATO AND HERB RISOTTO

1 tsp butter
1 small onion, finely chopped
2 garlic cloves, crushed
*12 oz **wholegrain rice***
¼ pint dries white wine
2 pints boiling vegetable stock
9 oz cherry tomatoes, halved
4 sun-dried tomatoes, chopped
3 tbsp grated fresh Parmesan cheese
4 tbsp chopped fresh herbs
sea salt and fresh ground black pepper

Heat the butter, add the onion and garlic and stir-fry gently for 2 minutes. Stir in the rice, turning it to coat it in the butter. Add the wine, bring to the boil, reduce heat, and simmer until the rice has absorbed the liquid.

Add a ladle of boiling stock and simmer until absorbed, stirring continuously. Continue this process until all the stock has been used, adding the tomatoes and tomato puree with the last ladle of stock. Stir the Parmesan and herbs through the rice, season to taste. [154]

SPINACH TORTILLA

1 lb potatoes, sliced
1 tbsp olive oil
1 onion, sliced
*7 oz **spinach***
3 eggs, beaten
3 tbsp fresh Parmesan, grated
*¼ tsp **apricot kernels***
¼ tsp nutmeg
Sea salt and fresh black pepper

---

[153] Ibid.
[154] Ibid.

Cook the potatoes in boiling water for 5 minutes, until almost tender. Drain. Heat the oil in a medium frying pan. Add the onion and fry for 2-3 minutes. Add the spinach and stir-fry until it has wilted and any moisture evaporated. Add the potato slices and turn them to combine with the other ingredients.

Mix together the remaining ingredients and pour into the pan. Cook over a low heat until almost set. Place under a pre-heated grill for 1-2 minutes, until the top is golden and the eggs have set.[155]

LAMB AND FLAGEOLET BEAN SALAD

10 oz lamb fillet
2 tbsp mixed peppercorns, crushed
2 tbsp butter
1 garlic clove, chopped
1 red onion, cut into wedges
13 oz canned pimentos, drained and sliced
*13 oz canned **flageolet beans**, drained and rinsed*
2 tbsp balsamic vinegar
Fresh herbs

Roll the lamb in the crushed peppercorns to coat well. Heat the butter in a frying pan. Add the lamb and fry over a high heat for 5-6 minutes, turning until cooked to your liking. Remove the lamb from the pan and set aside.

Add the garlic onion to the pan and fry for 2-3 minutes. Stir in the pimentos, beans and balsamic vinegar and heat through. Turn the bean salad out of the pan on to a warmed serving dish. Cut the lamb into thin slices and lay them on the bean salad. Garnish with fresh herbs. [156]

SPINACH AND RICOTTA-FILLED CHICKEN

4 boned and skinned chicken breasts
2 tbsp light vegetable oil
1 small onion, finely sliced
½ tsp grated nutmeg

---

[155] Ibid.
[156] Ibid.

½ tsp grated **apricot kernels**
4 oz **spinach,** chopped
7 oz ricotta
¼ pint chicken stock

Cut a slit in one side of the chicken breast to make a pocket for the stuffing. Heat half the oil in a frying pan. Add the onion and fry gently for 2-3 minutes, until softened. Add the nutmeg, apricot kernels and spinach and continue to fry for 3-4 minutes, until the spinach is cooked and any moisture has evaporated. Season well, and then stir in the ricotta.

Stuff the chicken breasts with the spinach mixture and secure the sides with cocktail sticks. Pre-heat the oven to 200C/400F/Gas Mark 6. Heat the remaining oil in a frying pan. Add the chicken breasts and fry until brown on both sides. Put in an ovenproof dish and add the stock. Bake for 25 minutes, until the chicken is cooked through.[157]

MOROCCAN VEGETABLES AND CHICKPEAS ON COUSCOUS

2 tbsp light vegetable oil
1 small aubergine, cut into chunks
2 courgettes (zucchini), cut into chunks
1 carrot, cut into chunks
½ cauliflower, cut into wedges
1 onion, chopped
Piece fresh root ginger, peeled, grated
2 garlic cloves, crushed
1 tbsp ground cumin
1 tsp chilli powder
13 oz canned chopped tomatoes
2 tbsp tomato puree
¼ pint vegetable stock
13 oz canned **chickpeas**
7 oz green beans, halved
sea salt and freshly ground black pepper
8 oz couscous

---

[157] Diabetes UK, *Diabetes Cookbook*, op. cit.

14 fl oz boiling water
strips of fresh red chilli, to garnish
chilli sauce to serve

Heat the oil in a large saucepan. Add the aubergine, courgettes, carrot, cauliflower, onion, ginger and garlic and fry gently, stirring for 3-4 minutes, until the vegetables begin to soften. Add the cumin and chilli powder and continue to fry for 1 minute. Add the tomatoes, tomato puree and vegetable stock and bring to the boil. Reduce the heat and simmer for 8 minutes, adding the chickpeas and beans halfway through the cooking time. Season well.

Place the couscous in a large bowl and pour the boiling water over it. Leave to soak for 8-10 minutes. Serve the vegetables on the couscous, garnished with the red chilli strips and with a little chilli sauce on the side.[158]

---

[158] Ibid.

DESSERTS

LEMON CAKE

A beautiful moist golden cake with an intense lemon flavour. It contains no flour and is perfect to serve with a berry or other fruit compote, or great on its own.

2 lemons, unwaxed, preferably organic
6 eggs
7 oz fructose (obtainable at most large supermarkets)
9 oz ground almonds
1 tsp **apricot kernels**

Pre-heat the oven to 150C/300F/Gas Mark 2. Line an 8-inch cake tin, preferably with a loose base. Wash the lemons, then put them into a pan, cover with water and bring to the boil. Leave to cook gently for about 45 minutes, or until the lemons are very tender when tested with a sharp knife. Leave to cool.

Drain the lemons and cut them open so you can remove the pips. Then place them into a food processor and whiz into a golden puree. Whisk the eggs and fructose together for about 5 minutes until they are pale and very thick. Pour the mixture into the tin then bake for 1¼ hours. Cool the cake in the tin. Turn out carefully.

YOGHURT DESSERT WITH APRICOT KERNELS

yoghurt (thick creamy Greek set or set live yoghurt with whey poured off)
nutmeg
chopped dates
ground **apricot kernels**
macedonia nuts
almond or fig fingers (optional)

Spoon the yoghurt into sundae glasses. Add chopped dates, ground apricot kernels and a sprinkling of nutmeg. Drizzle a little honey (or maple syrup) over the top and place a Macedonia nut in the centre. Chill thoroughly before serving. Place the sundae dish on a plate and serve with an almond or fig finger on the side.

ALMOND BISCUITS

*8 oz **ground almonds***
*(or 4 oz ground **walnuts**)*
1 heaped tsp baking powder
2 oz (3 tbsp) butter
approx. 3 tbsp goats' milk
½ tsp almond extract

Pre-heat oven to 190C/375F/Gas Mark 5. Combine the ground almonds, baking powder and almond extract in a bowl. Mix in the melted butter then add the milk, stirring in with a fork. Bring the mixture together with your hands to achieve a firm but moist dough. Roll out thinly on a surface sprinkled with some ground almonds. Cut into squares, fingers or rounds and lift carefully onto a lightly greased baking sheet. Leave cool and harden on the sheet for a few minutes, then transfer to a cooling o cool completely. (If you prefer savoury biscuits, omit the almond extract).

BAKED APPLES WITH APRICOT

4 medium eating apples
3 oz dried apricots
pinch of ground coriander
2 tsp pure honey
¼ pint apple juice

2 oz butter
*ground **apricot kernels***

Ideal to eat on its own! Core the apples and cut a shallow slit around the centre of each one to prevent the skins from bursting. Arrange the apples in a shallow ovenproof dish.

Mix together the apricots, honey and coriander. Pack the apricot mixture tightly into the apple cavities. Scatter the remaining filling around the apples so that it cooks in the sauce. Pour on the apple juice and dot the apples with pieces of butter.

Cook the apples uncovered in a pre-heated oven for about 30/40 minutes. (Do not overcook). Sprinkle with some ground apricot kernels. Traditionally baked apples are served hot but these are also delicious cold with cream.[159]

BAKED PEARS WITH ALMONDS AND HONEY
(serves 4)
4 large very ripe pears (Williams and Comice are the best)
2 tsp liquid honey
2 tsp fructose
60 g whole unskinned almonds
½ cinnamon stick, finely grated (use a grater or mortar and pestle)

Pre-heat oven to 200C/400F/Gas Mark 6. Cut each pear into 6 and remove the cores. Place the pieces in an oven-proof tray with the honey, fructose, almonds and cinnamon, then into the pre-heated oven for 10 minutes. Ground apricot kernels can be added to the ingredients before the dish is cooked. Serve immediately.[160]

PEACHES IN MARMALADE SAUCE
4 large ripe peaches (peeled, halved and stoned)
4 tbsp orange jelly marmalade (sweetened with fructose from health shops)

---

[159] Robinson, Barbara
[160] Adapted from Blanc, Raymond, *Blanc Vite*, op. cit.

1½ oz butter
¼ tsp ground cinnamon
2 tbsp blanched almonds
*ground peach and **apricot kernels***

Pre-heat oven at 180C/350F/Gas Mark 4. Arrange the peach halves, cut sides up in a shallow baking dish. Melt the marmalade, butter and cinnamon together in a saucepan, then pour the sauce over the peaches. Crack the peach stones and take out the kernels. Grind and scatter the nuts and kernels.

Cover with foil and cook for 35 minutes. Serve hot with fresh cream dairy-free ice cream (available from health shops) or yoghurt.[161]

ALMOND STUFFED FIGS

4 large ripe figs
1 tbsp ground almonds
*1 tbsp ground **apricot kernels***
2 tbsp orange juice
2 tbsp freshly chopped dried apricots

SAUCE
4 tbsp natural yoghurt
finely grated rind of half an orange

GARNISH
wedges of ripe fig
wedges of lime
ground cinnamon

Make a cross cut in each fig without cutting right down and through the base. Ease the four sections of each fig out, rather like a sunflower head. Mix the ground almonds and apricot kernels with the orange juice and chopped dried apricots and press into the centre of each fig.

For the sauce, mix the yoghurt with the orange rind and thin down with a little water. Spoon a pool of orange yoghurt sauce on to each of 4

---

[161] Robinson, Barbara

small plates. Sit a stuffed fig into the centre of each one. Decorate with wedges of fig and lime and a sprinkling of ground cinnamon.[162]

B17 COCKTAIL -1

*2 cups **watercress***
2 cups unsweetened pineapple juice
*1 tsp ground **apricot kernels***
6 ice cubes
4 sprigs mint

Put ingredients into a blender for 1 minute. Pour into frosty glasses and serve.[163]

B17 COCKTAIL - 2

*1 cup **alfalfa sprouts***
1 cup apple juice
*10 **apple seeds***
12 almonds
4 sprigs of parsley
4 sprigs mint
6 ice cubes and enough cold water to thin a little

Put ingredients into a blender for 1 minute and serve.

B17 COCKTAIL - 3

2 cups of papaya juice
2/3 cup of dried apricots
½ cup pineapple juice
*¼ cup **sorghum cane syrup** or honey*
*1 tbsp ground **apricot kernels***
6 ice cubes

Liquify in a blender for 2 minutes and serve.[164]

---

[162] Ibid.
[163] de Spain, June, *The Little Cyanide Cookbook*, op. cit.
[164] Ibid.

NON–GRAIN MUFFINS

beat 2 egg whites stiff
mix egg yolks, 1 tsp vanilla essence
4 tbsp 100% vegetable glycerine
sea salt
beat the above until yellow. Stir in 1 tsp baking powder
*grind 2 cups of **walnuts***

Pre-heat the oven to 190C/325F/Gas Mark 5. Combine the egg yolk mixture with whites, folding thoroughly. Can be eaten by themselves, with organic butter. Cinnamon may also be added.[165]

---

[165] Mercola, Joseph, *The Mercola Cookbook*, op. cit.

WHY ARE THE NATIONS DYING?

> **Degenerative diseases are taking hold of industrialised nations like never before. The following excerpted US Senate document warned of the health holocaust to come.**

Senate Document No. 264, 1936.

74th Congress, 2nd Session

"Our physical well-being is more directly dependent upon minerals we take into our systems than upon calories or vitamins, or upon precise proportions of starch, protein or carbohydrates we consume... Do you know that most of us today are suffering from certain dangerous diet deficiencies which cannot be remedied until depleted soils from which our food comes are brought into proper mineral balance?

The alarming fact is that foods (fruits, vegetables and grains), now being raised on millions of acres of land that no longer contain enough of certain minerals, are starving us - no matter how much of them we eat. No man of today can eat enough fruits and vegetables to supply his system with the minerals he requires for perfect health because his stomach isn't big enough to hold them.

The truth is, our foods vary enormously in value, and some of them aren't worth eating as food... Our physical well-being is more directly dependent upon the minerals we take into our systems than upon calories or vitamins or upon the precise proportions of starch, protein or carbohydrates we consume.

This talk about minerals is novel and quite startling. In fact, a realization of the importance of minerals in food is so new that the text books on nutritional dietetics contain very little about it. Nevertheless, it is something that concerns all of us, and the further we delve into it the more startling it becomes.

You'd think, wouldn't you, that a carrot is a carrot - that one is about as good as another as far as nourishment is concerned? But it isn't; one carrot may look and taste like another and yet be lacking in the particular mineral element which our system requires and which carrots are supposed to contain.

Laboratory test prove that the fruits, the vegetables, the grains, the eggs, and even the milk and the meats of today are not what they were a few generations ago (which doubtless explains why our forefathers thrived on a selection of foods that would starve us!)

No man today can eat enough fruits and vegetables to supply his stomach with the mineral salts he requires for perfect health, because his stomach isn't big enough to hold them! And we are turning into big stomachs.

No longer does a balanced and fully nourishing diet consist merely of so many calories or certain vitamins or fixed proportion of starches, proteins and carbohydrates. We know that our diets must contain in addition something like a score of minerals salts.

It is bad news to learn from our leading authorities that 99% of the American people are deficient in these minerals [this was in 1936!], **and that a marked deficiency in any one of the more important minerals actually results in disease. Any upset of the balance, any considerable lack or one or another element, however microscopic the body requirement may be, and we sicken, suffer, shorten our lives.**

We know that vitamins are complex chemical substances which are indispensable to nutrition, and that each of them is of importance for normal function of some special structure in the body. Disorder and disease result from any vitamin deficiency. **It is not commonly realized, however, that vitamins control the body's appropriation of minerals, and in the absence of minerals they have no function to perform. Lacking vitamins, the system can make some use of minerals, but lacking minerals, vitamins are useless. Certainly our physical well-being is more directly dependent upon the minerals we take into our systems than upon calories of vitamins or upon the precise proportions of starch, protein of carbohydrates we consume.**

This discovery is one of the latest and most important contributions of science to the problem of human health."

THE HUNZA LESSON
by Phillip Day

Upon embarking on a study of longevity, you don't get very far into the project before you come into contact with the Hunzas. This isolated people of north-eastern Pakistan, located in the Himalayan foothill valleys, were not discovered until the 1920s, when the British Army traversed the mountain passes and came into contact with one of humankind's longevity miracles for the very first time. One practitioner who went with them was Dr Robert McCarrison (later Sir Robert McCarrison), who was able to document in some detail the astonishing culture he discovered.

The society the army engineers found was open, warm, friendly and religious and had a tremendous sense of community. One of the things McCarrison noticed immediately was the astonishing lack of diseases and the fine condition of the people. In their indigenous, isolated environment, the Hunzas exhibited near perfect physical and mental health. There was no sign of cancer, heart disease, diabetes, ulcers, colitis, diverticulosis, high blood pressure or childhood ailments. Neither was there any juvenile delinquency or crime. Respect for elders and age was ubiquitous and the tribe's sense of community made it clear to all members that if one was to succeed, all had to succeed. The teamwork with which the Hunzas executed their daily chores was very evident in their happiness, peace of mind and conspicuous lack of strife. The Hunzas had no police, no jails, no judges and no doctors or hospitals.

Their teeth were in the finest condition - perfect dental arches full of even, white teeth with no disfiguration, dental caries or other tarnishments common to the industrialised societies. Many of their population were later estimated to be older than 100, fathering children at 100-plus, with some of the most vital apparently surviving to 150 and beyond. Hunza womenfolk too were of the finest condition. No birth problems were observed and those ladies of 80 looked the equivalent of 40, with fresh and remarkably unblemished complexions.

McCarrison, later to become Director of Research on Nutrition in India and Chairman of the Post-Graduate Medical Education

Committee at Oxford University, was so taken by these people that he spent years of his life uncovering the Hunzas' health secrets. He later wrote: *"These people are unsurpassed by any other race in perfection of physique. They are long-lived, vigorous in youth and age, capable of great endurance and enjoy remarkable freedom from disease in general."* [166]

Renee Taylor too studied the Hunzas and was told by their King, the Mir: *"The idleness of retirement is a much greater enemy in life than work. One must never retire from something, one must retire to something."* [167]

The Hunza workload was prodigious. It was common, researcher Roger French remarks, for a Hunza to walk the 200km return trip to Gilgit in neighbouring Pakistan, carrying a heavy load over mountain passes and dangerous terrain without any stops for rest other than meal breaks. The men regularly played vigorous games, including volleyball and polo. In a strenuous game of volleyball, the young men, aged 16 to 50, would play against the elders, who were well over 70 and, as observed in one game, included a man thought to be 125 years old. Hunza polo was ferocious and without rules and there were often teeth knocked out. As the Mir remarked: *"The men of 100 felt no more fatigue than the men of 20."* [168]

McCarrison got to the bottom of the Hunzas' success and roundly attributed it to super-nutrition and the absence of a toxic, industrially polluted environment. McCarrison set out to prove how diet was a major contributor to the Hunzas' success by taking rats and feeding them a staple Hunza diet – fresh fruits and vegetables (especially the apricot, along with its kernel), dried fruits, legumes, whole-grain foods and goat's cheese and butter. Meat was a rarity, and the meat and dairy components of their diet were low, in contrast to Westernised diets today.

---

[166] **French, Roger** *The Man Who Lived in Three Centuries*, Natural Health Society of Australia, 2000, p. 29
[167] **Taylor, Renee** *Hunza Health Secrets*, Keats Publishing, 1964
[168] French, Roger, op. cit. p.30

Hunza water was later found to be highly mineralised, with a full spectrum of nutrients derived from fresh mountain streams and glaciers. The Hunzas also irrigated their crops with this mineral-rich mixture, greatly benefiting the crops that were subsequently harvested and eaten. McCarrison also noted that the Hunzas ate a high percentage of their foods raw and as close to nature as possible. Biochemist Ernst Krebs, along with other researchers, would also remark that the Hunzas, proud farmers of apricots, always consumed the seeds (kernels) of their fruits along with the pulp. This practice is widely condemned in Western societies today because of a supposed danger of cyanide poisoning (more details in a later chapter). McCarrison's Hunza rats were extremely long-lived and almost completely free of disease. Their condition was sleek. Their childbirth was easy and free of complications and the young ones were gentle, good-natured and healthy.

McCarrison then fed another sample of rats on the diet of the poor of the Bengal/Madras region: lots of pulses, rice, old vegetables, condiments and a little milk, together with city water. As described in his book, *Studies in Deficiency Diseases*, McCarrison's Bengal/Madras rats were not happy rodents. The list of diseases afflicting them included diseases of the ear, nose and throat, lungs and upper respiratory tract, gastrointestinal diseases, skin diseases, reproductive problems, cancer of the blood and lymph, heart disease and edema.

Finally McCarrison fed a third sample of rats the same diet consumed by the working-class Englishman of the day: refined, white bread and sugar, margarine, sweetened tea, boiled vegetables, tinned meats and jams. The same rash of diseases as previously reported with the Bengal/Madras group broke out among the rats, this time with severe additional complications; namely nervous diseases and pronounced delinquency among the rodents, which bit their attendants constantly and finally, by the 16th day of the experiment, began turning upon their own, killing each other and cannibalising the weaker among them. McCarrison's summary was succinct:

"I know of nothing so potent in producing ill-health as improperly constituted food. It may therefore be taken as a law of life, infringement of which shall surely bring its own penalties, that the single greatest factor in the acquisition of health is perfectly

<u>constituted food</u>. *Given the will, we have the power to build in every nation a people more fit, more vigorous and competent; a people with longer and more productive lives, and with more physical and mental stamina than the world has ever known."* [169]

[169] Quoted from French, Roger, op. cit. p.32

THE ANTI-*CANDIDA* DIETARY REGIMEN
Prepared by Nikki Zalewski

Although appearing to be extremely strict, after following this diet for a few days, you should notice increased energy, easier movement, better sleep, and less digestive problems

Foods to avoid:

All cow's milk products: cheese, yoghurt, whey – all cow's milk derivatives

All yeast products: alcohol, bread, (soda bread is allowed), Marmite, Oxo, Bovril, vinegars, mushrooms, processed and smoked fish and meats

All sugar products: honey, fructose, lactose, glucose, dextrose, Nutrasweet, Canderel, Equal and all aspartame and saccharin products

Nearly all fruit: over-ripe fruits are full of sugar and yeast (hence they go mouldy when over-ripe)

High-sugar root vegetables such as carrots, parsnips, sweet potatoes, beetroots. *NB: If you really can't live without potatoes, wean yourself off them slowly and try to end up with one a day.*

The list below shows you the foods *Candida* loves and thrives on. These need to be eliminated from your diet for between three to six months to start with.

Too much carbohydrate turns to glucose *rapidly*

Avoid:
- Sugar, and sugary foods
- Bread of all kinds and all of its pastry relatives: crackers, pastries, doughnuts, pies, muffins, cookies, etc.
- Cereals, hot or cold, sweetened or unsweetened
- Fast-food snacks, including crisps and pretzels
- White rice, potatoes and corn
- Products made with white flour such as pasta

- Most fruit
- Root vegetables such as carrots, turnips, parsnips and beetroot
- Chick peas, dried beans, lentils and pinto beans
- Coffee and other caffeine containing beverages
- Fizzy, canned drinks
- Alcohol in all forms
- Fruit juices and squash
- All convenience/junk foods, as they contain hidden sugars and other undesirable ingredients
- Cheeses (except non-cow's milk cheeses), milk and yoghurt
- All soy products
- Processed meats such as bacon, sausage, ham, salami, bologna, pastrami and hot dogs
- High salt foods such as processed meats and fish. Smoked fish contains unnecessary levels of sodium that can contribute to water retention
- Mushrooms and fungi, including quorn
- Condiments, such as pickles, toppings and all shop-bought sauces
- Hydrogenated fatty acids and partially hydrogenated fatty acids as contained in stick margarines and man-processed foods
- Saturated fats from tropical oil such as coconut oil
- Saturated fats, primarily from meat, dairy and eggs
- Health supplements containing lactose, gluten, citric acid

The following fruit and vegetables are best avoided until the *Candida* is under control:

Apricots, artichokes, asparagus, aubergine, avocado, blackberries, courgettes (zucchini), grapefruit, kumquats, okra, passion fruit, peaches, peas, plums, pumpkin, raspberries, sauerkraut, sugarsnap peas, squash, strawberries, tomato, watermelon.

SO what do I eat?!
Good food choices

The foods below have the lowest possible sugar/yeast content and are your best choices. You will notice there are several oils included as certain 'good fats' are vital for health (omegas 3, 6 and 9 essential fatty acids) (See **A Guide to Nutritional Supplements**).

Eat plenty of the following foods:

- Alfalfa sprouts, bean sprouts, bell peppers, (sweet peppers), Bok choy, broccoli, Brussels sprouts, cabbage, cauliflower, celery, cucumber, endive, fennel, garlic, green beans, greens, hot chili peppers, kale, lettuce, onions, parsley, radishes, spring onions, spinach, swiss chard, yellow beans
- Free range eggs, fresh fish (deep and cold caught) and sea food (**not shellfish**), lamb and veal, poultry, chicken, turkey, (particularly skinless white meat), in **small** amounts. Cancer patients should avoid all animal/fish proteins apart from those discussed in the cancer section of *The ABC's of Disease*
- Culinary herbs and spices

Fats (in moderation)

Avocado oil, cod liver oil, fish oil, flaxseed oil, grape seed oil, hemp oil, monounsaturated fats, olive oil, primrose oil.

Fluids

Try to drink 8 glasses of water each day: the body is 70% water, so needs fresh supplies daily for optimal hydration and to help flush out toxins. If you can get into the habit of drinking more water, the benefits are many – you'll notice increased energy, better concentration and clearer skin, to name but a few.

Herbal teas, especially Essiac and peppermint, are ideal

Although most fruits are taboo on the anti-*Candida* program, you may have one piece of *firm* fruit a day: apple, pear or kiwi. However, don't take fruit juice as well.

THE *FOOD FOR THOUGHT* LIFESTYLE REGIMEN

- Little or no meat in the diet. Any meat consumed should be hormone and pesticide-free. White meat is better than red. Avoid pork
- Avoid sugar, dairy, coffee and alcohol
- Eat properly constituted, organic, whole, living foods, a high percentage raw. If you want hot, briefly steam your veggies. Do not murder them. Remember that heat kills enzymes. Excellent recipes are provided in our companion guide, *Food For Thought*.
- The ideal balance is: 80% alkali/20% acidic ash foods. Most diets today comprise 90% acid/10% alkali!
- Some broiled fish, deep and cold caught, eaten sparingly is OK
- Avoid the foods below
- Hydrate the body (2 litres (4 pints) of clean, fresh water a day)
- Keep high-glycaemic fruit intake down. Eat more fruits that have low sugar-conversion, such as pears and apples
- Eat six *small* meals a day, ensuring a) that you don't go hungry, and b) that the body has a constant supply of nutrients
- **THE BASIC SUPPLEMENT PROGRAM** will consist of ionised colloidal trace minerals, antioxidant tablets, Vit C and B complexes and essential fats (see **A Guide to Nutritional Supplements**)
- Exercise (to get everything moving and assist in detoxing the body in an oxygen-rich environment). A regular walk in the early morning air is also healthy and very invigorating
- Rest. Rest. Rest. Rest. Rest
- Reduce environmental toxicity (avoid jobs using dangerous chemicals, radiation, etc.)
- Use safe personal care products*
- Use safe household products*

Foods to avoid

> - Pork products (bacon, sausage, hot-dogs, luncheon meat, ham, etc.) These are high in nitrites and are known homotoxins which can cause high blood urea and dikitopiprazines, which cause brain tumours and leukaemia.[170]
> - Scavenger meats (inc. ALL shellfish and other carrion-eaters – see Leviticus 11 in the Bible). Carrion-eaters, pork and shellfish in particular, concentrate toxins of other animals in their tissues, which we then consume to our detriment. The same goes for the elimination organs of commercially raised animals, such as liver and kidney, which can be high in drug and pesticide residues
> - Aspartame/saccharin, artificial sweeteners. These are known mental impairment problems and cancer risks.
> - Refined sugar/flour/rice. SUCROSE FEEDS CANCER Restricted amounts of wholegrain bread are OK. Use only wholegrain rice. No sugars should be consumed other than those contained naturally in whole foods
> - Hydrogenated & partially hydrogenated fats (margarine)
> - Junk (processed) food, including fizzy sodas and other soft drinks containing sugar, artificial sweeteners or phosphoric acid, which are drunk out of aluminium cans
> - Fat-free foods. Essential fats are *essential*!
> - Olestra, canola, soy, etc. Avoid fake or synthetic fats. Soy, in its unfermented state (meat and milk substitute products), disrupts the hormone (endocrine) system, blocks the absorption of calcium and magnesium, and acts like estrogen in the body. Small usage of unfermented soy and fermented soy products (soy sauce and miso) is OK. For more information on soy, see **The Shadow of Soy**
> - Polluted water (chlorinated or fluoridated – see *Health Wars*, 'Water Under the Bridge')
> - Caffeine products
> - Alcohol products
> - Excess refined salt. It's better to spice food with ground kelp to maintain a healthy iodine intake

---

[170] *Biologic Therapy*, "Adverse influence of pork consumption on human health", Vol. 1, No. 2, 1983

*Implementing Changes –
Convert Your Bathroom Pack

As many of the harmful ingredients we examined earlier can be found in the average bathroom, clear these out in one fell swoop and replace with safe alternatives. Neways' Convert Your Bathroom pack contains shampoo, conditioner, bath gel, shaving gel, deodorant, toothpaste and mouthwash that are not only free from damaging ingredients, but are of the highest quality. Whether you are undergoing nutritional therapy for cancer or are simply interested in cancer prevention, the cumulative toxic onslaught your body receives at the hands of harmful consumer products has to stop.

Exercise in Moderation

Research shows that those with a sedentary lifestyle are more prone to cancer and heart problems. A good exercise program will assist in cleansing the body and getting all the pieces of the body toned and in proper working order. Simply MOVE! Walking, a non-threatening hour in the gym twice or three times a week or cycling are ideal and immensely enjoyable once you get on the pro-active program. If you sit still all day long, you might as well not breathe! Life is about healthy action. Celebrate your life by looking, moving and feeling the way your body was designed to be.

THE FOUR PILLARS OF MENTAL HEALTH
- ➤ Eliminating allergies
- ➤ Maintaining blood sugar balance
- ➤ Avoiding toxins and pollution
- ➤ Ingesting optimum nutrition[171]

---

[171] **Day, Phillip** *The Mind Game*, Credence Publications, 2002

THE BASIC SUPPLEMENT PROGRAM

Remember that the body likes to take nutrients in collectively. Nutrition works best when the various components are allowed to work synergistically in combination with a natural, whole-food diet, the vast majority eaten raw. A basic, but comprehensive supplement program, such as my ideal one below, can have extremely good results, if carried out *consistently* over a period of time with suitable diet and lifestyle changes.

For many years, I have been disease-free and have not had a day off work (haven't got the time☺). I put this down to avoiding the minefields, boosting nutrients in the body, staying hydrated, getting exercise and rest, and having a moderately good attitude. The regimen below can hardly be described as a 'basic' supplement program, in view of the complexities of the nutrients involved, but here's the 'basic' version I use anyway!

> ➢ **Maximol (ionised mineral and vitamin supplement)**
> ➢ **B-complex supplement**
> ➢ **Vitamin E, 400 IU per day**
> ➢ **Zinc, 15 mg, am and pm**
> ➢ **Revenol (antioxidant)**
> ➢ **Essential fatty acid complex. Alternatively, 1 tbsp flaxseed oil per day**
> ➢ **Apricot kernels, 7 g per day**
> ➢ **Vitamin C complex (ascorbates plus bioflavonoids), 1-3 g per day**
> ➢

Once again, this program must be taken IN CONJUNCTION WITH **THE FOOD FOR THOUGHT DIETARY REGIMEN** and adequate hydration. A supplementation program is not a substitute for a good diet!

An advanced supplement program

Can contain any of the above components, plus other items discussed in the following section, **A Guide to Nutritional Supplements**. Please consult a health practitioner who is qualified to diagnose and recommend a comprehensive nutritional program for your particular circumstances.

A GUIDE TO NUTRITIONAL SUPPLEMENTS

The following section outlines nutritional components that have been studied and used for specific purposes in relation to nutritional support for those who have disorders or those wishing to exercise prevention. The purpose of this section is to inform, not to recommend any particular course of action or product. Health advice from a qualified health practitioner trained in nutrition is always advised. If you would like more details on any of the following, or have a question, please use the Contacts! section of this book to follow up

Smart nutrients and brain food

The human brain is responsible for man's superior mental power. It is the command centre for intellect, memory, awareness, motor control, and sensory perception - the internal regulator of all body processes. The brain's mental energies diminish as chronological age advances. The impact of aging, poor circulation, nutrient-depleted food, polluted air and water, toxic chemicals, and lifestyle stressors can severely impair your body's ability to supply nourishment to the brain. Increase blood flow is very important to the very narrow blood vessels throughout the body increasing the supply of oxygen to vessels that may receive very little oxygen due to their constricting size. The muscles and nerve cells of the brain are composed of phosphatidylserine and phosphatidylcholine. The following ingredients, both of ancient and recent discovery, are known to help enhance circulation and mental/physical energy.

DMAE (dimethylaminoethanol): DMAE is the precursor for choline, which in turn can cross the blood-brain barrier to manufacture the memory neurotransmitter molecule acetylcholine. DMAE has been shown to improve cognitive abilities when taken in doses ranging from 100–300mg. In a 1996 study in Germany, those patients taking the placebo showed no change in their EEG brain patterns, while those on DMAE demonstrated improvements in their brainwave patterns in those parts of the brain which play an important role in memory, attention and flexibility of thinking.[172]

DMAE supports the health of the brain's nerve fibres. Also known as centrophenoxine, it has been shown to decrease lipofuscin in the brain. With age, the number of lipofuscin-containing neurons in the cortex increases. An increase in lipofuscin results in a concomitant decrease in spontaneous

---

[172] **Dimpfel et al** "Source density analysis of functional topographical EEG: monitoring of cognitive drug action", *European Journal of Medical Research*, Vol.1, No.6 (19th March 1996): pp.283-290

neuronal action potentials and age-related neuro-pathies. Centrophenoxine is an anti-lipofuscin compound that prevents this age-related increase in lipofuscin. Centrophenoxine also increases acetylcholinesterase activity in the hippocampus thus reversing the age-related decline of the cholinergic system and possibly mediating its effects on cognitive and neuronal synaptic function.

DMAE, marketed as the drug Deaner or Deanol, was shown by Dr Bernard Rimland at the Autism Research Institute in San Diego to be almost twice as effective in treating children with ADD/ADHD than Ritalin, without the side-effects.[173]

5-HTP: 5-HTP (5-hydroxytryptophan) aids in maintaining healthy serotonin levels in the brain to combat feelings of depression, frequent headaches, and muscle aches and pain. 5-hydroxytryptophan is a compound native to the body and use to synthesise serotonin. Decreased levels of serotonin have been associated with depression, frequent headaches, and muscle aches and pain. Supplementation with 5-HTP has the potential to alleviate many of these ailments.

Ginkgo biloba extract: Contains the flavonone glycosides quercetin and kaempferol. It improves blood flow, especially in the microvasculature in the body. In the brain, this improves memory and capacity for learning.[174]

Bacopa monniera extract: Bacopin, the active chemical constituent found in the herb Bacopa monniera, is an excellent antioxidant that helps support mental function and memory. Bacopa monniera extract is used to improve mental performance, memory, and learning. It is useful when stress and nervous exhaustion are decreasing mental function. It acts as an adaptogenic, a tonic for the nervous system, a circulatory stimulant, and a cerebral stimulant. It is also used to promote longevity, and for nervous deficit due to injury and stroke. Other traditional uses include epilepsy, insanity, nervous breakdown and exhaustion.

Phosphatidylserine (PS): Phosphatidylserine contains the amino acid serine and is one of the brain's phospholipids. It plays a vital role in brain nerve cell membrane functions. Phosphatidylserine makes up approximately 105 of the total phospholipids in nerve cell membranes. Phosphatidylserine helps activate and regulate membrane proteins and play major roles in nerve cell functions, such as the generation, storage, transmission and reception of nerve impulses. As we age, our cellular membranes begin to change, and

---

[173] **Holford, Patrick & Hyla Cass** *Natural Highs*, Piatkus Books, 2001, p.139
[174] **Blumentahl, et al** Complete German Commission Monographs, *Therapeutic Guide to Herbal Medicine*, op. cit.

become stiffer. Proper functioning of the nerve cell membrane requires that it be more fluid, which phospha-tidylserine accomplishes. It also acts as a glutamate blocker, thereby preventing excitotoxic damage to the cell. Those having hypoglycaemia or a strong family history of one of the neurodegenerative diseases should avoid excitotoxins in their food and probably should take these supplements at an early age, beginning in their twenties or thirties. Phosphatidylserine boosts the brain's energy supply, thereby protecting vulnerable brain cells from injury.[175]

When Dr Thomas Crook, from the Memory Assessment Clinic in Bethesda, Maryland, gave 149 people with age-associated memory impairment a daily dose of 300 mg of PS or a placebo, those only taking PS experienced a vast improvement after 12 weeks in their ability to match names to faces – a recognised measure of memory and mental function.[176]

Centella asiatica extract: Centella asiatica, the ancient Ayurvedic herb commonly called gotu kola, maintains healthy blood flow, helps to balance the nervous system, and encourages proper brain function and enhanced mental capacity. It also contains compounds knows as asiaticosides. Asiaticosides are converted to Asiatic acid in vivo and have been researched thoroughly for their ability to elevate antioxidant levels in the blood and decrease the time necessary for wound-healing. The increase in antioxidant levels could be beneficial to those suffering from cerebral insufficiency. Centella asiatica, a source of vitamins A, B, E, and K, and magnesium, is used to support the improvement of memory, and enhance the body's fight against insomnia, fever, headache and inflammatory skin problems. It also promotes bloodflow by strengthening the veins and capillaries.[177] In India, the herb is used to assist against skin disease, syphilis, rheumatism, in the treatment of leprosy, for mental illness, epilepsy, hysteria, and for dehydration. In Southeast Asia, the herb supports prompt bladder activity, physical and mental exhaustion, diarrhoea, eye disease, inflammations, asthma, and high blood pressure. Additional effects of

---

[175] **Crook, T, et al** "Effects of phosphatidylserine in age-associated memory impairment", *Neurol.*, (1991), 41:664-649; **Cenacchi, B, et al** "Cognitive decline in the elderly: A double-blind, placebo-controlled multicenter study on efficacy of phosphataidylserine administration", *Aging Clin. Exp. Res.*, (1993), 5:123-133; **Engle, R, et al** "Double-blind, cross-over study of phosphatidylserine vs. placebo in subjects with early cognitive deterioration of the Alzheimer type", *Eur. Neurophycolpharmacol.*, (1992), 2:149-155; **Kidd, P M** "A review of nutrients and botanicals in the integrative management of cognitive dysfunction." *Altern. Med. Rev.* June, 1999, 4:144-61

[176] **Crook, T, et al** "Effects of PS in age-associated memory impairment", *Neurology*, Vol.41, No.5, (1991), pp.644-9

[177] Kidd, PM, op. cit.

Centella asiatica (gotu kola) include psychotropic and pharmacological effects. In forced swimming behavioural tests, an extract of Centella asiatica caused a significant reduction in the duration of the immobilisation phase. These tests show the sedative and antidepressive effects of Centella asiatica.

Pregnenalone: Pregnenalone, a steroid naturally produced in the body, supports the brain's natural capacity for recalling facts and events. Pregnenalone is synthesised in the body from cholesterol. The brain has the capacity to use cholesterol to make pregnenalone and other steroids. Pregnenalone can be metabolised into progesterone or converted into DHEA. DHEA in turn can be converted into androgens, estrogens and other steroids (as many as 150 different steroid hormones). Pregnenalone also improves visual perception - colours are brighter. Shapes and forms are more noticeable, increasing one's awareness of the environment. In addition, pregnenalone is a potent anti-depressant and can affect memory capabilities. Pregnenalone can accumulate in the body, especially the brain and nervous system, so effects may take time to manifest.

Phosphatidylcholine: Phosphatidylcholine contains phosphory-lated choline and is one of the brain's phospholipids. It plays a vital role in brain nerve cell membrane functions. Phosphatidylcholine makes up approximately 50% of the total phospholipids in nerve cell membranes. The cell membrane acts as a master switch controlling entry of nutrients, exit of waste products, movements of charged ions through the membrane, membrane shape changes, and cell-to-cell communications. The membrane-based ion pumps, transport molecules, enzymes, and receptors that manage these master-switch activities are the membrane proteins. These membrane protein concentrations and positioning are effected by the phospholipid composition and structure.

Phosphatidylcholine can come from the diet as phosphatidylcholine or choline. In addition, it can be synthesised in the body using free choline. Good dietary sources (in decreasing order of concentration) of phosphatidylcholine and choline are eggs, beef steak, cauliflower, butter, oranges, apples, whole-wheat bread, and lettuce. Dietary phosphatidyl-choline is cleaved by the pancreatic enzyme phospholipase B that leads to small amounts of choline entering the blood system. Phosphatidylcholine is synthesized in the body through two different pathways, the CDO-choline pathway and the PE methylation pathway. In the latter pathway, phosphatidylethanolamine is converted to phosphatidylcholine, freeing ethanolamine and consuming choline.

Phosphatidylethanolamine: One of the brain's phospholipids. It plays a vital role in brain nerve cell membrane functions. Phosphatidylethanolamine makes up approximately 25% of the total phospholipids in nerve cell membranes. Phosphatidylethanolamine is present in foods at approximately equal concentrations as phosphatidylcholine. Phosphatidylethanolamine can be converted to phosphatidylcholine in the liver, generating most ethanolamine in the body. Phosphatidylethanolamine can also be synthesized from free ethanolamine and diacylglycerol by the CDP-ethanolamine pathway. Smaller quantities of phosphatidylethanolamine can be reversibly converted to phosphatidylserine upon demand. Additionally, phosphatidylethanolamine can be converted from phosphatidylserine catalysed by a Vitamin B6-requiring enzyme.

Vinpocetine: Vinpocetine, the active compound in the herb periwinkle, helps the body maintain healthy circulation to the brain in support cerebral capacity. Found in the lesser periwinkle *Vinca minor*, vinpocetine has been shown to be an excellent vasodilator and cerebral metabolic enhancer. It improves glucose transport (uptake and release) through the blood-brain barrier throughout the brain, providing increased nutrients for cellular respiration. Vinpocetine is also a phosphodiesterase-1-inhibitor that in turn suppresses the production of TNF-alpha (responsible for inflammatory cytokines in the nervous system).

Researchers at the University of Surrey in the UK gave 203 people with memory problems either vinpocetine or a placebo. Those taking vinpocetine demonstrated a significant improvement in cognitive performance. Russian research has also shown that vinpocetine is potentially helpful for those with epilepsy.[178]

Phosphatidylinositol: Phosphatidylinositol contains the sugar inositol and is one of the brain's phospholipids. It plays a vital role in brain nerve cell membrane functions. Phosphatidylinositol makes up approximately 5% of the total phospholipids in nerve cell membranes. Phosphatidylinositol plays a vital role in the transmission of some hormonal signals. Phosphatidylinositol is the major source of inositol-1,4,5-triphosphate (IP3). IP3 is a modified sugar that has proven to be a versatile molecule participating in signalling events within many types of body cells (e.g., calcium signalling). Phosphatidylinositol is necessary to convert arachidonic acid to prostaglandins and thromboxanes.

NADH: NADH (niacinamide adenine dinucleotide) enhances proper neurotransmitter function - the electrochemical transmission of nerve

---

[178] **Hindmarch, I et al** "Efficacy and tolerance of vinpocetine in ambulant patients suffering from mild to moderate organic psychosyndromes", *Int'l. Clin. Psych.*, Vol.6, No.1 (1991): pp.31-43

impulses between the brain and body. Niacinamide adenine dinucleotide is required by the brain to synthesize various neurotransmitters. With age, the level of NADH diminishes resulting in a subsequent decrease in energy production and neurotransmitter levels. This in turn alters brain chemistry and can affect mental function. Theoretically, supplementation with NADH should improve one's mental capacities.

Huperzine: Also known as Huperzine A, is a purified alkaloid isolated from the Chinese club moss *huperzia serrata*. It inhibits the breakdown of the neurotransmitter acetylcholine. Acetylcholine is rapidly broken down in the brains of Alzheimer's patients and age-related memory disorders causing dementia. A shortage of acetylcholine appears to contribute to memory loss and other cognitive defects. Huperzine disrupts the enzyme acetylcholinesterase that breaks down acetylcholine. Current research is ongoing to use Huperzine to protect the brain against damage from strokes, epilepsy and chemical weapons. Studies conducted in China on Huperzine A have indicated its efficacy as an acetylcholinesterase inhibitor. Because cholinergic neurons are responsible for memory, theoretically an acetylcholinesterase inhibitor could improve memory.[179]

Ingenious (Neways International)

Enhanced brain nutritional support complex. The specially selected ingredients for Ingenious are well known in ancient Chinese, Ayurvedic, and western medicine for helping provide nutritional support to the brain's system to enhance circulation and revitalize mental energy. Ingenious is effective in supporting the body's natural processes, improving brain function and increasing cerebral and peripheral blood flow, circulation and oxygenation to the brain.

Ingredients: Vitamin B5 (calcium pantothenate), DMAE, 5-HTP, Ginkgo biloba extract, Bacopa monniera extract, Phosphatidylserine, Centella asiatica extract, Pregnenalone, Phosphatidylcholine, Phosphatidylethanolamine, Vinpocetine, Phosphatidylinositol, NADH, Huperzine.

Injectable B17/Laetrile/Amygdalin

Pharmaceutical grade vitamin B17 in metabolic therapy clinics is administered through injection for the first 21 days (Phase 1) and then orally afterwards (Home - Phase 2). 9 grams per day is used for the first 21 days in Del Rio Hospital. Dr Manner used this protocol. Injectable B17 is also

---

[179] **Xu, S, et al** "Efficacy of Tablet Huperzine-A on Memory, Cognition, and Behaviour in Alzheimer's Disease", *Acta Pharmacologica Sinica*, (1995), 16:391-395

invariably administered together with the tissue penetrating agent dimethylsulfoxide (DMSO).

Please note: Clinical tests have repeatedly shown that B17 is only truly effective when used in conjunction with pancreatic enzymes to break down the pericellular coating of the malignant cell.[180] Vitamins A and E in their emulsified form, along with high doses of C complex (ascorbates plus bioflavonoids), are then used in combination with B17 to attack the cancer cell. Clinics administering Metabolic Therapy to their patients always use these or similar supplements.

B17 Laetrile/Amygdalin Tablets
These pharmaceutical grade tablets contain the active B17 ingredient derived from the kernels of apricots. Usually available in 100 mg or 500 mg tablets. These tablets are always taken in conjunction with apricot seeds depending on body weight. For instance, manufacturers recommend:

- 2-4 100 mg tablets per day as a nutritional supplement for prevention (apricot seeds have been recommended by doctors in place of tablets for prevention also).
- 4-6 500 mg tablets per day as a nutritional supplement for clinical cancer sufferers, taken in conjunction with pancreatic enzymes (see below) and vitamins A & E (emulsified). When seeds are added, the B17 tablet dosage is reduced accordingly to avoid patient taking too much B17 at one time. If patient has cancer of the liver, a doctor should be consulted prior to dosing.

Pancreatic Enzyme Supplements
Specific enzymes used in B17 metabolic therapy include trypsin, chymotrypsin (human pancreatic enzyme), pancreatin and calf thymus (animal enzymes), papain (from papayas) and bromelain (from pineapples). Ernst Krebs has an opinion on this: *"The demasking effect of these enzymes against the pericellular layer of the malignant cell is something very concrete in the immunology of cancer. Now I prefer, rather than advising the use of bromelain or papaya tablets, that the individual seeking these enzymes get them directly from the fresh ripe pineapple and papaya fruit. As much as half a pineapple a day should be ingested."*

---

[180] **Manner, H W, Michaelson, T L, and DiSanti, S J** "Enzymatic Analysis of Normal and Malignant Tissues." Presented at the Illinois State Academy of Science, April 1978. Also **Manner, H W, Michaelson, T L, and DiSanti, S J** "Amygdalin, vitamin A and Enzymes Induced Regression of Murine Mammary Adenocarcinomas", *Journal of Manipulative and Physiological Therapeutics*, Vol 1, No. 4, December 1978. 200 East Roosevelt Road, Lombard, IL 60148 USA

If taking enzyme supplements as part of nutritional support for cancer and other illnesses, these should be consumed on an empty stomach, otherwise they just digest your food!

Emulsified Vitamin A (www.vitalminerals.org)

In 1963 when Dr Contreras initiated his activities as a clinical oncologist, the use of vitamin A as a useful agent in malignant neoplasm was considered illogical and absurd. Now vitamin A is accepted as an agent of great use for the major epithelial cancers as well as for epidermis carcinomas, chronic leukaemia and transitional cells.

The first formal studies of the possible anti-tumour effects of vitamin A were initiated in Germany, by investigators of Mugos Laboratories in Munich. It was a proven fact that lung cancer in Norwegian sailors was less common than in other groups, even though they smoked since childhood. Logic indicated that it had to be the opposite. After studying this phenomenon, it was discovered that they ate abundant quantities of raw fish liver, high in vitamin A, since childhood. The logical conclusion was that high doses of such a vitamin prevented the growth of lung cancer in heavy smokers. But it was also found that high doses of vitamin A were toxic, and could cause adverse reactions.

The main focus was to find out how to administer enough vitamin A to observe preventive or healing effects, without injuring the liver. The solution was found by one of the investigators, when he discovered that unprocessed milk had the vitamin, and children who were breast-fed never experienced toxic effects. Nature had the solution by including vitamin A in milk in the form of micro-emulsification.

Mugos investigators proceeded to prepare a variety of emulsified concentrations, formulating their famous High Concentration A-Mulsin. One drop contains 15,000 units. They were able to administer over a million units per day in progressive doses, without producing hepatic toxicity. The explanation is that, in emulsified form, vitamin A is absorbed directly into the lymphatic system without going through the liver in high quantities. Having solved the toxicity problem, it was possible to test the product in high doses. It was demonstrated that emulsified vitamin A has the following effects:

- In normal doses, it protects epithelium and vision
- In doses of 100,000 to 300,000 units per day, it works as a potent immune stimulant

- In doses of 500,000 to 1,000,000 units per day, it works as a potent anti-tumour agent, especially in epidermis and transitional carcinomas

Vitamin C Complex (Ascorbic acid/ascorbates plus bioflavonoids, etc.)

Dr Linus Pauling, often known as the 'Father of Vitamin C' and twice awarded the Nobel Prize, declared that large intakes of up to 10g of the vitamin complex each day aids anti-cancer activity within the body and also assists in repairing damaged arteries and removing arterial plaque (atherosclerosis) for heart disease sufferers. Pauling was largely derided for making these declarations (yet he lived to be 94!), but today, large doses of Vitamin C complex are used by many practitioners for cancer patients in nutritional therapy, who believe Pauling was right and that the popular nutrient is indispensable to the body in its fight to regain health from cancer.

Vitamin C is not one nutrient, but a complex of factors common in fruits, vegetables and many other foods. Several studies have suggested that Vitamin C may reduce levels of lead in the blood. Epidemiological studies have shown that people with elevated blood serum levels of Vitamin C had lower levels of blood toxicity. An examination of the data from the Third National Health and Nutrition Examination Survey, enrolling 4,213 youths aged 6 to 16 years and 15,365 adults 17 years and older from 1988 to 1994, found a correlation between low serum ascorbic acid levels and elevated blood lead levels. The authors conclude that high ascorbic acid intake may reduce blood lead levels.[181]

Ascorbic acid or the non-acidic ascorbates (calcium or magnesium ascorbates) should be taken along with bioflavonoids and a healthy, alkalising diet for optimum effects.

An analysis of the Normative Aging Study, which enrolled 747 men aged 49 to 93 years from 1991 to 1995, found that lower dietary intake of Vitamin C may increase lead levels in the blood.[182] A study of 349 African American women enrolled in the project Nutrition, Other Factors, and the Outcome of Pregnancy found that vitamin-mineral supplementation resulted in increased

---

[181] **Simon J A, Hudes E S** "Relationship of Ascorbic Acid to Blood Lead Levels." *Journal of the American Medical Association*, 1999;281:2289-2293

[182] **Cheng Y, Willett W C, Schwartz J, Sparrow D, Weiss S, Hu H** "Relation of nutrition to bone lead and blood lead levels in middle-aged to elderly men. The Normative Aging Study." *Am J Epidemiol* 1998 Jun 15;147(12):1162-1174

serum levels of ascorbic acid and decreased serum levels of lead. The authors concluded that maternal use of a vitamin supplement with ascorbic acid and Vitamin E might offer protection from lead contamination of the foetus during pregnancy.[183]

Because smoking lowers levels of ascorbic acid in the body, researchers theorised that Vitamin C supplementation may effect blood lead levels in smokers. A clinical study was performed on 75 adult men 20 to 30 years of age who smoked at least one pack of cigarettes per day, but had no clinical signs of ascorbic acid deficiency or lead toxicity. Subjects were randomly assigned to daily supplementation with placebo, 200 mg of ascorbic acid, or 1000 mg of ascorbic acid. After one week of supplementation, there was an 81% decrease in blood-lead levels in the group taking 1000 mg of ascorbic acid daily.[184]

Dosage recommended by Linus Pauling for prevention is between 600mg and 3g a day – or up to 10g/day for those who have been diagnosed with cancer. High levels of Vitamin C however can cause diarrhoea and may be contra-indicated with certain chemotherapy treatments. Vitamin C is especially useful when combined in moderate amounts with Calcium d-glucarate, as formulated in the Neways product D-Toxarate (see D-Toxarate in this section).

VITAMIN P (bioflavonoids): another part of the Vitamin C 'complex'. Dr Albert Szent-Gyorgi, 1937 Nobel Laureate for his isolation of Vitamin C, later found other factors intrinsic to the action of C. Originally believed to be a single nutrient, Vitamin C became the subject of further testing by Szent-Gyorgi, who fought long and hard to have the co-factor (bio)flavonoids included in the C complex. Coining the new bioflavonoids 'Vitamin P', Szent-Gyorgi argued that they were essential for proper functioning of the human organism, derived from plant pigments known as the flavonols and flavones. Bioflavonoids are widely accepted today for their health benefits and are available in hydroxylated and methoxylated forms. They are derived from the pith of fruits (mostly citrus). Quercetin, rutin, catechin, anthocyanidins and proanthocyanidins are examples of flavonoids. The term 'Vitamin P' has been less well received by our medical czars.

---

[183] **West WL, Knight E M, Edwards C H, et al** "Maternal low level lead and pregnancy outcomes." J Nutr. 1994 Jun;124(6 Suppl):981S-986S
[184] **Dawson E B, Evans D R, Harris W A, Teter M C, McGanity W J** "The effect of ascorbic acid supplementation on the blood lead levels of smokers." *J Am Coll Nutr.* 1999 Apr;18(2):166-170

B Complex
B, B, B1, B2, B3, B5, B6, B8, B9, B12, B15, B17
One of the most important groups of nutrients for mental health is the B-group. A dip in the intakes of any member of the group will cause problems, and fast. Together however, working in synergy with a sensible, varied diet, the great effects of the 'B's can be startling. B vitamins are water-soluble and rapidly pass out of the body, so a regular intake of a good B-complex is essential. We have variously looked at the B-Vits in my other books as we've made our way through the nutrition maze, so let's sum up.

Vitamin B (choline) is the base ingredient of lecithin. Choline helps in the formation of the 'memory' neurotransmitter molecule, acetylcholine, and has been used to great effect in treating Alzheimer's. It is often used medically in the form phosphatidylcholine (see section entitled 'Phosphatidylcholine').

Vitamin B (inositol) is another B nutrient used to treat mental illness. Bi-polar mental disorders, characterised by interchangeable periods of depression and euphoria, have responded well to high doses of the nutrient. Inositol is mentioned repeatedly in the scientific literature in connection with treating panic attacks and anxieties.[185]

Vitamin B (PABA), also known as paraaminobenzoic acid, is a component of B9 (folic acid) and acts as a co-enzyme in the body. PABA assists other B vitamins in making red blood cells, metabolising proteins, and helping with skin disorders. Nasty red bumps caused by the sun respond well to PABA applied externally or 400 mg internally. Many skin lotions have PABA to help prevent wrinkling of the skin and greying of the hair. A facial mask comprised equal parts of PABA, aloe vera and honey left on the face while sleeping will tighten loose skin and help some wrinkles to vanish. The face mask is removed the following morning with cotton balls saturated in rubbing alcohol followed by warm water. Not for nothing is this nutrient referred to as the 'Cosmetic B'![186]

Vitamin B1 (thiamine) deficiency leads to beriberi. The nutritional pioneer Dr W Henry Sebrell attributed his razor-sharp memory to a daily supplementation of 150 mg of B1 for almost 29 years! Sebrell explains that thiamine is often severely lacking in up to 50% of psychiatric patients. Thiamine binds to lead molecules, thereby assisting in excreting the heavy

---

[185] **Heinerman, John** *Encyclopaedia of Nature's Vitamins and Minerals*, Prentice Hall, 1998, p.15
[186] Ibid, p.18

metal from the body. Sebrell estimated that a daily intake of 100 mg of B1 would afford protection against lead poisoning.[187]

Vitamin B2 (riboflavin) appears under the microscope as a yellow, crystalline substance. This vitamin assists in body growth, repair and cell respiration. It's excellent too in maintaining the health of the nervous system, the assimilation of iron and, along with vitamin A, for great vision. Those suffering from chronic fatigue, oily skin and intestinal gas may test positive for low levels of this nutrient and iron.

Vitamin B3 (niacin) deficiency causes depression and psychosis. Subjects of various ages taking 141 mg of niacin a day demonstrated a measurable improvement in memory of 10-40% in all age groups.[188] Its RDA is only 18 mg in the UK, and yet studies, as we have seen, demonstrate that mega-doses can prove extremely beneficial to 'schizophrenics'. This nutrient is also sometimes prescribed with great effect for rheumatoid arthritis in doses between 150-300 mg to improve joint function and mood. May cause skin flushing. B3 can be purchased bound with inositol, which prevents flushing. Regular use of B3 will cause flushing to cease. B3 is also reported in the scientific literature to be useful in treating and preventing certain forms of cancer.[189]

Vitamin B5 (pantothenic acid), as it is also known, has been hypothesised to increase cholinergic activity in the body, specifically the central nervous system. This increase in cholinergic activity could result in increased memory, learning, and cognitive abilities. B5 (pantothenate) is another potent memory enhancer, assisting in the creation of the essential memory neurotransmitter, acetylcholine. Supplementing 250-500 mg of B5 along with choline may improve memory.

Vitamin B6 (pyridoxine) is essential for making neurotransmitters. It converts amino acids into serotonin, a deficiency of which brings on irritability, violence, poor memory and a dive in overall cognitive and social performance. Folic acid deficiency encourages anxiety and depression. One study showed that about a fifth of depressed people are deficient in pyridoxine.[190] Supplementation is ideally between 30-100 mg a day or more

---

[187] Ibid.

[188] **Loriaux, S, et al** "The effects of niacin and xanthinol nicotinate on human memory in different categories of age – a double-blind study", *Psychopharmacology*, 87, 390-395, 1985; also Heinerman, John, op. cit. p.28

[189] Heinerman, John, op. cit. p.29

[190] **Stewart, JW, et al** "Low B6 levels in depressed patients", *Biological Psychiatry*, Vol.141 (1982): pp.271-2

for normal dream recall (B6 can be toxic at high doses. Do not exceed 8000-1,000 mg).

Vitamin B8 (biotin) is known as the energy and beauty nutrient and assists our cells' mitochondria in producing the energy molecule adenosine-triphosphate (ATP). Biotin is used in the transformation of consumed carbohydrates, fats and proteins into energy, which is then stored in the liver and muscle tissue in the form of glycogen. Glycogen, when needed, is released from these stores and readily converted into glucose, which the body then chemically 'burns' as a fuel to produce physical energy. Biotin is very much an enzyme helper and catalyses many enzymatic reactions in the body.

Vitamin B9 (folic acid) was discovered almost simultaneously with B12 and indeed works in conjunction with this essential nutrient. Folic acid is well known in helping to avoid birth defects, such as spina bifida and neural tube defects. Folic acid, like B12, is essential for oxygen delivery to the brain. A deficiency in either causes anaemia. Ideal supplementation for folic acid is around 400 mcg daily.

Vitamin B12 (cyanocobalamin) has been shown to improve the rate at which rats learn. Lack of B12 leads to anaemia, confusion and poor memory.[191] Several of these nutrients can be raised to larger doses as part of a program to eradicate chronic shortages, as we have seen, with spectacular results. B12 supplementation is between 10-100 mcg a day. Some people have poor absorption of B12 and can benefit from amounts up to 1,000 mcg a day.

Vitamin B15 (pangamic acid) is another controversial nutrient, traditionally pilloried by the establishment. B15 has been described as 'instant oxygen', and has been used by Russian athletes for years to gain a competitive edge. Almost all research into this nutrient has come from Russia and has been viewed with outright scepticism by the American medical establishment. Pangamic acid has been variously described as the *"hottest substance to hit the ergogenic scene in recent memory,"* and was apparently capable of delivering *"flashy brilliance"* to orgasms and mopping up free radicals *"like mad"*. It is used in certain clinics today as part of the nutritional support for cancer patients. Some mainstream nutritional references still carry information about pangamic acid; others mention it, but disassociate themselves from its B-vitamin status.

Vitamin B17 (Laetrile, laetrile and amygdalin) is often referred to as the anti-cancer vitamin. Like B15, this nutrient has been clouded with controversy

---

[191] **Pearson, D & S Shaw** *Life Extension: A Practical, Scientific Approach*, Warner Books, 1982

and been the subject of repeated attacks by the medical establishment. Nevertheless, unlike B15, there is an impressive track record of success with B17, which is contained in the seeds of the common fruits, excluding citrus, and a wide variety of grasses, legumes, pulses, vetches and vegetables. I deal with the subject of vitamin B17 in some detail in my books *Health Wars*, *Cancer: Why We're Still Dying to Know the Truth*, and *B17 Metabolic Therapy: A Technical Manual*. B17 is renowned for its analgesic qualities and its ability selectively to target and kill cancer cells, while nourishing non-cancerous tissue. Broken down in the body, one of its by-products, sodium thiocyanate, reacts with the liver precursor, hydroxycobalamin, to form the other vitamin with a cyanide radical, vitamin B12. (see also 'Apricot Kernels')

Essential fats (inc. Vitamin F)
EFA Recovery Plus &
Omega-3 EPA (Neways International)

EFA Recovery Plus is a daily essential fatty acid mix that contains omega-3 and omega-6 fatty acids. It was designed to help balance one's diet with a 40/30/30 caloric ratio of the three macronutrient sources, carbohydrate, protein and fat, for optimal health and better performance. EFA refers to the 'essential fatty acids' required in our diet, because these fatty acids cannot be synthesised by our body. 'Recovery' refers to EFA's role in restoring and maintaining general health as well as biochemical recovery following physical exercise and work.

The two major energy sources for the production of ATP energy during exercise are carbohydrates in the form of muscle glycogen and fats in the form of fatty acids. Fat is the most misunderstood of the three macronutrient sources. The association between a high-fat diet and serious health problems is widely advertised. This is the reason for today's trend to buy 'fat-free' food products. However, it is important to know that dietary fat consists of three basic types of fatty acids: (1) saturated, (2) monounsaturated, (3) polyunsaturated.

Saturated fat, 'bad fat', found in most animal fat, margarine, shortening, etc. can raise blood cholesterol levels. Partially hydrogenated oils contain trans-fatty acids that are also classified as 'bad fats'. Unsaturated fat, 'good fats', are composed of cis-fatty acids typically found in vegetable oils, cold-water fatty fish (e.g., salmon, herring, etc.), avocado, nuts and some beans. These foods are known for their ability to reduce blood cholesterol levels.[192]

---

[192] **Siguel, E** "A new relationship between total-high density lipoprotein cholesterol and polyunsaturated fatty acids", *Lipids*, 1996 Mar;31 Suppl:S51-6

It is just as important to regulate the kinds of fat we ingest as the amount of fat itself. Unsaturated fats play a beneficial role in our body. Fats are the most concentrated source of energy in the diet. Many sources of fat provide important nutrients, carry fat-soluble vitamins, A, D, E, and K through the bloodstream, maintain healthy skin, and are crucial for foetal brain development. The typical western diet does not include a sufficient amount of EFAs, especially those referred to as omega-3 fatty acids. EFA Recovery Plus is a combination of the natural sources of all cis-fatty acids as: alpha-lipoic acid, linoleic acid (omega-6), EPA (omega-3) and DHA (omega-3). These fatty acids are essential. Essential fatty acids are involved in a variety of biochemical processes. EFAs are vital in the role of energy production for muscle cells during exercise and assisting in muscle relaxation.[193]

In addition, EFAs affect the control of blood coagulation.[194] They also affect the release of CCK, a hormone that signals the brain that you're full and to stop eating.[195] EFAs are involved in maintaining conduction velocities for sensory and motor nerves.[196] EFAs are also present in cell membranes and support suppleness of skin[197] and help to lower high blood pressure.[198]

Alpha-lipoic acid is a sulfur-containing essential fatty acid. Alpha-lipoic acid is directly involved in the availability of brain and skeletal energy during exercise.[199] Alpha-lipoic acid has been used in Europe to help the body control diabetic effects.[200]

---

[193] **Barbiroli, B, Medori R, Tritschler H J, Klopstock T, Seibel P, Reichmann H, Iotti S, Lodi R & P Zaniol** "Lipoic (thioctic) acid increases brain energy availability and skeletal muscle performance as shown by in vivo 31P-MRS in a patient with mitochondrial cytopathy", *J. Neurol.* 1995 Jul;242(7):472-7

[194] **Andriamampandry, M, Freund, M, Wiesel, M L, Rhinn, S, Ravanat, C, Cazenave J P, Leray, C, Gochet, C** "Diets enriched in (n-3) fatty acids affect rat coagulation factors dependent on vitamin K", *C. R. Acad. Sci. III* 1998 May;321(5):415-21

[195] **Matzinger, D, Degen, L, Drewe, J, Meuli, J, Duebendorfer, R, Ruckstuhl, N, D'Amato, M, Rovati, L, Beglinger, C** "The role of long chain fatty acids in regulating food intake and cholecystokinin release in humans", *Gut* 2000 May;46(5):689-94

[196] **Julup, O, Mutamba, A** "Comparison of short-term effects of insulin and essential fatty acids on the slowed nerve conduction of streptozoticin diabetes in rats", *J. Neurol. Sci.* 1991 Nov;106(1):56-9

[197] **Horrobin, D F** "Essential fatty acid metabolism and its modification in atopic eczema", *Am. J. Clin. Nutr.* 2000 Jan;71(1 Suppl):367S-72S

[198] **Lee, R M** "Fish oil, essential fatty acids, and hypertension", *Can. J. Physiol. Pharmacol.* 1994 Aug;72(8):945-53

[199] **Barbiroli, B, Medori, R, Tritschler, H J, Klopstock, T, Seibel, P, Reichmann, H, Iotti, S, Lodi, R, Zaniol, P** "Lipoic (thioctic) acid increases brain

Alpha-linolenic acid is an omega-3, polyunsaturated, cis-fatty acid found in flax seed oil. Alpha-linolenic acid is converted to EPA and DHA.

Linoleic acid is an omega-6, polyunsaturated, cis-fatty acid found in safflower oil. Linoleic acid in incorporated in phospholipids – phospholipids are key components of healthy cell membranes.[201] Linoleic acid is converted to special prostaglandins[202] – prostaglandins control blood-clotting.

Omega 3 Fats

Food processing has wrought havoc on daily intakes of Omega 3 fats. It is estimated that the population today may be consuming around one sixth of the Omega 3s that our ancestors ingested back in 1850, due mainly to today's food choices and processing.[203] Omega 3 fats are more susceptible to corruption during the cooking process. EPA and DHA are omega-3 polyunsaturated fatty acids – the 'good fats'. Eicosapentaenoic acid (EPA) and docosahexaenoic acid (DHA) are in high concentrations in cold-water fish (e.g. salmon, tuna, mackerel and herring). EPA is used to support against high cholesterol and to form membranes surrounding cells.[204] EPA is required for the production of prostaglandins, which control blood clotting and other arterial functions.[205] DHA is a component of human brain tissue[206] and the

---

energy availability and skeletal muscle performance as shown by in vivo 31P-MRS in a patient with mitochondrial cytopathy", *J. Neurol.* 1995 Jul;242(7):472-7

[200] **Ziegler, D, Reljanovic, M, Mehnert, H, Gries,** F A "Alpha-lipoic acid in the treatment of diabetic polyneuropathy in Germany: current evidence from clinical trails", *Exp. Clin. Endrocrinol. Diabetes* 1999;107(7):421-30

[201] **Raederstorff, D, Moser,** U "Influence of an increased intake of linoleic acid on the incorporation of dietary (n-3) fatty acids in phospholipids and on prostanoid synthesis in rat tissues", *Biochim. Biophys. Acta* 1992 Dec 2;1165(2):194-200

[202] **Mentz, P, Hoffmann, P, Lenken, V, Forster,** W "Influence of prostaglandins, prostaglandin-precursors and of a linoleic acid rich and free diet on the cardiac effects of isoprenaline and vasodilators", *Acta. Biol. Med. Ger.* 1978;37(5-6)801-5

[203] Ibid.

[204] **Mizota, M, Katsuki, Y, Mizuguchi, K, Endo, S, Miyata, H, Kojima, M, Kanehiro, H, Okada, M, Takase, A, Ishiguro, J,** et al. "Pharmacological studies of eicosapentaenoic acid ethylester (EPA-E) on high cholesterol diet-fed rabbits", *Nippon Yakurigaku Zasshi* 1988 Apr;91(4):255-66

[205] **Bell, J G, Tocher, D R, MacDonald, F M, Sargent,** J R "Diets rich in eicosapentaenoic acid and gamma-linolenic acid affect phospholipid fatty acid composition and production of prostaglandins E1, E2 and E3 in turbot (Scophythalmus maximus), a species deficient in delta 5 fatty acid desaturase", *Prostaglandins Leukot Essent. Fatty Acids* 1995 Oct;53(4):279-86

[206] **Ward, G R, Huang, Y S, Xing, H C, Bobik, E, Wauben, I, Auestad, N, Montalto, M, Wainwright,** P E "Effects of gamma-linolenic acid and

retinal tissue.[207] DHA serves in the transmission of nerve impulses in the nervous system.

Omega 3 Deficiency Symptoms: Dry skin, lack of co-ordination or impaired vision, inflammatory health problems, allergic reactions, memory or learning ability impaired, tingling in the arms or legs, hard to lose weight, high blood pressure or triglycerides, prone to infections.

Omega 6 Fats

Gamma-linolenic acid (GLA) is an omega-6 polyunsaturated cis-fatty acid found in evening primrose oil that helps to increase circulation. Research has shown that it aids in the reduction of platelet aggravation, lowers cholesterol and may reduce the risk of cardiovascular disease.[208] Evening primrose oil added to the diet of alcoholics undergoing withdrawal dramatically reduces symptoms and, in the long-term, improves memory.[209] This feature prompted researchers to see whether the oil would improve the memory of Alzheimer's patients. During a controlled trial, significant improvements were seen.[210] Other sources of Omega 6 fats are the seeds of hemp, pumpkin, sunflower, safflower, sesame, corn, walnut and wheatgerm oil. Omega 6 fats must have adequate levels of zinc, magnesium, B6 and biotin accompanying them to drive the enzyme that makes the conversion to GLA.[211]

Omega 6 Deficiency Symptoms: High blood pressure, eczema or dry skin, PMS or breast pain, dry eyes, blood sugar imbalance or diabetes, chronic fatigue, multiple sclerosis, alcoholism, depression and mood swings, excessive thirst.

Prostaglandins

Essential fats are, as their name suggests, essential for creating prostaglandins. These are extremely active, hormone-like substances which variously keep blood thin, relax blood vessels, thereby assisting in lowering

---

docosahexaenoic acid in formulae on brain fatty acid composition in artificially reared rats", *Lipids* 1999 Oct;34(10):1057-63

[207] **Neuringer, M** "Infant vision and retinal function in studies of dietary long-chain polyunsaturated fatty acids; methods, results, and implications", *Am. J. Clin. Nutr.* 2000 Jan;71(1Suppl):256S-67S

[208] **Scheer, James F** "Evening primrose oil – It's essential", *Better Nutrition*, 1998 Jun;60(6)60-64

[209] **Pfeiffer, Carl & Patrick Holford** *Mental Illness – The Nutrition Connection*, ION Press, London: 1996, p.31

[210] Ibid.

[211] Ibid.

blood pressure, boost immunity, assist in maintaining the water balance in the body, decrease inflammation, and assist the operation of insulin for correct blood sugar balance. Prostaglandins (series 1 & 3) themselves cannot be supplemented, due to their short-lived and volatile nature. However, an adequate intake of essential fats will equip the body with the raw materials it needs to create them. These two supplements from Neways assist in doing just that. The intake ratio between Omegas 6 and 3 should ideally be around 2:1.

EFA Recovery Plus ingredients: Alpha-lipoic acid, Linoleic acid, Alpha-linolenic acid, Gamma-linolenic acid, Eicosapentaenoic acid (EPA), Docosahexaenoic acid (DHA).

Omega 3 EPA ingredients: Eicosapentaenoic acid (EPA), Docosahexaenoic (DHA), Vitamin E, natural D-alpha tocopherol.

VITAMIN F: The polyunsaturated fatty acids (PUFA's) have been described as 'Vitamin F', a classification that once again hit rough waters with the medical establishment. Saturated fats have no hydrogen atoms missing in their carbon chains, whereas PUFA's may have two, three, four, or more double-bond linkages in the carbon chain with four, six, eight, or more hydrogen atoms missing. PUFA's are long-chain and extra-long-chain fatty acids which naturally occur in nature and are used by the body to prevent hardening of the arteries, normalise blood pressure, enhance glandular activity and assist in physical growth early in life. Despite the American Medical Association loudly denouncing the moniker 'Vitamin F' as quackery, PUFA's have rightly gained prominence in recent years as essential, life-sustaining nutrients. And what are essential, life-sustaining nutrients if not a vitamin?

Essiac

In 1923, a Canadian nurse, Rene Caisse, came upon an ancient Ojibway Indian herbal concoction that appeared to have remarkable powers to offer the sick. In the years since, thousands of patients, many considered beyond hope, have testified that this simple, natural treatment saved their lives where modern medicine had failed. Reported benefits of Essiac include:

1. Preventing the build up of fatty deposits in artery walls, heart, kidney and liver
2. Regulating cholesterol levels by transforming sugar and fat into energy
3. Destroying parasites in the digestive system and throughout the body
4. Counteracting the effects of aluminium, lead and mercury poisoning
5. Nourishing and stimulating the brain and nervous system
6. Promoting the absorption of fluids in the tissues

7. Removing toxic accumulations in the fat, lymph, bone marrow, bladder, and alimentary canals
8. Neutralising acids, absorbing toxins in the bowel and eliminating both
9. Clearing the respiratory channels by dissolving and expelling mucus
10. Relieving the liver of its burden of detoxification by helping to convert fatty toxins into water-soluble substances that can then be eliminated through the kidneys
11. Increasing the body's ability to utilize oxygen by raising oxygen level in the tissue cell
12. Increasing the production of antibodies like lymphocytes and T-cells in the thymus gland, which is the defence of our immune system
13. Inhibiting and possibly destroying benign growths and tumours

For more information on Essiac, please obtain a copy of the Credence title, *The Essiac Handbook.*

Apricot Seeds/Kernels

Apricot kernels are an inexpensive, rich and natural source of vitamin B17. They also deliver the vitamins, minerals and enzymes not found in the pharmaceutical derivative of B17. Consumption should be spread throughout the day, not taken in one sitting.

- 7 g of seeds per day for life are recommended by Ernst Krebs as a nutritional supplement for those exercising cancer prevention. (This equates to 10-12 of the larger kernels or 20-25 of the smaller 'Shalkur' type).
- 20 g of seeds per day are recommended by Ernst Krebs as nutritional support for clinical cancer sufferers.

In a minority of cases, cancer sufferers may experience nausea when taking seeds. In this event, clinics recommend that dosage is reduced and then gradually increased as tolerance is gained. Intake should commence with four apricot seeds a day (spread throughout the day) for the first four days, increasing up to 10-15 a day for a further four days and then to a maximum of 20 - 28 g a day. If of low body weight, then scale down intake accordingly.

Not all apricot seeds are effective. They must have the characteristic bitter taste indicating that the active ingredients are present. Not to be eaten whole. May be pulped, grated or crushed.

Please note: Some cancer sufferers believe that apricot kernels alone are all that is required to fight cancer. Consultation with a qualified health practitioner familiar with Metabolic Therapy is advised for further information. Apricot kernels are usually part of the nutritional support for those exercising cancer prevention *for life* as well as cancer patients undergoing Phase 1 or Phase 2 Metabolic Therapy.

Maximol (Neways International)

The huge rise in incidences of cancer and other degenerative diseases is primarily due to the depleted vitamin/mineral content in today's western diet coupled with environmental/chemical toxin factors. Among many nutrients invariably missing for cancer are B17, vitamin C, vitamin A and the trace mineral selenium. A recent US study showed an overall drop of 50% in cancer deaths and a fall of 37% in new cancer cases, especially lung, bowel and prostate – among 1,300 volunteers taking supplements for four years. [212]

Mineral supplementation is most effective in the ionised 'liquid suspension' form, assisted by fulvic acid, where an unusually high percentage of assimilation by the body can be expected. Our bodies use minerals as raw material. These cannot be manufactured by the body, and so have to be present in the food and liquids we ingest. Sadly, as mentioned previously, our food chain is severely depleted of minerals, resulting in over 150 nutritional deficiency diseases that are now striking our societies with increasing intensity.

To combat this very real threat, mineral and vitamin supplementation, far from being a quaint health fad, is essential for everyone and can literally make the difference between life or death, especially for those with cancer. To combat this threat, Neways has formulated Maximol Solutions, which contains 67 essential and trace minerals, 17 essential vitamins, 21 amino acids, three enzymes, and *lactobacillus acidophilus*.[213] To provide greater absorption of all these ingredients, Maximol contains nature's natural chelator, used by plants and animals for the absorption of minerals and nutrients - organic fulvic acid. It is known that fulvic acid aids in the transport and assimilation of minerals and nutrients into living cells. This may in part be due to its low molecular weight, its electrical potential, and its bio-transporting ability. Fulvic acid aids in the selective trading or supply of minerals and other nutrient stacks inside the cell. Fulvic acid is effective at neutralising a wide range of toxic material - from heavy metals and radioactive waste to petrochemicals.

Before minerals can be utilised, they must first be converted from their particular colloidal state to a micro-colloidal state. Thus, for greater bio-

---

[212] *Daily Mail*, 28th July 1999, p.31
[213] Contents may vary by country.

availability, Neways has formulated Maximol Solutions as an organic fulvic acid complexed micro-colloidal solution. In this form, Maximol provides higher percentages of easily assimilated minerals than non-ionised colloidal mineral supplements, whose particles are often too large for easy absorption.

Revenol (Neways International)

Scientists tell us that vitamins A, C, and E, as well as beta-carotene and other antioxidant bioflavonoids, are vitally important to good health. But there are antioxidant formulae around now that have many more times the power of Vitamin C and Vitamin E. Revenol contains antioxidants that are broad-spectrum, including those derived from maritime pine bark and grape seed pycnogenols extracts - up to 95% in concentration and bioavailability. Revenol also contains curcuminoids, nature's most powerful and aggressive antioxidant, which is around 150 times more powerful than Vitamin E, about 60 times more powerful than Vitamin C, and about 3 times more powerful than antioxidants from maritime pine bark and grape seed pycnogenols extract in neutralising harmful oxidation elements in our bodies. [214]

Revenol also contains ginkgo biloba for the brain and circulatory system; alpha and beta carotene to increase potency; esterfied Vitamin C - a bonded form of Vitamin C that increases its power and residual retention in the body (up to 3 days); natural Vitamin E for greater absorption and effectiveness. Micro-spheres are also included which bond to the intestinal wall, allowing up to 400% more of the ingredients to be digested and absorbed. Each tablet of Revenol supplies over 60 milligrams of curcuminoids and maritime pine bark and grape seed extract.

Cascading Revenol (Neways International)

Neways has also released an exciting, further version of Revenol, named Cascading Revenol. Oxidation elements, or free radicals as they are sometimes known, are unstable molecules hungry to scavenge additional electrons, thereby damaging healthy cells. These factors are especially dangerous for cancer sufferers. Antioxidants such as Vitamin C can help prevent the damage caused by free radicals by completing their compounds, thus rendering them inert. The problem is, after having entered the body, most antioxidant molecular structures will grab one free radical and then change into an inert state, ceasing to be of further radical-scavenging value. The additional problem is that even when an antioxidant neutralises a free radical, the process creates an off-shoot free radical that is slightly different and less potent in variety, which in turn creates another, and so on. Typical

---

[214] **Majeed, Muhammed, et al** *Curcuminoids – Antioxidant Phytonutrients*, Nutriscience Publishers, 121 Ethel Road West, Unit 6, Piscataway, NJ 08854 USA

antioxidants have a linear application and thus show no ability to address this free radical cascading effect.

However Cascading Revenol's formulation has been designed to regenerate these scavenging molecules so that they can neutralise multiple free radicals. So, instead of only one free radical being destroyed per antioxidant molecule, each molecule is able to change structure and repeat the process again and again. Thus the value of each individual antioxidant molecule increases exponentially. Cascading Revenol's unique action is devastating to the free radical onslaught that damages cancer sufferers. In my opinion, it is an essential component in any nutritional support program.

Hawaiian Noni Juice (Neways International)

The fruit juice of *Morinda citrifolia* contains a polysaccharide-rich substance with marked anti-tumour activity, according to recent studies into the famous fruit.[215] This research, performed at the University of Hawaii, has resulted in exciting new and scientifically reputable evidence for the potential benefits of Noni fruit juice in the treatment of cancer. Neways Authentic Hawaiian Noni features all the health-enhancing benefits of the noni plant as well as raspberry and blueberry extracts – both powerful antioxidants.

Parafree (Neways International)

Researchers state that the majority of people, especially those with cancer, play host to one form of parasite or another. One of the most troublesome for those with cancer is *Candida albicans*, a normally beneficial yeast found as part of our gut flora that invariably proliferates tremendously in the anaerobic, acidic system of a cancer patient. *Candida's* waste products especially can fuel the fermentation process that drives cancer throughout the body. Fungal infections too can damage tissue which the body then attempts to heal, often with the result of causing cell mutations.

This formula contains: Pumpkin (seed), garlic, black walnut (bark), grapefruit seed extract, clove, citrus seed extract, ginger root wild, slippery elm bark, Sweet Annie (*Artemesia annua*), cranberry concentrate, pomegranate, butternut bark, pau d'arco, red clover, olive leaf, ginseng

---

[215] **Hirazumi, A & Eiichi Furusawa**, "An Immunomodulatory Polysaccharide-Rich Substance from the Fruit Juice of *Morinda citrifolia* (Noni) with Anti-tumour Activity", Dept of Pharmacology, John A Burns School of Medicine, Hawaii, HI 96822 USA

(American), gentian root, hyssop, cramp bark, peppermint powder, fennel seed.

Magnesium oxide (www.vitalminerals.org)

Colon cleansing, while not a pleasant topic to address, is a subject that cannot be overlooked in the quest for extended youth, weight loss, and total health. Mucoid plaque, parasites and impacted toxic metabolites can be removed with a modified diet as well as with certain purgative agents that can assist in restoring the colon and intestines to full function. It is essential to allow the body to clean itself of detritus that has collected in the digestive system over the years, hampering the body's ability to absorb the nutrients it craves through the intestinal lining. Magnesium oxide, when used as directed, hydrates the colon and assist in flushing the entire length of the digestive tract.

D-Toxarate (Neways International)

As we have already learned, every day we are exposed to harmful substances in our environment. The air we breathe, the food we eat, and even objects we touch are contaminated by substances that threaten our health in many ways we are only just beginning to understand. D-Toxarate is formulated with two important ingredients to help many of these substances pass through the body without harmful effects. Calcium d-glucarate, the first ingredient, can help eliminate some agents that potentially harm our cells. The second ingredient is ascorbic acid (Vitamin C), an antioxidant with the interesting property we examined earlier - it reduces blood-lead levels.

Chelamin (Neways International)

This calcium, magnesium and Vitamin D supplement is one of my favourites, and is ideal for those seeking to bolster levels of these particular minerals and vitamins in the body for supreme health. Calcium, as we learned earlier, is a vital precursor to so many chemical reactions in the body and should be present abundantly in our diets along with *reasonable* sunlight for optimum effects.

SUPERMARKET SMARTS

Below is a list of the main products available at any supermarket (this list is from an English store). Bolded items can be purchased with the appropriate comments listed. When considering the validity of this list, keep in mind the food your ancestors would have consumed three hundred years ago. Also imagine the diets of those peoples who do not suffer from the degenerative and toxin diseases afflicting the Western world today.

ITEM	COMMENTS	
Birthday Cakes	No	Processed food
Cakes	No	Processed food
Flan and Pastry	No	Processed food
Rolls	No	Processed food
Speciality Bakery	No	Processed food
Bread	**Wholegrain, sparingly**	
Cream Cakes and Desserts	No	Processed food
In Store Bakery	No	Processed food
Savoury Morning Goods	No	Processed food
Sweet Morning Goods	No	Processed food
Alcopops	No	
Bitters and Ales	No	
Cider	No	
Light Spirits	No	
Rum	No	
Whisky	No	
Beer	No	
Brandy	No	
Gin	No	
Liqueurs	No	
Vodka	No	
Fresh Pasta, Sauces and Soup	No	Processed food
Pies, Quiche and Savoury	No	Processed food
Ready Meals and Pizza	No	Processed food
Meat Free	No	Processed food
Prep Meats, Fish and Poultry	No	Processed food
Sandwiches, Sushi and Snacks	No	Processed food
Butter and Margarine	**Real butter, sparingly**	
Cream	No	
Home Cooking	No	Processed food

Organic	Yes, be selective	
Cheese	No	Processed food
Eggs	**free range, sparingly**	
Milk	No	Processed food
Yogurts and Dairy Desserts	No	Processed food
Bacon	No	Processed food
Chicken	**only organic, sparingly**	
Fish	**deep-sea cold fish, sparingly**	
Offal	No	
Prep Meats, Fish and Poultry	No	Processed food
Speciality Meat and Poultry	No	Processed food
Beef	No	Processed food
Cooked and Continental Meat	No	Processed food
Lamb	No	Processed food
Pork	No	Processed food
Sausage	No	Processed food
Turkey	No	Processed food
Frozen Desserts	No	Processed food
Frozen Meat Cuts	No	Processed food
Frozen Natural Fish	No	Processed food
Frozen Pies and Savouries	No	Processed food
Frozen Potato Products	No	Processed food
Frozen Ready Meals	No	Processed food
Large Tub Ice Cream	No	Processed food
Frozen Fish Products	No	Processed food
Frozen Meat Products	No	Processed food
Frozen Natural Vegetables	No	Processed food
Frozen Pizza and Bread	No	Processed food
Frozen Poultry	No	Processed food
Frozen Peas, corn, mixed veg	No	Processed food
Apples	No	possibly contaminated
Berries and Rhubarb	No	possibly contaminated
Cucumbers and Peppers	No	possibly contaminated
Grapes	No	possibly contaminated
Luxury and Exotic Vegetables	No	possibly contaminated
Organic Fruit	**Yes**	
Other Salad	No	possibly contaminated
Potatoes	No	possibly contaminated
Salads, Dressings and Dips	No	processed food
Tomatoes and Fresh Herbs	No	possibly contaminated
Bananas and Melons	No	possibly contaminated
Citrus	No	possibly contaminated
Exotic Fruit	No	possibly contaminated
Lettuce	No	possibly contaminated

Mushrooms, Onion and Garlic	No	possibly contaminated
Organic Vegetables	**Yes**	
Pears	No	possibly contaminated
Prepared Fruit, Veg and Salad	No	possibly contaminated
Stone Fruit	No	possibly contaminated
Traditional Vegetables	No	possibly contaminated
Baked Beans and Pasta	No	possibly contaminated
Breakfast Cereal	No	processed food
Cooking Sauces	No	processed food
Desserts and Baking Mixes	No	processed food
Ethnic and Kosher	No	processed food
Gravy and Pour Over Sauces	No	processed food
Meat and Fish	No	processed food
Oils	**cold press organic only**	
Pasta	**wholewheat pasta only**	
Rice and Pulses	**organic only**	
Savoury and Sweet Spreads	No	processed food
Soup	No	processed food
Sugar	No	processed food
Vegetables	No	processed food
Baking Aids	No	processed food
Canned Fruit	No	processed food
Custard	No	processed food
Dried Fruit and Cooking Nuts	**organic only**	
Flour and Suet	**organic w'wheat flour only**	
Herbs and Spices	**organic only**	
Mincemeat, Milk and Cream	No	processed food
Organic sundries	**so long as they are!**	
Pickles and Condiments	No	processed food
Sauces, Vinegars and Dressings	No	processed food
Snack Meals	No	processed food
Stuffing and Breadcrumbs	No	processed food
Tomato Puree and Pizza	No	processed food
Baby Food and Care	No	processed food
Haircare	non-toxic versions are not avail here	
Male Grooming	non-toxic versions are not avail here	
Personal Grooming	non-toxic versions are not avail here	
Bathroom	non-toxic versions are not avail here	
Healthcare	no unnecessary drugs	
Oral Hygiene	non-toxic versions are not avail here	
Skincare	non-toxic versions are not avail here	
Cleaning Products	non-toxic versions are not avail here	
Gifts	**yes please...**	
Laundry Products	non-toxic versions are not avail here	

Foils, Wraps and Bin Liners	non-toxic versions are not avail here	
Household Sundries	non-toxic versions are not avail here	
Tissues and Towels	**non-scented**	
Chilled Fruit Juice	Possibly contaminated	
Filter and Ground Coffee	No	
Milk Based Drinks	No	processed food
Soda Stream	No	
Squash	No	processed food
Water	**uncontaminated only**	
Coffee Whiteners	No	processed food
Fizzy Drinks	No	processed food
Longlife Fruit Juice	No... ask why it has a long life...	
Mixers	No	processed food
Single Drinks	No	processed food
Tea	sparingly	
Boxed Chocolates and Sweets	No	processed food
Chocolate Biscuit Bars	No	processed food
Crisps	No	processed food
Everyday Treats	No	processed food
Kids Biscuits	No	processed food
Savoury Nibbles	No	processed food
Snacks	No	processed food
Sweets	No	processed food
Chocolate Bars	No	processed food
Crackers and Crispbreads	No	processed food
Everyday Biscuits	No	processed food
Healthy Biscuits	No	processed food
Popcorn and Nuts	No	processed food
Single Packets of Chocolate and Sweets	No	processed food
Special Treats	No	processed food
Cigarettes and Cigars	No, sorry...	
Champagne and Sparking Wine	**every now and then...**	
Rose Wine	**every now and then...**	
Wine Accessories	No	processed food
Red Wine	**every now and then...**	
White Wine	**every now and then...**	

Small amounts of the above 'No's' are not going to land you in court. The purpose of this illustration is to make the point that our food supply, in the main, is processed, often contaminated with pesticides, and devoid of the 'whole foods' once eaten by our ancestors. Our emphasis should be on these 'whole foods', organically grown, which should comprise 80-90% of our diet. 80% of our diet should be water-based foods, such as fruits and vegetables. **Organic** meat, fish or dairy products should not comprise more than 5-10% of the total food we consume.

COMMON ALKALI ASH FOODS

(help to control acid in your internal environment)[216]

Almonds
Apples
Apricots
Avocados
Bananas
Beans, dried
Beet greens
Beet
Blackberries
Broccoli
Brussels sprouts
Cabbage
Carrots
Cauliflower
Celery
Chard leaves
Cherries, sour
Cucumbers
Dates, dried
Figs, dried
Grapefruit
Grapes
Green beans
Green peas
Lemons
Lettuce

Milk, goat*
Millet
Molasses
Mushrooms
Muskmelons
Onions
Oranges (small amounts)
Parsnips
Peaches
Pears
Pineapple
Potatoes, sweet
Potatoes, white
Radishes
Raisins
Raspberries
Rutabagas
Sauerkraut
Soy beans, green
Spinach, raw
Strawberries
Tangerines
Tomatoes
Watercress
Watermelon

* Recommended for infants only when mother's milk is not available.
Note: Some of the above foods may seem acidic, but in reality leave an alkali ash in the system.

Convert your diet to 80% alkali ash/ 20% acid ash foods. Ensure that your diet is predominant high-water content foods that are fresh and organic. Supplementation with trace minerals and vitamins is also advised.

---

[216] Morter, E T, op. cit.

COMMON ACID ASH FOODS

Bacon
Barley grain
Beef
Blueberries
Bran, wheat
Bran, oat
Bread, white
Bread, whole wheat
Butter
Carob
Cheese
Chicken
Cod
Corn
Corned beef
Crackers, soda
Cranberries
Currants
Eggs
Flour, white
Flour, whole wheat
Haddock
Lamb
Lentils, dried
Lobster
Milk, cow's ^

Macaroni
Oatmeal
Oysters
Peanut butter
Peanuts
Peas, dried
Pike
Plums ^
Pork
Prunes ^
Rice, brown
Rice, white
Salmon
Sardines
Sausage
Scallops
Shrimp
Spaghetti
Squash, winter
Sunflower seeds
Turkey
Veal
Walnuts
Wheat germ
Yoghurt

^ These foods leave an alkaline ash but have an acidifying effect on the body.

NEUTRAL ASH FOODS THAT HAVE AN ACIDIFYING EFFECT

Corn oil   Corn syrup   Olive oil   Refined sugar

45 FOODS RICH IN VITAMIN B17

apple seeds
alfalfa sprouts
apricot kernels
bamboo shoots
barley
beet tops
bitter almond
blackberry
boysenberry
brewer's yeast
brown rice
buckwheat
cashews
cassava (tapioca)
cherry kernels
cranberry
eucalyptus leaves
currants
fava beans
flax seeds
garbanzo beans
gooseberry
green peas
huckleberry
kidney beans
lentils

lima beans
linseed meat
loganberries
macadamia nuts
millet
millet seed
mulberry
nectarine kernels
peach kernels
pear seeds
pecans
plum kernels
quince
raspberry
sorghum cane syrup
spinach
sprouts (alfalfa, lentil, mung bean, buckwheat, garbanzo)
squash seeds
strawberry
walnuts
watercress

ON THE MOVE
(why we must exercise – yes, even me)
by Phillip Day

Natural Hygiene also promotes exercise to get oxygen into the system to encourage a dynamic circulation, elimination and mobility for your marvellous human machine. Quite simply, if you are doing good for your body, you will feel so darned fine, you will quit your job and begin promoting the Natural Hygiene lifestyle full-time like the dedicated nutritional evangelical you have become, for the rest of your extended happy days.

I love exercise, having lived in California for a number of years. But before you can come to terms with the need for it (exercise, not California), you have to see, like swimming, how far you will sink without regular movement. I am hardly a zealot with exercise, as many are, but I do my part and have developed a discipline over the years that has served me well, and I have been disease-free for the last fifteen years, not only as a result of exercise, but also thanks to the other factors covered in this book.

I have to say though, the one thing that impressed me most about Californians who lived healthy outdoor lives down in those beach communities like Malibu, Santa Monica, Playa del Rey and Redondo Beach, was that they actually enjoyed themselves, looked great and were living life to the full. Months later, I too was part of that euphoria that is healthy Southern California.

I was amazed when, as a pale Englander, I had first arrived in Los Angeles to see tanned and fit octogenarian men sailing by on roller-blades and vital, pretty ladies in their seventies playing volleyball on the sandy beaches before picking up their bikes and cycling along the famous bike-path to one of the great restaurants along Santa Monica Bay for a scrumptious chow-down, consisting of - you guessed it - platefuls of high-water-content, unrefined plant dietary.

Exercising is something we all must do, because living things DO move, and the more they move, the more alive they feel. Look at a Jack Russell puppy. It's bouncing off the walls with excitement and couldn't get into more drawers and mischief if you paid it. Inactivity is a relatively recent phenomenon with humans, ever since the abandonment of the horse and the advent of mass transport earlier in the 1900s. Many facets affecting health, like high meat and dairy consumption, drug abuse, environmental contamination and polluted food, water and air, are also quite new to us, and so are the health tragedies we are suffering as a result. It often helps to put these things in perspective. We haven't always done many of the things we do or don't do today. And with health and sickness, we are very much reaping the results of our activity or inactivity. Obesity is at an all-time high, as we examined earlier. Our convenience society, coupled with our new chemical junk diets and personal toxin fripperies, is, as they say where I'm from, doing us in. And exercise has all but gone out the window.

The key with exercise is don't overdo it, just work the muscles progressively and get cycling to raise a light sheen for a hour or so, and genteelly glow if you are a female. If you are a man, go ahead and sweat and stink all you want. Sweating's good, because the body is eliminating from the lymph massage with the exercise you are giving it. Do not use antiperspirants EVER AGAIN, as the aluminium and other compounds block up your lymph nodes, giving rise to major problems down the road when internal toxins can be driven back into the body, denied any means of escape and damage the lymph and breast. A deodorant with safe ingredients, such as the one marketed by Neways International, is ideal. Remember, the idea is to get everything moving both inside and outside the body with your exercising.

Health Wars contains an ideal beginner's exercise regimen to follow, along with the dietary recommendations covered in some detail. Start today. You'll be glad and feel better that you did!

RECOMMENDED FURTHER READING

In addition to the sources quoted in this book, several ideas for recipes came from the following excellent sources, which we highly recommend:

Diamond, Marilyn *Fit For Life* Cookbook, Bantam, 1991
De Spain, June *The Little Cyanide Cookbook*, Amercian Media, CA USA, 1999
Barnard, Neil *Foods That Fight Pain*, Bantam Books, 1999
Habgood, Jackie *The Hay Diet Made Easy*, Souvenir Press, 1997
Marsden, Kathryn *Food Combining Diet – Lose Weight The Hay Way*, Harper Collins, 1993
Carrier, Robert *New Great Dishes of the World*, MacMillan, 1997
Lawson, Nigella *How To Eat*, Chatto & Windus, 1998
Blanc, Raymond *Blanc Vite*, Headline Books, 2000
Elliott, Renee & Eric Treuille *Organic Cookbook*, Dorling Kindersley, 2000
Oliver, Jamie *Return of the Naked Chef*, Penguin, 2000

CONTACTS! CONTACTS! CONTACTS!

If you wish to purchase more copies of this book or find out where you may obtain any of Credence's other book and tape products, please use the contact details below. Credence has local sales offices in a number of countries. Please see our website at **www.credence.org** for further details on how to contact them:

UK Orders: (01622) 832386
UK Fax: (01622) 833314
www.credence.org
e-mail: sales@credence.org

Obtaining health products

If you need more information or help on any of the materials discussed in this book, such as where to find them, please use the above contact details. Alternatively, you may contact us at:

Credence Publications
PO Box 3
TONBRIDGE
Kent TN12 9ZY
England
infopack@credence.org

OTHER TITLES BY CREDENCE

CANCER: WHY WE'RE STILL DYING TO KNOW THE TRUTH
by Phillip Day

The book that has become a classic. This is Phillip Day's simple but stunning overview exposing the ongoing medical, political and economic scandal surrounding cancer and what you can do about the disease YOURSELF.

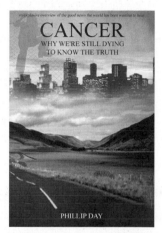

Science has known for 100 years that cancer is a healing process that has not terminated upon completion of its task. This book details the amazing track record of nutrition and its role within the simple protocol of Vitamin B17 metabolic therapy, a science which has been researched to the highest levels of biochemistry, used by leading doctors around the world today to control and eliminate cancers of all kinds.

- Hear the simple facts of the natural treatments from the medical experts themselves.
- Can cancer be treated at home today for just dollars/pounds a day?
- If nutritional therapy works so well with cancer, why doesn't everybody know about it?
- Why aren't chemo and radiotherapy cancer treatments working?
- Why is diet so important?
- Uncover why more people are making a living from cancer than are dying from it.
- Read the amazing testimonies of those like you who have decided to take control over their illness and are now cancer-free.

Whether you have cancer, or are exercising prevention for you and your family, PLEASE get educated on this vital issue today.

B17 METABOLIC THERAPY IN THE PREVENTION AND CONTROL OF CANCER

- a technical manual -
compiled by Phillip Day

B17 METABOLIC THERAPY

in the prevention and
control of CANCER

a technical manual

compiled by
PHILLIP DAY

From the desks of some of the world's leading cancer scientists comes the empirical proof of vitamin B17 and its associated protocols in the treatment and prevention of cancer. These explosive findings have been the cause of the real cancer war, where vested interests have moved to vilify and denigrate nutrition in order to protect their highly lucrative cancer incomes.

- Find out why 18 'primitive' cultures do not get cancer in their isolated state
- What nutritional components have been found vital in the prevention and the treatment of cancer?
- What can you do to change your diet in ways which will give you maximum protection from cancer and other associated ailments?
- Why do animals not get cancer in the wild, yet succumb to it when 'domesticated' by humans?
- Discover the amazing research of Professor John Beard of Edinburgh University and American biochemist Ernst T Krebs Jr. which shows what cancer actually is. Remove your fear of this disease forever
- Examine the actual technical theses and trials carried out by doctors and scientists that validate this amazingly simple anti-cancer system
- Read the fabulous case histories of those who recovered using these simple methods

GREAT NEWS
on cancer in the 21st century
by Steven Ransom

THERE IS TIME!

A cancer diagnosis calls for decisions – decisions that, because of circumstances, are so often made in haste. *Great News on Cancer in the 21st Century* is the first book that tells us there is time to consider the options! Within these pages is everything you need to know about taking the next step.

Did you know, for instance, that vested interests in the cancer industry have a direct impact on the advice you are receiving from your doctor? Why aren't we being told about the validated, non-conventional treatments that are saving and enhancing lives daily?

Instead, we are offered profitable chemotherapy and radiation treatments that damage the immune system – sometimes irreparably. Get informed on the dangers associated with these treatments, including the facts and figures they don't tell you. Learn how to interpret misleading information for yourself.

Take mammography, for example. How dangerous is it? Find out about the simple breast self-examination procedures that are just as effective and pose no danger to women's health, and discover the great news that will lift the current fear associated with breast cancer. Read the powerful testimonies of people who are being helped tremendously with various non-conventional treatments - stories of doctors unable to believe the disappearance of supposedly incurable cancers! This summary represents just a fraction of the wealth of information you will uncover in *Great News on Cancer in the 21st Century*.

HEALTH WARS
by Phillip Day

WHY IS OUR HEALTHCARE SERVICE KILLING US?

One of the most significant health books to come out in the new millennium, *Health Wars*, compiled by UK health researcher Phillip Day, tears the lid off the shameful medical and corporate scandals that are killing our nations. The author also reports the exciting and straightforward results of research into cancer, heart disease, osteoporosis and a host of other diseases, which we can simply and cheaply prevent or treat with nutrition and lifestyle changes.

- *The proof that western healthcare has become the third leading cause of death in western nations*
- *What simple measures can you take to avoid heart disease and cancer, the two leading killers?*
- *Find out why diets fail and how best to lose weight effortlessly and permanently*
- *Why is WHEN you eat almost as important as WHAT you eat?*
- *What is the truth about vaccinations?*
- *Why are at least 18 cultures living effortlessly to 100 and beyond when we die in the industrialised nations from diseases that do not afflict these long-lived peoples*
- *And much, much more*

Phillip Day: "This entirely pointless and unnecessary global medical catastrophe is growing worse with each passing year, but people are finally beginning to wake up and take action. By necessity, this new century must be the age of the Health Wars."

THE ESSIAC HANDBOOK
by James Percival

In 1923, a Canadian nurse, Rene Caisse, came upon an ancient Ojibway Indian herbal concoction that appeared to have remarkable powers to offer the sick. In the years since, thousands of patients, many considered beyond hope, have testified that this simple, natural treatment saved their lives where modern medicine had failed. Essiac has been studied in detail, research reporting that the benefits of this herbal tea include:

1. Preventing the build-up of fatty deposits in artery walls, heart, kidney and liver
2. Regulating cholesterol levels by transforming sugar and fat into energy
3. Destroying fungi and parasites in the digestive system and throughout the body
4. Counteracting the effects of aluminium, lead and mercury poisoning
5. Neutralising acids, absorbing toxins in the bowel and eliminating both
6. Clearing the respiratory channels by dissolving and expelling mucus
7. Relieving the liver of its burden of detoxification by helping to convert fatty toxins into water-soluble substances that can then be eliminated through the kidneys
8. Increasing the body's ability to utilize oxygen by raising oxygen level in the tissue cell
9. Increasing the production of antibodies like lymphocytes and T-cells in the thymus gland, which make up the defence of our immune system
10. Inhibiting and possibly destroying benign growths and tumours

This book also cites great testimonies of recovered patients, even from Dr Charles Brusch, physician to President J F Kennedy!

FOOD FOR THOUGHT

Compiled by Phillip Day

Much of what we buy from the supermarkets today is actually not food at all, but highly processed commercial material palmed off on the public as 'food'.

Foodstuffs today are often repositories for a daunting host of harmful additives, artificial sweeteners that cause cancer, high levels of hidden sugars, fungi, hormones, pesticides, and other chemicals. The untold health damage that has been wrought on our societies in the name of shelf-life and convenience has been staggering.

The Credence crusade to better health and a disease-free life begins with what we put in our shopping carts each week. *Food for Thought*, our official recipe book, is the ideal companion to our other titles and offers practical and fun advice on healthy eating and disease prevention. This delightful guide takes you through the main concepts of

- acid/alkali
- Vitamin B17 dishes
- the proper combining of foods
- the problems with meat and dairy in excessive amounts
- fruit consumption techniques
- a host of detox menus
- 5-10% meat and dairy recipes
- healthy snacks
- pro-active sickness foods
- children's dishes
- proper supplementation, and much, much more!

Whether you are suffering, or just want to make a change for your extended future, sensible nutrition comes to life in *Food For Thought*, bringing you the most delicious foods that WON'T KILL YOU!

246

WAKE UP TO HEALTH
in the 21ˢᵗ Century
by Steven Ransom

Despite our increasingly toxic world and the various threats to our health, we CAN live healthily. Spending only a little time educating ourselves in these matters is all that is needed to reap a very healthy return. Discover for yourself:

· **The full and fascinating history of vaccination:** read information never before in the public domain. Discover the dangers and the sensible way forward

· **The truth about antibiotics:** how they are supposed to work and what alternatives there are to this 'magic bullet'

· **Painkillers:** those little pills in your cupboard. Are they doing more than just killing pain?

· **New insight into the 'fast food' industry:** just what *are* those burgers and fries? Educate your friends towards enjoying healthier alternatives

· **The truth about many so-called 'infectious' diseases:** In so many instances, despite the media say-so, the true cause of most serious illness is not viral, but environmental. Much illness can be easily avoided

· **The 'germ theory' of disease:** Was Louis Pasteur correct in his assumptions about illness and disease? Did you know that on his death-bed, Pasteur recanted much of his work? Has money-making germ theory had its day? Discover a fascinating, yet simple approach to the cause, treatment **and prevention** of much illness and disease today

· **Can we be too clean?** Discover how our unquestioning acceptance of germ theory has led us into carrying out some quite extraordinary and unhealthy actions as part of our daily 'health' routine

· **Allergies and allergy testing:** What we're not told about this new diagnostic tool and what we need to know

· **The health of our pets:** Our furry friends are just as much part of the family as we are. Discover some simple facts about commercial pet food and pet care that will improve the health and wellbeing of our animals tremendously

And much, much more!

THE MIND GAME
by Phillip Day

Every new year brings incredible new inventions, advances in technologies, new medicines, further discoveries in physics, chemistry and the other sciences. There are also new political challenges and military threats. News channels such as ABC, CNN, the BBC and Sky report 24 hours a day on the problems besetting this complicated, restless and fretting planet.

But today, ordinary, decent citizens feel imprisoned – witnesses to unprecedented levels of terrorism, street violence, illiteracy, crime and disastrous school standards. We also have the exploding drug culture, the tide of sleaze in our media, corruption in our governments and the misery of what is termed 'mental illness'. Is there a common thread?

- Find out why there is no such thing as a 'mental disease'
- Uncover natural treatments, dietary and lifestyle changes that have a proven track record in reversing so-called 'mental illness'
- Read how psychiatry has killed some of our best loved film and pop stars with its brutalising treatments
- What is the truth behind the rash of schoolyard shootings we have seen in America?
- Why are millions of children being given mind-altering drugs after being diagnosed with the bogus disorders ADD/ADHD?
- How can you improve your attitude and general peace of mind with a few simple but telling techniques?

Phillip Day shines a critical light on the problems besetting 21st century society and leads us to the tremendous answers available for those who seek them. Absolutely do not miss this fascinating, penetrating political and medical insight into our times.

WORLD WITHOUT AIDS

by Steven Ransom and Phillip Day

THE DOOMSDAY VIRUS—THE 10 YEAR INCUBATION PERIOD—THE CHILLING DIAGNOSIS—AFRICA RAVAGED—THE MILLIONS WE MUST RAISE—THE FRANTIC RACE AGAINST TIME. AND THE WORLD BOUGHT IT ALL...

World Without AIDS dismantles one of the world's greatest fears and exposes the deceit, fraudulent science and needless fear-mongering lying at the heart of this supposed global epidemic.

Over ten years in the making, this impeccably researched book gives an eye-opening account of what vested interests can get away with, given a trusting public, an almost limitless supply of money, and scant scruples.

- Read about the hoax of HIV from the experts themselves
- Find out about the fraudulence of the HIV test and how it can trigger a false positive with over 60 different causal factors
- Uncover the real causes of immune suppression
- Expose the AIDS-devastating-Africa myth
- Discover the appalling dangers of the establishment-approved medications prescribed to those who have been written off as 'HIV positive'
- Read the amazing stories of those who had 'AIDS' and are now completely healthy.
- Find out the simple, natural regimens they used.

"Ransom and Day are the Woodward and Bernstein of AIDSgate, exposing the corruption, fraud and lies on which the multibillion-dollar HIV industry is based." Alex Russell, Continuum Magazine

TOXIC BITE
by Bill Kellner-Read

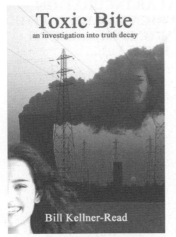

Most people go to the dentist at some point in their lives, and many go regularly. But who really questions what happens when we are in the dentist's chair? Can we be sure that we are receiving the best, long-term treatment for such an important and necessary part of our body? And what are the long-term implications of poor dental hygiene and health?

Finally there's a new book that demystifies dentistry and lets you take control of your own dental health. *Toxic Bite*, by British dentist Bill Kellner-Read, gets to the bottom of some startling questions:

- Could your gum disease be responsible for heart disease or stroke?
- What products are we using every day that contribute to wider toxic illnesses?
- And what about extractions? Do we really need that tooth pulled?
- Should we really be extracting children's teeth for orthodontic correction?
- What are the longer-term consequences of having less teeth in our mouth?
- What about the other correctional work being carried out today?
- Is there a link between nutrition and gum disease?

For the best in toxin-free tooth, mouth and body care, read *Toxic Bite* - the latest addition to the Credence roster of top-selling healthcare titles.

TEN MINUTES TO MIDNIGHT
by Phillip Day

During the coming months, Britain as a nation may cease to exist. If the British people can be talked into joining the euro and the new EU constitution, they will discover that they have been fooled into giving up a lot more than the pound.

Increasingly, Great Britain has been governed from Brussels by an unelected cabal of foreign committees dictating what British citizens can and can't do down to the last detail. Yet the extent of the EU's incompetence, fraud and criminal activity is hardly reported to the citizens soon to be governed completely by this autocratic, unaccountable new superstate. Did you know that:

- Britain is the EU's biggest customer? We don't need to be in the EU to trade with Europe. Other nations not in the EU, such as Switzerland, trade freely and are doing well
- 10% of the EU's total budget disappears on fraud every year?
- The EU Court of Auditors has been unable to sign off the EU's accounts for eight years running because of gross irregularities?
- All agents and officers of the EU's new quasi-FBI police force, Europol, have been granted a blanket immunity from prosecution?
- Joining the euro will be irreversible, even if it proves is a disaster?
- Joining the euro will entail Britain handing over her gold and currency reserves to the EU apart from a small working balance?
- The EU is in the process of restricting a huge cross-section of nutritional products and herbs once widely available?

Yet, in spite of all the problems, *Ten Minutes to Midnight* also explores the heartening character of the British, and why we must, at all costs, face up and fight this second Battle of Britain in order to regain our independence and avoid a new European war.

VIGILANCE
by Ashley Mote

VIGILANCE
A defence of British liberty

Ashley Mote

"What a demolition job!
Vigilance smashes huge holes in the walls which have long
hidden the squalid truth about the European Union."

Some people think the United Kingdom has effectively been abolished already. It will certainly cease to exist as a free and sovereign nation unless we reverse the erosion of our ancient rights, freedoms and customs by endless interference in British affairs by the European Union.

In 1975, as new members of the EEC, we thought we were voting for a free trade area. What we have today is an undemocratic, unaccountable police state that makes laws behind closed doors and seeks by stealth to destroy the UK as an independent nation. The European Union is being increasingly rammed down British throats in pursuit of a dream we never voted for. That dream has become a living nightmare. Silent discontent is no longer an option.

If you are concerned about the activities of the EU and its impact on the British way of life, then this book is for you.

Vigilance is not a book about politics in the usual sense. Nor is it academic. It is a simple, clear and horrifying account of what is being done to our country by the EU, why it matters, and why it must be stopped.

Vigilance also paints a vivid picture of the thriving, wealthy, confident and outward looking Britain that will quickly emerge from the ruins of the EU disaster.

The EU issue is of monumental proportions.

Ultimately, it is about British liberty.

Videos

Healthy at 100! - The video

The absolutely NOT TO BE MISSED documentary from Down Under, featuring Phillip Day's tour of Australia, some great slices of his talk in Melbourne before a capacity crowd, and interviews with doctors, practitioners and those who have recovered from serious illness. Funny, poignant, thoughtful and the most highly informative 65 minutes you will spend all year. (PAL format, 65 minutes)

Health Wars - The video

We are told we have the brightest and the best-trained doctors in the world looking after us. So why is western healthcare now the third leading cause of death in our nations today? In this fascinating, independently produced documentary, Phillip Day brings us great news on successful, non-toxic treatments for cancer and other degenerative illnesses, along with expert medical and political opinion which supports his heart-warming, exciting information. Find out how you and your family can triumph over the major disease killers and help others to do the same. (PAL format, 75 minutes)

Audio Cassettes

Cancer, The Winnable War, cassette

(90 minutes) The best highlights of Phillip Day's US tour on cancer, recorded in Seattle, WA, on the prevention of, and nutritional treatments for cancer. This tape also deals with why this information is continuing to be suppressed. A must-have for all the family – even the stubborn ones! Great for distributors and health practitioners. The "Dead Doctors Don't Lie" of the cancer industry.

Health Wars, the truth behind cancer and AIDS, cassette

A 60-minute studio-quality tape featuring two 30-minute overviews on cancer and AIDS by UK author and researcher Phillip Day. This tape is an ideal tool for educating your distributorship and members of the public on the important issues of cancer, AIDS and the toxins wilfully used in our environment, that lead to misery, sickness and death.

Cancer / Politics The Real War, cassette

Total time 63 minutes. In this live US radio interview with Phillip Day, host Tom Mischke asks the tough questions about cancer, the medical industry and the political / financial forces driving it. This is a no-holds-barred expose of the current state of the medical industry and the historical background that puts it all into perspective. Although cancer is the main subject, it is ultimately western healthcare that is on trial. The verdict is a tough pill to swallow.

THE CAMPAIGN FOR TRUTH IN MEDICINE

WHAT IS CTM?

The Campaign for Truth in Medicine is a worldwide organisation dedicated to educating the public on health issues and pressing for change in areas of science and medicine where entrenched scientific error, ignorance or vested interests are costing lives. Our ranks comprise doctors, scientists, researchers, biochemists, politicians, industry executives and countless members of the world public, all of whom have made at least one observation in common. They have recognised that, in certain key areas of global disease, drug treatments and overall healthcare philosophy, the medical, chemical and political establishments are pursuing the wrong course with the maximum of precision, even when their own legitimate scientific research has illustrated the dangers of pursuing these courses.

CTM STANDS FOR CHOICE IN HEALTHCARE

Millions today use nutritional supplements and alternative health strategies for themselves and their families, and yet, increasingly, the public's freedom to choose is being eroded by government legislation and attempts by the pharmaceutical conglomerates to 'buy out' the massive alternative health market. CTM stands for the people's right to choose the healthcare system they feel is right for them, free of big business interference, pointless government regulation, and coercion by the medical establishment which often attempts to compel its own dubious remedies upon an unwilling public.

CTM STANDS FOR SPREADING THE GOOD NEWS

Every month, CTM sends out EClub, its global online magazine, which is forwarded free to CTM subscribers around the world to keep them informed of the latest news, developments, scandals and great news in healthcare and other relevant issues. Within EClub, doctors, researchers, journalists, scientists, leading healthcare advocates, researchers and members of the public share their tips, views and strategies with hundreds of thousands around the world. EClub represents the news you are not being told; information that can literally change or save lives. Don't miss out on this vital resource, forwarded FREE to you every month, containing the very latest in news and views on vital health issues for you and your family.

WHAT YOU CAN DO NOW

Why not add your voice immediately to the hundreds of thousands around the world who are getting united, mobilised and making a difference through CTM in so many lives. Join for FREE today by completing the form in this brochure and sending it in. Alternatively, you may wish to join via our web-site at www.campaignfortruth.com.

Let's be part of a different future. One that celebrates life!

HOW TO ORDER CREDENCE PRODUCTS

Credence has offices and distributors in many countries around the world. If you would like more information, or wish to purchase any of the Credence titles described, please use the details in the **Contacts!** section of this book. Alternatively, why not visit Credence's comprehensive web-site at **www.credence.org**, which contains secure on-line global stores, our famous testimonies section, and many other great features.

Please note: Items not available in your regional shop may be obtained through the Rest of World store.

INDEX

Crime, 165, 195
Crohn's disease, 172
Curcuminoids, 226
Cushing's disease, 88
Cycling, 237

D

Daidzen, 58
Deanol, 207
Delaney Clause, 174, 175
Delinquency, 195, 197
Dementia, 211
Dentistry, 250
Depression, 87, 207, 216, 217, 222
Dextrose, 166
Diabetes, 172, 173, 195, 220, 221, 222
Diarrhoea, 87, 89, 208, 215
Dikitopiprazines, 203
Dimethylaminoethanol (DMAE),
206, 207, 211
Diverticulosis, 195
Docosahexaenoic acid (DHA), 220,
221, 222, 223
Dogs, 203
Drug abuse, 237
Dry skin, 222
D-Toxarate, 215, 228

E

Echinacea, 90
Eczema, 220, 222
Edema, 197
Eicosapentaenoic acid (EPA), 221
Elimination cycle, 20, 21, 22, 23, 26
Endometriosis, 87
Enzymes, 85, 86, 88, 202, 209, 212,
224, 225
EPA (Environmental Protection
Agency), 178
Epilepsy, 207, 208, 210, 211
Equal, 176
Essential fatty acids (EFA's), 205, 219,
220
Estrogen, 203
Europe, 220

Evening primrose oil, 222
Exercise, 172, 173, 205, 219, 220, 236,
237

F

FDA (Food & Drug Administration),
170, 176, 177, 178, 179
Feelin' Good, 227
Feflux, 87
Fennel, 201, 228
Fibre, 24
Fish, 219, 221
Flax, 221
Flour, 231
Food Science and Nutritional
Laboratory, 178
Formaldehyde, 178
Formic acid, 178
Free radicals, 168, 226, 227
Fructose, 166
Fulvic acid, 225, 226
Fungal infections, 85, 87, 91

G

Gamma-linolenic acid (GLA), 222
Genistein, 58, 62
Germany, 221
Gingko biloba, 207, 211, 226
Glaciers, 197
Glucose, 24, 166, 167
Glutamate, 177
Glutamic acid, 171
Gluten, 138, 200
Glycogen, 218, 219
Goat's cheese, 196
Gout, 87

H

Hair, 216
Hall, Richard, 216
Hawaii, 227
Hawaiian noni, 227
Hayes, Jr., Arthur Hull, 179

Headaches, 207
Healing, 171, 176
Health Wars, 203, 219
Heart disease, 23, 195, 197, 250
Hemp, 222
Herpes, 88
Herxheimer's Reaction, 90
High blood pressure, 195
High-glycaemic foods, 202
Holford, Patrick, 222
Hunzas, 195, 196, 197
Huperzine, 211
Hydrogenated fats, 203
Hyperactivity, 170
Hypoglycaemia, 208

I

India, 195
Inflammation, 89, 223
Insomnia, 208
Insulin, 172, 173, 220, 223
Intestines, 21, 85, 171, 228
Ionised calcium, 225, 226
Iron, 217
Irritable bowel syndrome, 87
Isoflavones, 58, 59, 60, 61, 62, 63, 64, 65, 66

J

Jock itch, 87

K

Kidneys, 170
Krebs Jr, Ernst T, 197

L

Lactobacillus acidophilus, 89, 225
Lactose, 166
Leukaemia, 203
Linoleic acid, 221, 223
Liver, 85, 169, 170, 203, 210, 218, 219

London, 222
Longevity, 23, 180, 195
Los Angeles, 236
Lungs, 85, 197
Lupus, 87
Lymph, 21, 86, 170, 197, 224, 237
Lymphatic system, 85

M

Madras, 197
Magnesium, 203, 208, 222
Magnesium oxide, 228
Malic acid, 26
Maltose, 166
Martin, William Coda, 165, 167
Maximol, 225
McCarrison, Dr Robert, 195, 196, 197
Mercola, Joseph, 168, 173, 179
Metabolic therapy, 211, 212, 224, 225
Metabolites, 169, 171, 178, 228
Methanol, 177
Milk, 199, 200, 203, 213
Monsanto, 177
Monte, Woodrow C, 178, 179
Morinda citrifolia, 227
Multiple sclerosis, 86, 87, 222

N

Natural Hygiene, 20, 23, 236
Nausea, 224
Neurons, 177
Neurotransmitters, 177, 206, 210, 211, 216, 217
NIEHS (National Institute for Environmental Health Services), 175
Nobel Prize, 214
NTP (National Toxicology Program), 175
Nutrasweet, 176
Nuts, 219

O

Obesity, 237

Olney, John W, 176, 177
Osteoporosis, 169
Oxford University, 196
Oxidation, 168

Y

Z

W